FROMMER'S

LISBON, MADRID, & THE COSTA DEL SOL

DARWIN PORTER

1989–1990

Published by Prentice Hall Trade Division
A Division of Simon & Schuster, Inc.
Gulf + Western Building
One Gulf + Western Plaza
New York, NY 10023

ISBN 0-13-047482-7
ISSN 0899-2932

Manufactured in the United States of America
Text Design: Levavi & Levavi

*Although every effort was made to ensure the accuracy
of price information appearing in this book,
it should be kept in mind that prices
can and do fluctuate in the course of time.*

CONTENTS

MAPS

INFLATION ALERT: The author of this book has spent many hours researching to ensure the accuracy of prices appearing in this guide. As we go to press, we believe we have obtained the most reliable data possible. However, we cannot offer guarantees for the tariffs quoted. In the lifetime of this edition—particularly its second year (1990)—the wise traveler will add *at least* 20% to the prices quoted.

CURRENCY CONVERSIONS: The currency conversions from escudos to dollars and from pesetas to dollars, which appear in parentheses throughout these pages, were prepared on the basis of 133 escudos and 110.4 pesetas to $1 (U.S.). These rates may not be accurate by the time you travel, as they do change from day to day, depending on the relative values of both currencies on world markets. Use our currency conversions, therefore, only as a gauge of what you'll be spending and check with a banker before you leave for Iberia to determine what the actual rates of exchange are at that time.

CHAPTER I

AN INTRODUCTION TO IBERIA

□ □ □

As your jet descends over the port of Lisbon or sweeps above the golden plains of Castile on its way to Madrid, you'll be embarked on a unique travel adventure—the conquest of Iberia.

Long isolated from mainstream Europe by nature and man— the Pyrenees mountains and the Moors—Iberia developed and grew in its own very individual, very distinct way. Exotic is the word for it. Where else in Europe will you come across anything like the bold, sensuous rhythm of flamenco, the mournful wailing strains of fado, or the truly long, lazy siesta? And above all, the fascinating sport of bullfighting.

These are aspects of Iberia every person has heard of or seen, but to experience them firsthand is something else, something no traveler should miss. But Iberia is much more than this—indeed, it is a continent in miniature.

SPAIN—QUEEN OF A LOST EMPIRE: Castles, mostly in ruins, dot the Spanish countryside, hollow reminders of Spain's Golden Age, when she dispatched her fleet to conquer the New World and return with its riches. Columbus sailed to America, Balboa to the Pacific Ocean. Cortés conquered Mexico for her glory and the glory of the Church; Pizarro brought her Peru.

The conquistadores too often revealed the negative side of the Spanish soul, the brutality in the name of honor and glory, but they also embodied the positive side, the belief that "the impossible dream" was possible—Don Quixote's tilting at windmills on the plains of La Mancha, and often conquering them.

It's difficult to see Spain today without recalling its golden past, for there are many, many reminders. Spain today is a perfect mixture of the old and the new, and its images constantly float by you—silvery olive trees in the south; mantilla-wearing Carmens in Andalusia; Moorish palaces; harsh Basque fishing villages along the northeast coast; the luxurious sandy beaches from the Costa de la Luz to the Costa Brava, thronged with bikini-clad tourists; the orange groves of Valencia; the hard-working industrial city of Barcelona, the largest of the Mediterranean ports; the elegance and serenity of Madrid.

So how can a traveler in Spain go wrong? Here you'll have the glories of the past and the excitement of the present.

AND PORTUGAL—IN ITS OWN RIGHT: Portugal suffers
from one of the most widespread misconceptions in European travel: that it's really "another Spain." This completely erroneous judgment exists even today, because Portugal is still relatively unknown and unexplored by the mass of foreign travelers, who, at best, know only Lisbon and the famous resort of Estoril.

Victorian guidebook writers called Portugal an "island," even though it's obviously connected to Spain. The marriage of this Iberian couple, which lasted for 60 years, was never successful. Spain was too large, too dominant, too intent on protecting its own interests, which conflicted with those of its reluctant bride. Although ruled by their powerful neighbor, the Portuguese staunchly maintained their identity during the captivity and zealously waited for the moment when they could throw off the yoke and reassert their independence.

Despite its small size—only 140 miles in width, 380 miles in length—Portugal is one of the most rewarding adventures on the European docket. Exploring its towns, cities, villages, and countryside takes far longer than expected, because there is so much richness, such variety, along the way.

The people are the friendliest in Europe. The land they inhabit is majestic—almond trees in the African-looking Algarve; cork forests and fields of golden wheat in Alentejo; ranches that raise the brave black bulls in Ribatejo; the narrow, winding streets of the Alfama in Lisbon; ox-drawn carts crossing the plains of Minho; apron-clad *varinas* (the wives of the fishermen) carrying baskets of wiggling eels on their heads; and the vineyards of Douro.

Azaleas, rhododendrons, and canna grow for miles on end; the sound of fado drifts out of small cafés; windmills clack in the Atlantic breezes; rare, intricate *azulejos* (tiles) line churches and buildings; sardine boats bob in the bay; gleaming whitewashed houses; and the sea . . . always the sea.

Kaleidoscopic scenery, sandy beaches, mild climate, and

unique man-made attractions such as Manueline architecture have contributed to the recent tourist boom in Portugal. But what made the land initially popular with its many English visitors—and later the German multitude pouring into the Algarve—is its low tariffs, not only in its hotels and restaurants, but in its shops as well. Portugal charges some of the lowest prices in Western Europe. Inflation, however, is the rule here too, and the people are hard-pressed. Nevertheless, Portugal is still a soothing breeze to those who've been to Rome and Stockholm lately.

Focusing on the unique features of each of these two countries is one goal of this guide. The other is finding those special hotels and fine restaurants that will make your trip to Iberia memorable.

CHAPTER II

GETTING ACQUAINTED WITH LISBON

□ □ □

Narrow, cobblestone streets . . . pastel-washed houses . . . cable cars clacking down to the river . . . a black-shawled *fadista* singing of unrequited love . . . floodlights illuminating an ancient castle . . . boats loaded with fresh seafood . . . mosaic sidewalks . . . ferryboats plying the Tagus . . . laundry flapping in the wind . . . the crowing of a rooster early in the morning.

This is Lisbon, an ancient city, whose people fancifully like to claim Ulysses as their founder. If this legendary figure did indeed possess a character of "experience, tenacity, and intelligence," then he is the appropriate father symbol for Lisbon, Europe's western-most capital, sprawling across seven hills on the right bank of the Tagus.

HISTORY IN BRIEF: Those cynical of the Ulysses legend claim (no history backs them up) that the seafaring Phoenicians founded Lisbon. In time, the Carthaginians sailed into the port. Romans oc-cupied the city from the beginning of the 3rd century B.C. to the 4th century A.D., during which time it was known as "Felicitas Ju-lia." After Rome's decline, Lisbon was a Visigoth stronghold, then a Moorish city before it was liberated by the Catholic Portuguese from the north in 1147. But it wasn't until 1256 that Afonso III felt safe enough to move his court there, forsaking Coimbra, now a uni-versity city.

During the Age of Exploration some of the greatest names, such as Vasco da Gama and Magellan, embarked from Lisbon on their voyages of discovery. Like Ulysses, the captains of those long-ago crews had to contend with widely held beliefs that their ships would be consumed by huge sea monsters, or else be swallowed up by the fiery mouth (*boca*) of Hell.

In time, the discoveries and exploration, the opening of new worlds to the west and east, created a mother city of Lisbon, called in its Golden Age the "eighth wonder of the world." Ivory and slaves from Africa; spices, silks, rubies, pearls, and porcelain from China and the East Indies; ginger and pepper from the Malabar Coast—all these riches were funneled through the thriving port of Lisbon. Shopkeepers literally had more money than they knew how to spend. Their wives hired servants more for ostentation than need. The sea captain's spouse wore finery fit for a princess.

And then came the earthquake. At the peak of Lisbon's power, influence, and wealth, it suffered one of the greatest earthquakes of all time. Two-thirds of the city was destroyed. At 9:40 on the morning of November 1, 1755, most of the city's residents were at church, celebrating an important religious observance, All Saints' Day, when the earthquake struck. In minutes, the glory that was Lisbon became a thing of the past. The great earthquake was felt as far north as Scotland, causing damage even in North Africa. Ambassadors and slaves, merchants and sailors, courtesans and priests added to a death toll estimated at 20,000 to 60,000 people. A fire raged for nearly a week, destroying much that the quake left undamaged, but thankfully sparing the heart of the Alfama district.

After the ashes had settled, the Marquês de Pombal, the prime minister, ordered that the dead be buried, the city rebuilt at once. To accomplish that ambitious plan, the king gave him the power of a virtual dictator.

What Pombal ordered constructed was a city of wide, symmetrical boulevards leading into handsome squares dominated by fountains and statuary. Bordering these wide avenues would be black-and-white mosaic sidewalks, the most celebrated in Europe.

LISBON TODAY:
The mixture of the old (pre-earthquake) and the new (post-earthquake) was done so harmoniously that travelers consider Lisbon one of the most beautiful cities on earth.

Despite its sprawling size and population near the one-million mark, a shopkeeper laments, "It's really a village—everybody knows everybody else. You can't even look at a pretty girl without your wife finding out."

Many who don't know Lisbon from actual fact know it well from all those World War II spy movies. It would be only natural, you'd assume, to see Hedy Lamarr slinking around the corner any moment. In World War II, Lisbon, officially neutral, was a hotbed of intrigue and espionage. It was also a haven for thousands of refugees. Many of those—such as deposed royalty—remained, settling into villas in Estoril and Sintra.

ORIENTATION

THE DISTRICTS OF LISBON: As conceived by the Marquês de Pombal, the gateway to Lisbon is the **Praça do Comércio** (Commerce Square), also known as the Terreiro do Paço (Palace Grounds) in memory of the days when the royal court was located here before the earthquake destroyed it.

However, in the past century the English dubbed this same square **Black Horse Square,** and the name stuck (even some Portuguese refer to it in this way). The appellation is derived from the equestrian statue on the square of King José I, dating from 1775, the work of Machado de Castro, the leading Portuguese sculptor of his day. It was on this square in 1908 that the king, Carlos I, and his son, Prince Luís Filipe, were killed by an assassin's bullets.

To the east of the square lies the sector known as the **Alfama,** the ancient Moorish district of Lisbon spared from the earthquake. It is crowned by St. George Castle, once a Visigoth stronghold, although the present structure dates from the 12th century. This eastern quarter of Lisbon consists of narrow streets (some really stairways) and medieval houses, where neighbors could, if they wanted to, reach out and shake hands with the people next door. Old street lanterns and flower-draped balconies, barefoot children, and fishwives selling the latest catch from the sea add to the local color.

To the north of Black Horse Square lies the **Rossio,** more formally known as Praça Dom Pedro IV. A riot of neon, it draws the devotee of the sidewalk café, who sits talking, getting a shoeshine, and sipping the black, aromatic coffee of Angola. Again, tourists have bestowed a nickname on it: Rolling Motion Square. The undulating patterns of the black-and-white mosaic sidewalks certainly do give that impression.

A statue there honors Pedro IV, emperor of Brazil. The Estação do Rossio, the railway station on one side—one of the most bizarre in Europe—is built in what many have described as "Victorian Gothic" or "neo-Manueline." Also opening onto the square is the Teatro Nacional Dona Maria II.

Proceeding north, you arrive at the Praça dos Restauradores, with an obelisk commemorating the Portuguese overthrow of Spanish domination in 1640.

Beginning here is Lisbon's main boulevard, the **Avenida da Liberdade** (Avenue of Liberty), dating from 1880. Graced with

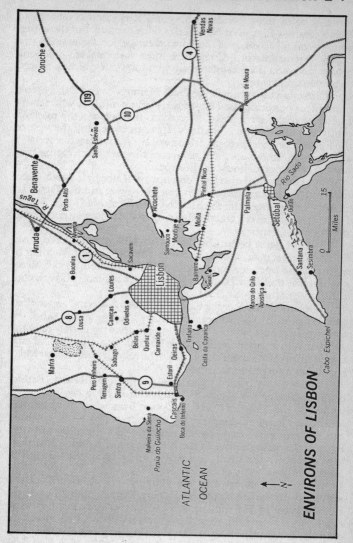

ENVIRONS OF LISBON

gardens, palm trees, ponds with swans, it is often compared to Paris's Champs-Élysées or New York's Fifth Avenue. But those suggestions are misleading, as the Portuguese avenue maintains a distinctly original flavor. Along this most fashionable, mile-long promenade, you'll encounter many outdoor cafés, airline offices, restaurants, and shops.

Crowning the avenue is the Praça Marquês de Pombal, a heroic monument honoring the 18th-century prime minister who rebuilt Lisbon after the earthquake. Directly to the north is the magnificently laid-out Parque Eduardo VII, commemorating the visit of the English king to Portugal. It's one of the most attractive spots in all of Lisbon. In the northern section of the park is the Estufa Fria, one of the best greenhouses in Europe.

The commercial district ("downtown" Lisbon) is **Baixa,** a sector which is centered mainly between the Rossio and the Tagus. Its three principal streets are the Rua do Ouro (Street of Gold), Rua da Prata (Street of Silver), and the Rua Augusta. All three streets lead to the Praça do Comércio.

West of Baixa is the **Chiado,** higher up and considered more fashionable. Its main street is known as the Rua Garrett, in honor of a Portuguese poet, an appropriate commemoration, as this street has been the traditional gathering place for the literati. Today it contains some of the city's finest stores.

Looking down over the Chiado is **Bairro Alto** (the upper quarter). When many visitors see the laundry flapping in the wind, the fishwives, the narrow, cobblestone streets, they think they're in the Alfama. Not so, but much of this district was, like the Alfama, spared from the destruction of the earthquake. It is of interest today because of its excellent fado cafés.

The western quarter of Lisbon is known as **Belém** (Bethlehem). In reality, it's a suburb, characterized by its world-famous landmark, the Tower of Belém, the point from which the explorers set out in the age of discovery (at Belém, the Tagus—after a long run beginning in Spain—pours into the sea). Opening onto the Praça do Império (Square of the Empire) is the Jerónimos Monastery, and down the street, on the Rua de Belém, is the Coach Museum.

Lisbon is connected to the working-class district, **Cacilhas,** which lies on the left bank of the Tagus, by the Ponte 25 de Abril. Built at a cost of $75 million, it is the longest and most expensive suspension bridge in Europe. Before it was opened, Lisbon was cut off from the south, except by ferryboat connections. The bridge is 7,473 feet long, its towers rising to a height of 625 feet. A herculean statue of Christ, his arms stretching out to the sky, stands watch over the southern banks of the Tagus. Tourists and Portuguese alike, by the way, visit Cacilhas because of its seafood.

FLYING TO LISBON: If you wish to fly directly to Lisbon from North America, as most visitors will, there are two major airlines that do so: **TAP** (the Portuguese international airline) and **Trans World Airlines.** TAP gives passengers the option of stopping midway across the Atlantic in the Azores and makes baggage transfers and seat reservations on connecting flights within Portugal easier.

Like the early Portuguese explorers, the airline goes to four continents, touching down in New York, Boston, Toronto, and Montréal, plus nine destinations within Portugal. TAP flies frequently on much-used routes originating in most of the major capitals of Western Europe. Its routes to Lisbon from London are especially value-conscious, sometimes priced so attractively that a client might combine a sojourn through England with an inexpensive side excursion to Portugal.

Several ticket options exist for transatlantic passengers eager to experience both Portugal and its national carrier. Winter bargains, when certain restrictions apply, are available between January and March, when Lisbon is arguably at its most serenely untrammeled.

Most passengers, however, prefer to travel in Portugal in the spring, summer, and autumn. At those times, TAP's most popular and lowest-priced ticket is called a midweek APEX fare. Its price varies with the season, but is competitive with similar fares carrying similar restrictions on other airlines. Tickets must be purchased 14 to 21 days before your departure, depending on the day you intend to leave. In some cases, a $100 penalty is imposed for any changes made after payment of either leg of a passenger's itinerary. For families, one strong attraction is the fact that children under 12 traveling with a parent pay between 50% and 67% of the adult fare.

Travelers who prefer not to specify when they will return home, or who can't purchase their tickets 14 or 21 days prior to takeoff, usually opt for an excursion fare. Costing more than either of the APEX options, it requires that passengers delay using the return half of their ticket from 10 to 180 days before jetting back to North America. On this ticket, peak season lasts from June 15 to August 15.

For exact departure dates and up-to-the-minute tariffs, you can phone a reservations clerk at **TAP Air Portugal** (tel. 212/944-2100, or toll free 800/221-7370 outside New York City) or consult a travel agent. In Lisbon, for ticket sales, flight reservations, and information about the city and the country, you can get in touch with the polite and efficient personnel of TAP Air Portugal at 3 Praça

Marquês de Pombal (tel. 54-40-80, the airline's reservation number).

Charter Flights

Strictly for reasons of economy, some travelers may wish to accept the numerous restrictions and possible uncertainties of a charter flight to Portugal. Charters require that passengers strictly specify departure and return dates, and full payment is required in advance. Any changes in flight dates are possible (if at all) upon payment of a stiff penalty. Any reputable travel agent can advise you about fares, cities of departure, and most important, the reputation of the charter company.

Airports

Both foreign and domestic flights arrive at Lisbon's **Portela Airport,** which lies about four miles from the heart of the city. For all airport information, telephone 80-20-60 or 80-45-00. A green line bus, called *Ligne Verte,* carries passengers into the city for 95$ (70¢) to 190$ ($1.70), depending on how many zones you cross. However, I'd recommend a taxi instead, as the cost is only about $5 (U.S.), which is certainly worth it considering the comfort and convenience.

GETTING AROUND LISBON: If all the attractions lay on the
Avenida da Liberdade, getting around Lisbon would be easy. As it is, many of the most charming nooks lie on streets too steep or too narrow for automobiles. Thus a good pair of walking shoes is essential for the explorer who really wants to get to know Lisbon.

Lisbon is suitably endowed with a quite adequate public transportation system that is cheap if not always convenient. At any rate, some form of public or private transportation is necessary, as most of the major attractions of Lisbon are in such suburbs or neighboring centers as Belém, Queluz, or Sintra. Also, many visitors prefer to anchor into hotels along the nearby Costa do Sol (Estoril, Cascais) and make frequent trips into Lisbon, so mastering the transportation network is essential—even for short-time visitors.

Taxis

Taxis in Lisbon tend to be cheap and are a popular means of transport for all but the most economy-minded of tourists. The taxis are usually diesel-engine Mercedes, charging a basic fare of 70$ (55¢) for the first 400 yards. After that, you'll be assessed another 6$ (5¢) for each additional 180 yards, with 20% additional for night fare from 10 p.m. to 6 a.m. The driver is allowed by law to tack on another 50% to your bill if your total luggage weighs in at more than

66 pounds. If you travel outside Lisbon, the driver is allowed to charge you 31$ (25¢) per kilometer. Most Portuguese tip about 20% of an already-modest fare.

Many visitors anchor at one of the Costa do Sol resort hotels, perhaps in Estoril or Cascais. If that is your situation, then you'll probably find taxi connections from Lisbon prohibitively expensive. Far preferable for Costa do Sol visitors is the electric train system (see below).

Trams and Buses

These are among the cheapest in Europe. The trolley cars, such as those that make the steep run up to the Bairro Alto, are usually painted a rich Roman gold. The double-decker buses, on the other hand, come from London and look as if they need Big Ben in the background to complete the picture. If you're trying to stand on the platform at the back of a jammed bus, by the way, you'll need both hands free to hold on.

At the foot of the Santa Justa elevator on the Rua Aurea, a stand will give you a schedule pinpointing the zigzagging route of these trams and buses. Your hotel concierge also should be of help to you.

You will pay a flat fare of 90$ (70¢) on a bus and a basic fare of 72$50 (55¢) on a streetcar if you buy your ticket from the driver. There are now a very limited number of buses and streetcars with conductors. These tickets allow you to ride through the five zones of the public transportation system within the city limits. Almost every passenger now purchases books of 10 or 20 tickets, with which a person pays for rides as follows: On buses, for one zone, one ticket costing 20$25 (15¢); two to four zones, two tickets costing 40$50 (30¢); five or more zones and also express buses, three tickets costing 60$75 (45¢). On streetcars, for one zone, use one ticket costing 20$25 (15¢); for two or more zones, two tickets costing 40$50 (30¢).

Subways

Lisbon's Metro stations are designated by large **M** signs lit at night, but some readers have reported difficulty in locating them, as several are missing. A single fare purchased at a vending machine is only 37$50 (30¢). A series of ten tickets costs only 30$ (25¢) per ride. One of the most popular trips, and likely to be jam-packed on corrida days, is from the Avenida da Liberdade to the Campo Pequeno, that brick bullring away from the center of the city.

Electric Trains

Lisbon is connected with all the towns and villages along the Portuguese Riviera by a smooth-running electric train system. You can board the train at the waterfront **Cais do Sodré** station in Lisbon, heading up the coast all the way to Cascais, the end of the run.

Only one class of seat is offered, and the rides are cheap. For example, if you go all the way—that is, Lisbon to Cascais—the one-way fare is 100$ (75¢). From Lisbon to Estoril, the one-way fare is also 100$. Sintra, that third major destination in the environs, is not reached by the electric train. You must go to the Estação do Rossio railway station, opening onto the Praça Dom Pedro IV or the Rossio, where frequent connections can be made.

For information about rail travel in Portugal, telephone 87-60-25 in Lisbon.

Portugal doesn't have a vast railway network. It is possible, however, to travel by electrified train to Porto in the north, leaving from Sta. Apolonia Station in Lisbon. Reservations are absolutely necessary.

Daily express trains in summer depart Lisbon for the Algarve (except on Sunday). These leave from the Barreiro Station (across the Tagus—take one of the ferries departing frequently). Off-season service is reduced to four times weekly.

Ferryboats

Long before the advent of the Ponte 25 de Abril (see below), the reliable ferryboats chugged across the Tagus, connecting the left bank with the right. They still do, as popular as ever, as many Portuguese find the bridge too expensive to traverse with their automobiles. Therefore they leave their cars at home and take the ferryboat to work.

Most of the boats leave from the Praça do Comércio, heading for Barreiro and Cacilhas. The one-way fare on the ferryboat is 55$ (40¢) per passenger. You can take your car over on the ferry as well for 80$ (60¢) to 140$ ($1.05), depending on the car. Or else you can drive on the:

Ponte 25 de Abril

As mentioned, this suspension bridge, the largest ever built in Europe, connects Lisbon with its left bank and the district south of the Tagus. For a small car, the toll charge is 35$ (25¢), increasing to 70$ (55¢) for a larger automobile. A van pays 120$ (90¢). Not only can you take the bridge to reach Cacilhas, but you can use it for such cities as Setúbal in the south and Évora, the old Roman city in the east.

Car Rentals

So many of the scenic parts of Portugal are so isolated from a train or bus station that having a private car is almost mandatory if

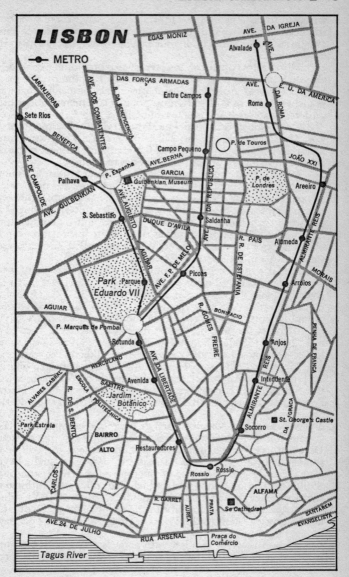

you plan to do much serious touring. That way, you're your own free agent, unhindered by the somewhat fickle timetables of trains and buses, which often limit your excursions to places close to the beaten track.

Most visitors opt for an auto-rental plan providing weekly vehicle use with unlimited kilometers included in the overall price. Some of North America's major car-rental companies maintain branches at each of Portugal's most popular commercial and tourist centers, at rates that are usually competitive.

On my most recent trip, I used the services of **Budget Rent-A-Car.** The staff volunteered to deliver my car to any location I specified in Lisbon and sent a personal representative to meet me at the airport upon my arrival early on a Sunday morning.

Like the other companies, Budget requires at least a 48-hour advance reservation period to guarantee their low rates on a variety of cars. If you plan to travel as economically as possible, Budget's rate in high season for their smallest car, a Renault 4, is about $179 per week with unlimited mileage. Budget (and its competitors) must add a 17% tax on all rentals. Up-to-date information can be obtained prior to your trip directly from the staff at Budget's reservation center in Dallas (tel. toll free 800/527-0700).

Avis has an office at the airport in Lisbon, plus as many as ten convenient offices in Lisbon and Estoril. The main office is at 12-C Avenida Praia da Vittoria in Lisbon (tel. 56-11-77). Unlimited mileage is only available by the week at a rate of 25,270$ ($189.50) in high season, 22,540$ ($169) in shoulder season, and 17,990$ ($140) in low season. These prices are for cars in class A. They go up to 112,140$ ($841), 100,l00$ ($751), and 98,840$ ($740) for vehicles in the most luxurious category, depending on the season.

Likewise, **Hertz** is represented throughout Portugal, offering well-maintained cars which tend to be slightly more expensive than those at Budget. For reservations and information about Hertz's Portuguese facilities, call toll free within the U.S. 800/654-3001.

A WARNING ABOUT INSURANCE. Each of the rental companies offers a certain amount of coverage automatically built into the contract. Despite this coverage, in the event of an accident you will be responsible for a certain dollar amount of damage (usually beginning, according to the value of the car you've rented, at around $500). Most companies (Budget included) offer an additional insurance policy, called a collision damage waiver (CDW), which eliminates all financial liability in the event of an accident. If in doubt, buy it—I always do. Prices begin at $4.35 (U.S.) per day.

GAS. Lisbon is well provided with garages and gasoline pumps; some are open around the clock. If you're motoring in the provinces, best fill up, as in some parts of the country gasoline stations are few and far between.

Hitchhiking

There's no law against it, yet it isn't commonly practiced. If you decide to hitchhike, do so with discretion.

THE ABCs OF LISBON

It's maddening to have your trip marred by an incident that could have been avoided if you'd been tipped off previously. Seeking medical care, getting your hair cut, or ferreting out the nearest toilet can at times become a paramount problem. Although I don't promise to answer all your questions, there are a variety of services in Lisbon that can ease your adjustment into the city.

The concierge in your hotel is a usually reliable dispenser of information, bullfight tickets, general advice, or assistance in pleading with your wife (or husband) to speak to you again after your too-friendly attention to a *fadista*. However, should your hotel not be staffed with an English-speaking person, or should you desire more detailed answers to your questions, the following brief summary of some of Lisbon's "facts of life" may prove helpful.

The **telephone area code** for Lisbon is 01.

AMERICAN EXPRESS: The representative of American Express in Lisbon, **STAR Travel Service,** can accommodate most banking and mailing needs, providing you're a client. Its offices are at 4-A Avenida Sidónio Pais (tel. 53-98-71). It's open from 9 a.m. until 12:30 p.m. and 2 to 6 p.m. weekdays; closed on Saturday and Sunday. The offices are near Pombal Square and easily reached by bus. There you can buy traveler's checks and tickets for tours, exchange currency, and cash American Express traveler's checks.

BABYSITTERS: Check with the staff of your hotel for arrangements. Most first-class hotels can provide competent women or girls for babysitting from lists that the concierge keeps. At smaller establishments, the girl is likely to be the daughter of the proprietor. Rates are low. Remember to request a babysitter no later than in the morning if you're going out that evening.

BANKS: Check with your home bank before your departure, as many banks in Canada and the United States have affiliates in Lisbon. The majority of the banks open at 8:30 a.m., closing at 11:45 a.m. Afternoon hours are from 1 to 2:45 p.m. A trio of major Portuguese banks are **Banco Português do Atlântico,** 112 Rua Aurea (tel. 36-64-15); the **Banco Espírito Santo e Comercial de Lisboa,** 195 Avenida da Liberdade (tel. 57-80-05); and at the airport a branch of **Banco Totta & Açores** (tel. 88-40-11), which is open at all hours of the day and night, including holidays.

CIGARETTES: The price of American-brand cigarettes (which varies) is always lethal. Bring in at least 200 cigarettes as allowed by Customs. If you're saving money, try as an adventure one of the Portuguese brands. Many smokers have found Portuguese tobacco excellent.

CLIMATE: The climate of Portugal is most often compared to that of California, with the rainfall occurring mostly in the winter, the summers tending to be dry. Where the border touches Spain's Galicia, Portugal is on the same latitude as New York—but there the resemblance ends, thanks to the mitigating force of the Gulf Stream.

For most tastes, spring through autumn is the best time for a Portuguese vacation. But many visitors head to the Algarve in the south in winter. At Madeira, winter is high season.

From November through March, the average temperatures in Lisbon and Estoril range between 46° and 65° Fahrenheit. June through August, the range is 60° to 82° Fahrenheit.

LISBON: AVERAGE MONTHLY TEMPERATURES

	HIGH	LOW		HIGH	LOW
January	56	46	July	81	63
February	59	47	August	82	64
March	62	50	September	78	62
April	66	53	October	72	58
May	69	55	November	63	52
June	76	60	December	57	47

CLOTHING SIZES: See "The ABCs of Madrid" in Chapter IX.

CURRENCY: Portugal is one of the most inexpensive countries in which to travel in Europe. But first-time American visitors often panic at price quotations because Portugal uses the same dollar sign ($) to designate its currency. The Portuguese **escudo** is written as 1$00—the dollar sign between the escudo and the **centavo**. Banknotes are issued for 20, 30, 50, 100, 500, and 1,000 escudos. In coins of silver and copper, the denominations for escudos are 1,

2.50, 5, 10, and 20. In centavos (100 to the escudo), the denominations are 10, 20, and 50.

It is possible to exchange your money at your arrival at Portela Airport; the bank there is open all the time.

CUSTOMS: You may be asked how much tobacco you're bringing in: the limit is 200 cigarettes or 50 cigars. One still camera with five unexposed rolls of film is allowed duty free; also a small movie camera with two reels, a portable tape recorder, a portable record player with ten "used" records, a portable typewriter, a portable radio, a portable musical instrument, and a bicycle (not motor bikes). Campers and sporting types are allowed to bring in one tent and camping accessories (including a kayak not exceeding 18 feet), a pair of skis, two tennis rackets, a tackle set, and a small firearm (for hunting only) with 50 bullets. A normal-size bottle of wine and a half-pint of hard alcohol are permitted, as are a "small quantity" of perfume and a half-pint of toilet water.

Upon leaving Portugal, citizens of the United States who have been outside the U.S. for 48 hours or more are allowed to bring in $400 worth of merchandise duty free—that is, if they have claimed no similar exemption within the past 30 days. Beyond this free allowance, the next $1,000 worth of merchandise is assessed at a flat rate of 10% duty. If you make purchases in Portugal, it's important to keep your receipts. On gifts, the duty-free limit has been increased to $50.

DENTIST: Place a call to **Centro de Medicina Dentaria,** 1 Calçada Bento da Rocha Cabral (tel. 68-41-91).

DOCUMENTS FOR ENTRY: Canadians, Americans, and the British need only a valid passport to enter Portugal.

ELECTRIC CURRENT: Many North Americans find that their plugs will not fit into sockets in Portugal, where the voltage is 200 volts AC, 50 cycles. Adapters and transformers may be purchased once you're in Lisbon. It's always best to check at your hotel desk before plugging in any electrical equipment.

EMBASSIES: If you lose your passport, or have some other pressing problem, you'll need to get in touch with the **U.S. Embassy,** on the Avenida das Forças Armadas (à Sete Rios) (tel. 726-66-00). Hours are 8:30 a.m. to 12:30 p.m. and 1:30 to 5 p.m. If you've lost a passport, a photographer will be recommended who can provide the proper size photos for American passports. The **Canadian Embassy** is at 2 Rua Rosa Araujo (tel. 56-38-21); the **British Embassy,**

37 Rua São Domingos à Lapa (tel. 66-11-91); and the **Australian Embassy,** 244 Avenida da Liberdade (tel. 53-91-08).

EMERGENCIES: For the police (or for an ambulance) in Lisbon, telephone 115. In case of fire, call 32-22-22. The Portuguese Red Cross can be reached at 61-77-77.

FILM: This is so expensive that I suggest you bring in all that Customs will allow. There are no special restrictions on photographs, except in certain museums.

HAIRDRESSERS: Men are advised to go to any of the big barbershops in the deluxe hotels, such as the Ritz Inter-Continental in Lisbon. For women, three hairdressers in Lisbon are particularly recommendable: **Cabeleireiro Martins,** 31-1° Dt. Avenida Defensores de Chaves (tel. 54-89-33); **Cabeleireiro Isabel Queiroz do Vale,** 35-1° Avenida Fontes Pereira de Melo (tel. 54-82-38); and **Lúcia Piloto,** 12 Avenida da Liberdade (tel. 32-05-35).

HOLIDAYS AND FESTIVALS: Watch those holidays and adjust your banking needs, or whatever, accordingly. Aside from the regular holidays such as Christmas, Portugal has a few all its own: Universal Brotherhood Day on January 1; a Memorial Day to the country's greatest poet, Camões, on June 10; Assumption Day, August 15; the anniversary of the republic, October 5; All Saints' Day on November 1; Independence Day on December 1; and the Feast of the Immaculate Conception on December 8. Good Friday and the Feast of Corpus Christi are also holidays, but their dates differ every year.

LANGUAGES: One writer suggested that Portuguese has "the hiss and rush of surf crashing against the bleak rocks of Sagres." If you don't speak it, you'll find French, Spanish, and English commonly spoken in Lisbon, along the Costa do Sol, and in Porto, as well as in many parts of the Algarve. In small villages and towns, hotel staffs and guides usually speak English. The native tongue is difficult, but the Portuguese people are helpful and patient. Gestures often suffice.

LAUNDRY: Most hotels in this guide provide laundry services, but if you want your garment returned on the same day, you'll often be charged from 20% to 40% more. Simply present your maid or valet with your laundry or dry cleaning (usually lists are provided). Note: Materials needing special treatment (such as certain synthetics) should be called to the attention of the person handling your laundry. Some establishments I've dealt with in the past treated every fabric as if it were cotton.

Do-it-yourselfers in Lisbon may want to take their clothes to a self-service laundry, **Lavimpa,** 22-A Avenida de Paris (tel. 89-03-88). Metro: Alvalade. The laundry is part of a chain.

LIBRARIES: If you're looking for a library for research or whatever, the **Biblioteca Nacional de Lisboa,** 83 Campo Grande (tel. 76-77-86), near University City, contains more than a million volumes (books, periodicals, non-book material). It is open from 9:45 a.m. to 5:30 p.m. Monday to Friday, mid-July to mid-September; from 9:45 a.m. to 8 p.m. Monday to Friday and from 9:45 a.m. to 5 p.m. on Saturday in winter. In addition, the **American Cultural Center** at 22-B Avenida Duque de Loulé (tel. 57-01-02) has a library of some 8,000 volumes and 132 periodicals. It is open from 2 to 6 p.m. on Tuesday, Wednesday, and Friday, to 7 p.m. on Monday and Thursday.

LIQUOR LAWS: You have to be 18 years of age to drink liquor in the bars of Portugal. Liquor is sold in most markets, as opposed to package stores in the United States. In Lisbon you can drink till dawn. There's always some bar or some fado club open serving alcoholic beverages.

MAIL DELIVERY: While in Portugal you may have your mail directed to your hotel (or hotels), to the American Express representative, or to General Delivery (*Poste Restante*) in Lisbon. Your passport must be presented for mail pickups. Open 24 hours a day, the general post office in Lisbon is at Praça dos Restauradores (tel. 37-00-51).

MEDICAL CARE: Portugal does not have free medical service. The concierge at your hotel can usually put you in touch with the house doctor, or summon him or her in case of emergencies. You can also call the **U.S. Embassy,** Avenida das Forças Armadas (à Sete Rios) (tel. 726-66-00), and ask the consular section there to give you a copy of its list of English-speaking physicians; or the **British Hospital,** 49 Rua Savaiva Carvalho (tel. 60-20-20), where the telephone operator, staff, and doctors all speak English, naturally.

METRIC MEASURES: See "The ABCs of Madrid" in Chapter IX.

NEWSPAPERS: The *International Herald Tribune* is sold at most newsstands in Lisbon, either in major hotels or else along the street.

OFFICE HOURS: Hours in general are from 9 a.m. to 5 or 5:30 p.m., with a two-hour break for lunch between 1 and 3 p.m.

PETS: Pets brought into Portugal must have the okay of the local veterinarian and a health certificate from their home country.

PHARMACIES: The Portuguese government requires selected pharmacies (*farmácias*) to stay open at all times of the day and night. This is effected by means of a rotation system. So check with your concierge for locations and hours of the nearest drugstores, called *farmácias de serviço*. In general, chemists in Portugal are open from 9 a.m. to 1 p.m. and 3 to 7 p.m. A popular one is the **Farmácia Azevedos,** 31 Rossio (tel. 32-74-78).

POLITICS: The dust of the revolution has long settled. The Portugese Republic, after years of dictatorship, is a democratic state, and tourists can travel without restrictions into every province of the land.

RADIO AND TV: In Lisbon there are two major TV channels— Channel 1 (VHF) and Channel II (UHF). Many foreign films are shown, often in English with Portuguese subtitles. Visitors to Portugal may want to listen to the radio every day at 8:15 a.m. when a 45-minute program—called "Holidays in Portugal"—is broadcast on the Metropolitan wavelength in English. Much helpful advice is offered for touring the country.

RELIGIOUS SERVICES: Portugal is a Catholic country, and there are places of worship in every city, town, and village—far too numerous to document here. If you're a Protestant, a Baptist evangelical church exists in Lisbon. It's the **Igreja Evangélica Baptista de Lisboa,** 36-B Rua Filipe Folque (tel. 53-53-62), with Sunday services (in Portuguese) at 10 and 11 a.m. and 7:30 p.m. (also at 7:30 p.m. on Wednesday). For Jewish readers, services are usually held twice weekly at the **Shaare Tikua Synagogue,** 59 Rua Alexandre Herculano (tel. 68-15-92), on Friday at 7 p.m. and on Saturday at 10:30 a.m.

REST ROOMS: All major terminals (airports and railways) have such facilities, and Lisbon has several public ones. However, you can often use one at a café or tavern, as one of these establishments exists practically within every block. It is considered polite to purchase something, however—perhaps a small glass of wine or whatever.

TAXES: Since Portugal and neighboring Spain simultaneously joined the European Economic Community (EEC), or Common Market, on January 1, 1986, Portugal has imposed a Value Added Tax on most purchases made within its borders. Known in Portugal as the **I.V.A.**, its amount is almost always written into the bottom line on the bill of any purchase a foreign visitor might make. With many exemptions, goods fall into three categories. The essential commodities of life for the average Portuguese are taxed at 8%. Car rentals and hotel bills automatically include an additional 16% tax (less than in some other European countries). Such deluxe goods as jewelry, furs, and expensive imported liquors include a 30% built-in tax. Because a scotch and soda in a Portuguese bar carries this high tax, many imbibers have changed their choice of alcohol from scotch to Portuguese brandy and soda or, more prosaically, beer.

TELEGRAMS: At most hotels the receptionist will help you send a cable or telegram. If not, there is a cable dispatch service, open 24 hours a day, at **Marconi** (the Portuguese Radio Communications Office), 131 Rua S. Julião (tel. 36-45-38). To send international telegrams, telephone 113.

TELEPHONES: If you're calling locally in Lisbon, you can place your call at any number of telephone booths. However, you'll need some 1$00 coins, and preferably some 5$00 coins if you plan to talk more than three minutes or telephone long distance in the country. For most long-distance telephoning, particularly transatlantic calls, go to the central post office in Lisbon at the Praça dos Restauradores (tel. 37-00-51). Give an assistant there the number you wish, and she'll make the call for you, billing you at the end.

TELEX: Ask your hotel for assistance.

TIME: Portugal is six hours ahead of the United States (Eastern Standard Time). For the local time in Lisbon, phone 15. Daylight Saving Time (standard time plus one hour) is in effect from the last Sunday in March to the last Sunday in September.

TIPPING: The following tips on tipping are merely guidelines.
The **hotels** add a service charge (known as *serviço*) which is divided among the entire staff. But individual tipping is also the rule of the day: 50$ (40¢) to the bellhop for errands run, 50$ (40¢) to the doorman who calls you a cab, 50$ (40¢) to the porter for each piece of luggage carried, 150$ ($1.15) to the wine steward if you've

dined often at your hotel, and 150$ ($1.15) to the chambermaid for stays of less than a week. However, in deluxe hotels, the chambermaid should get 200$ ($1.50) and the wine steward 300$ ($2.25) if you've dined at the hotel. Porters get 70$ (55¢) for each piece of luggage.

In first-class or deluxe hotels, the concierge will present you with a separate bill, outlining your little or big extras, such as charges for bullfight tickets, etc. A gratuity is expected in addition to the charge, the amount depending entirely on the number of requests you've put to him.

Hairdressers: For a normal haircut, you should leave 50$ (40¢) behind as a tip to the barber. But if your hair is cut at the Ritz, don't dare leave less than 100$ (75¢). Beauticians get 150$ ($1.15); a manicurist, around 100$ (75¢).

Taxis: Figure on about 20% of the regular fare for short runs. For longer treks—for example, from the airport to Cascais—15% is adequate.

Porters: The porters at the airport or train stations generally charge you 25$ (20¢) per piece of luggage. In addition, you should tip another 25$ (20¢).

Restaurants: Restaurants and nightclubs include service charge and government taxes. As in the hotels, this service is distributed among the entire staff, including the waiter's mistress and the proprietor's grandfather—so extra tipping is customary. Add about 5% to the bill in a moderately priced restaurant, up to 10% in deluxe or first-class establishments.

Services: Hatcheck women in fado houses, restaurants, and nightclubs expect at least 50$ (40¢). The women who stand on sentinel duty in washrooms usually get no more than 25$ (20¢). The shoeshine boys of Portugal are the most undertipped creatures in Portuguese society. Here I recommend greater generosity, providing the shine was good.

TOURIST INFORMATION: The **Portuguese National Tourist Board** is at 86 Avenida António Augusto de Aguiar in Lisbon (tel. 57-50-86). The public information section is housed at the Palácio Foz at Praça dos Restauradores (tel. 36-33-14), and at the Lisbon airport (tel. 88-59-74). For information or facts about Portugal before heading there, you can make contact with the **Portuguese National Tourist Office**, 548 Fifth Ave., New York, NY 10036 (tel. 212/354-4403).

WEATHER INFORMATION: If you don't speak Portuguese, ask someone at your hotel desk to translate one of the weather reports that appear daily in the leading newspapers of Lisbon.

CHAPTER III

HOTELS IN AND AROUND LISBON

□ □ □

In searching for a hotel, it's best to think of the Portuguese capital as "Greater Lisbon." For Lisbon differs from most European capitals in that it can be visited on a day trip (or several day trips) from one of several attractive resorts along the Costa do Sol, such as Estoril or Cascais. Few capitals in Europe offer such resort-style accommodations so close to metropolitan life.

If you're arriving anytime between April 1 and October 1 and planning a fairly long stay, you may want to find an attractive resort hotel on the sea, venturing into Lisbon only for sightseeing excursions, fado singing, shopping, or whatever. If your stay is for only two or three days, you'll want to stay in Lisbon proper, as it takes more time to adjust to life in a resort hotel. And if your visit is in off-season, you'll doubtless prefer a city lodging.

When staying along the Costa do Sol, the matter of transportation to Lisbon is taken care of by either renting a car or using the electric train system running from Cascais along the coast to Lisbon.

GOVERNMENT-CONTROLLED PRICES: In my selections —the majority of which are within Lisbon city limits—I have mainly kept to establishments the Portuguese government rates as "first-class." First-class hotels in Portugal, however, are moderate in price. Many would even be considered "budget" by some. In some cases, there is a slight distinction made between a first-class "A" hotel and a first-class "B" hotel. But often this is only a legal, technical difference that's of interest more to badge-wearing bureaucrats than to tourists.

At the reception desk of your hotel, you'll see (or should see) a sign on which the official tariffs are quoted. In Portugal, the Directorate of Tourism regulates the price a hotel owner may charge clients. To that official rate, a 10% charge is added for service, plus an additional 3.1% "tourist tax," which is another way the government has of earning a bonus from the influx of foreign visitors.

OFF-SEASON DISCOUNTS: Off-season visitors find that the government requires hotels or inns along the coast—and especially in the southern province of the Algarve—to give you a reduction of at least 15% on room charges. Off-season is November to February. Many establishments, of course, grant greater reductions than this, often extending the time limit from mid-October to April 1. From November to March, hotels in Estoril grant reductions that average around 15%. Few Lisbon hotels grant off-season discounts; rates are the same year round.

The recommendations in this guide include a few of the older, more established lodgings, but generally the hotels are products of the 1960s, 1970s, and 1980s, and come complete with modern equipment and furnishings.

If the expense of a first-class accommodation is too much for a lean budget, you have an ample choice of smaller hotels and pensions or boarding houses (listed further on) where you can live inexpensively, the more so if you take all three meals at your lodging place.

REMINDER: When telephoning for information or reservations, the telephone area code for Lisbon—and for all the hotels listed in this chapter—is 01.

LISBON'S HOTELS

DELUXE HOTELS: The **Ritz Inter-Continental,** 88 Rua Rodrigo da Fonseca, 1000 Lisboa (tel. 69-20-20). You can't lose with a name like "the Ritz," especially when such a hotel lives up to its tradition. This is Lisbon's most prestigious accommodation, now a part of Inter-Continental Hotels Corporation. "The Ritz, please," is all you need to tell your cab driver. Close to everything, the 12-story modern structure faces the capital's Edward VII Park.

Four elevators serve the 254 rooms and 50 suites of the hotel, where an entire floor (30 rooms and five suites) has been allotted for use of nonsmokers. Suites at the Ritz are top-drawer, furnished with antiques such as fringed canopy beds, fine Italian and Portuguese wood pieces, and inlaid desks and chairs. All the rooms are comfortable, spacious, and well kept, each equipped with a balcony, marble bath with complete facilities and amenities, hairdryer, mini-bar, radio, color TV (both local and satellite), direct-dial phone, and air conditioning. The price of singles ranges from 18,000$ ($135) to 23,000$ ($173); doubles rent for 20,000$ ($150) to 27,000$ ($203). Suites, which include a sitting room and boudoir, cost more.

The hotel offers a wide variety of dining pleasure in its three restaurants. In the Grill, classical music accompanies dinner, while music in the Varanda is furnished by Portuguese guitar players. In the Snack Ritz, guests can enjoy a fast and light meal in an agreeable atmosphere. Near the lobby is the Piano Bar.

An Executive Service Center is part of the hotel's facilities, for use by business people as a meeting place and working site. It is equipped with all the communications devices and services modern business requires.

The **Lisboa-Sheraton Hotel & Towers,** 1 Rua Latino Coelho, 1000 Lisboa (tel. 57-57-57), is one of the tallest buildings in Portugal, rising 30 stories. Opened in 1972, the hotel boasts 400 bedrooms in a fine position on a prominent boulevard near Edward VII Park. The bedrooms all have temperature control, satellite TVs, direct-dial phones with message alert, and hi-fi radios. Singles range in price from 16,000$ ($120) to 23,000$ ($173). Two people pay 19,000$ ($143) to 26,000$ ($195) for a twin-bedded room. The tariffs include tax and an American-style buffet breakfast. Crowning the tower room complex is the Panorama Room and Bar overlooking the city, with a stunning view of old and new Lisbon. A buffet lunch and à la carte dinners are served in the Caravela Restaurant, and the Alfama Grill features regional Portuguese dishes. Among the facilities of the hotel are a health club, open-air heated swimming pool, shopping arcade, beauty parlor, and barbershop.

The **Hotel Meridien,** 149 Rua Castilho, 1000 Lisboa (tel. 69-09-00), opened in 1985, takes advantage of the nearby Edward VII Park, whose verdancy is reflected in the wrap-around windows that fill each of the bedrooms with Iberian sunshine. The air-conditioned lobby glitters with talc-white marble, polished chromium, and mirrors. A symmetrical entranceway frames the tile-bottomed fountains where the splashing rises to the top of the sunlit atrium.

You'll find lots of attractive and interesting public rooms, including a tea room awash with Portuguese tiles, a ground-floor brasserie with a view of the park and the adjacent boulevard, and the formally glamorous Restaurant Atlantic. The hotel has a piano bar, plushly upholstered in maroon velvet, and a health club. The facilities are operated by a competent staff who combine French expertise with Portuguese capability. Depending on the season, the 331 handsomely furnished bedrooms rent for 17,000$ ($128) to 23,000$ ($173) in a single and 20,000$ ($150) to 27,000$ ($203) in a double, all tariffs including a continental breakfast.

The **Hotel Alfa Lisboa,** Avenida Columbano Bordalo Pinheiro, 1000 Lisbon (tel. 72-21-21), removed from the commercial center of the city, is a five-star hotel that has gained popularity with business travelers. The staff, young and charming, works hard to make visitors comfortable. At the imposing reception desk in the marble-floored lobby, you will be quoted rates of 10,500$ ($79) to 16,500$ ($124) for a single, 12,700$ ($95) to 20,000$ ($150) for a twin or double, with breakfast included.

The occupants of the hotel's 355 well-furnished rooms and junior suites can enjoy an array of drinking and dining facilities. The most formal is the Pombalino Restaurant, with an 18th-century Portuguese palatial décor and an international cuisine. On the second floor, A Perola is less formal, offering a selection of dietetic food. The most popular and least expensive selection is A Aldeia, a coffeeshop and restaurant decorated in regional Portuguese style. The Labirinto Bar, with a piano player nightly, is the most popular drinking spot, while Zacarias, on the 24th floor, is a night restaurant together with a bar and disco open till 3 a.m. Visitors appreciate the health club and massage facilities in the complex.

The **Avenida Palace,** 123 Rua 1 de Dezembro, 1100 Lisboa (tel. 36-01-54), is Lisbon's leading hotel-link to the past, a world reflected in crystal and antiques. The second-floor drawing room attracts those partial to the age of silk-brocade wall paneling, fringed velvet draperies, crystal chandeliers, marquetry tables, consoles, and hand-woven Portuguese carpets. Five tall windows in the dining room overlook the avenue. The location is noisy, right at the Rossio, minutes from fado clubs, restaurants, and some of Lisbon's major shops. Most of the rooms have been redone. The redecorated bedrooms are furnished in a traditional manner, with 18th-century antiques or artwork (most often reproductions), and are air-conditioned and centrally heated, with TV, mini-bar, and music. The walls are paneled, often with gilt trim. The spacious bathrooms are faced in Portuguese marble. A single room rents for $80 (U.S.), rising to $85 in a double room, and all tariffs include a continental breakfast. A lunch or dinner costs $15, taxes and service included.

The **Hotel Altis,** 11 Rua Castilho, 1200 Lisboa (tel. 52-24-96), is a five-star deluxe hotel with 225 rooms, including 13 suites, overlooking the city, in the commercial and cultural center of Lisbon. The hotel has a pleasant décor, an intimate European atmosphere, and high-quality, personalized service. The fully air-conditioned rooms are equipped with direct-dial phones, mini-bars, radios, and color TV via satellite. A new wing contains another 80 rooms. Singles cost from 14,000$ ($105); twins, from 16,000$ ($120). On the ground floor is a piano bar with live music. The Panoramic Bar and Grill Room on the top floor and the spacious Girassol Restaurant are attractive features that make your stay at the Altis a good one. The hotel also has a fully equipped health club, an indoor heated swimming pool, a coffeeshop, and a disco.

The **Hotel Tivoli,** 185 Avenida da Liberdade, 1200 Lisboa (tel. 53-01-81), has a choice location on the main boulevard of Lisbon. Large enough to accommodate more than 600 guests, it has bountiful public facilities. The two-story reception lobby has a mezzanine lounge with comfortable islands of furniture and Oriental rugs. Room prices are scaled according to position, the larger and more expensive ones facing the boulevard. Singles start at 16,000$ ($120), and doubles at 18,000$ ($135), the tariffs including a continental breakfast, service, and taxes. The air-conditioned rooms contain a mixture of modern and traditional pieces, with solid fabrics and walls. Each has a private bath, direct-dial phone, radio, color TV, and mini-bar.

The hotel's wood-paneled O Zodiaco restaurant is decorated with Easter egg–colored chairs and a wall plaque depicting astrological signs. Meals are all à la carte. On the top floor, O Terraço offers a view of Lisbon, plus à la carte meals with emphasis on steaks and chops that you select and have cooked on a tile charcoal grill. Adjoining the restaurant is a home-like salon with a wood-burning fireplace, Oriental rugs, and restrained décor.

Guests have access to the Tivoli Club, shared with patrons of the Tivoli Jardim (see below), surrounded by a beautiful garden, with a swimming pool (heated in winter), a tennis court, a solarium, and a bar. Light snacks are served.

The **Tivoli Jardim,** 7-9 Rua Júlio C. Machado, 1200 Lisboa (tel. 53-99-71), is the Tivoli's sister hotel, with a more contemporary design in the lounges and bedrooms. Positioned behind the Tivoli away from the traffic noises of the Avenida da Liberdade, it features a free parking area for guests. The air-conditioned structure is graced with balconies, two shafts of elevators, and well-styled accommodations. The rooms have a restrained décor, with rough white plaster walls and built-in furniture. Each unit has a color TV, mini-bar, direct-dial phone, radio, and a bathroom with patterned tile, bidet, shower, and tub. A glass wall, curtained at night, leads to the room's balcony, furnished in rattan. For a room with a continental breakfast, service, and taxes, a single costs 10,000$ ($75); a double 12,000$ ($94).

There are public lounges and a cathedral-high, glass-walled lobby dominated by a ceiling-high tapestry in sunburst colors. The tile and marble floors are peacock blue and emerald green. The dining room is tasteful, with white brick walls and green tables, its wall niches filled with Portuguese ceramics. The main decorative piece is a convoluted bronze sculpture. Guests of the Tivoli Jardim can use the facilities of the Tivoli Club, described above.

The **Príncipe Real,** 53 Rua da Alegria, 1200 Lisboa (tel. 36-01-16), is that intimate and highly personalized little hotel the traveler hopes to find in every big city. One *Los Angeles Times* newspaper columnist called it "one of the finest small hotels in Europe." It's in the neighborhood of the Botanical Gardens, in the center of Lisbon. The Príncipe Real is like a villa home, with a wood-burning fireplace, comfortable armchairs, and a windowseat nook. Well-selected antiques and reproductions have been placed throughout the hotel. Tiles, gilt and woodcarvings, ecclesiastical figures, an Empire lamp, a pieces-of-eight chest, an Oriental rug—all create the comfortable ambience. The little wood-paneled bar with its black leather chairs and red tile tables is one of the coziest spots in Lisbon for a before-dinner drink. The staff is superbly trained, one of the most helpful you're likely to encounter.

When you see the bedrooms, you'll understand why the Ritz sometimes sends overflow guests here. Each room has its own personality. Although each is compact, everything desirable seems to be there: fresh flowers in each room, unusual older-style beds, coordinated printed or solid fabrics at the windows and on the beds, tall mahogany swivel mirrors, an inlaid desk—all backed up by private baths, direct-dial phones, satellite TVs, bathrobes, and a newspaper if you stay more than one night. Rates are 10,000$ ($75) in singles, 12,500$ ($94) in doubles, and 14,000$ ($105) in triples. All tariffs include a continental breakfast, taxes, and service. The morning meal is served in the picture-window room on the top floor, with a slanted beamed ceiling, red velvet chairs, and a mahogany jewel box at the entrance.

The **Hotel Flórida,** 32 Rua Duque de Palmela, 1200 Lisboa (tel. 57-61-45), suits those desiring a first-class anchor in the center of Lisbon life, convenient to boutiques, shops, restaurants, and discos. From the restaurant, you overlook the circular Praça de Marquês de Pombal, with its statue of the 18th-century prime minister and a bronze lion guarding the top flank of the Avenida da Liberdade.

Modernized, the Flórida is decorated with vibrant colors to bring warmth to every room. For example, the main lounge—with walls of glass, a checkerboard floor of Portuguese marble, and comfortable sofas—draws constant lobby devotees. The 112 bedrooms —each with private bath, radio, air conditioning, and phone—have color-coordinated décor. A double room begins at 8,600$ ($64.50) and a single at 7,200$ ($54), with service, breakfast, and taxes included. There are a bar and a large lounge on the second floor, plus a winter garden.

The **Hotel Lutécia,** 52 Avenida Frei Miguel Contreiras, 1700 Lisboa (tel. 80-31-21), lies in the direction of the airport. This 12-story structure incorporates much comfort. There is air conditioning in its 151 rooms and suites, each unit has a private bath, and every guest has a private balcony. Twin beds are set against walls of fine-grained wood paneling, and the rooms all have color TV and a mini-bar and are filled with all sorts of "built-ins." The baths are tiled, the draperies soft and filmy, the furnishings up-to-date. Singles average 8,500$ ($63.75), and doubles run 9,500$ ($71.25), including a buffet breakfast, taxes, and service.

The reception area is spacious and smartly designed, as are the public rooms. The preferred place to dine is the rooftop lounge, with its grand vista; select one of the chef's specialties, cheese or meat fondues, or perhaps the smoked swordfish. Those in a hurry gravitate to the attractive snackbar on the second floor.

The **Hotel Mundial,** 4 Rua Dom Duarte, 1100 Lisboa (tel. 86-31-01), is a modern hotel in the heart of Lisbon, close to the Alfama. The hotel is properly manicured and serviced by a capable staff. The bedrooms are good, with restrained dignity enhanced by color coordination. A room with a gold-and-white-striped bedcover, for example, might have yellow draperies and a matching headboard wall to blend with herringbone parquet floors. Each of the 147 rooms is equipped with a tile bath, phone, radio, color TV, and air conditioning. Double rooms cost 9,600$ ($72), and singles go for 8,000$ ($60), including a continental breakfast and all taxes. The most expensive rooms have a private terrace.

On the top floor is a dining room offering a panoramic view of Lisbon, with St. George Castle in the background. The skilled chef prepares a four-course dinner, including, perhaps, gazpacho, grilled swordfish, braised veal tongue in madeira wine, and dessert.

OTHER TOP CHOICES: The **Dom Manuel I,** 187-189 Avenida Duque d'Avila, 1100 Lisboa (tel. 57-61-60), is for those who desire a high standard of living at a reasonable price. Its location is a little off-center, but not its taste level. A little hotel, it has a rear lounge styled as in a fine private home, with an Aubusson tapestry, a raised fireplace, and sofas and armchairs. A window looks out onto a planter of subtropical greenery. The intimate mezzanine cocktail lounge, with decorative brass fixtures, overlooks the living room. The lower-level dining room is in the typically Iberian style, with leather armchairs, tall candle torchères, and a large stained-glass rose window. The bedrooms, although small, are consistently winning. Singles go for 6,500$ ($48.75); doubles, 7,200$ ($54). A continental break-

fast is included in the rates. The accommodations contain many
built-in features and unusually fine bedcovers, color coordinated.

The **Hotel Dom Carlos,** 121 Avenida Duque de Loulé, 1000
Lisboa (tel. 53-90-71), is a cool and inviting choice, set back from a
busy boulevard and separated from the street by a small garden in
which canna and daisies bloom. An all-modern, 73-room, glassed-in
structure, the Dom Carlos lies just off Marquês de Pombal Square,
in the center of Lisbon. Around the corner is a service station and a
garage belonging to the hotel. A favorite spot is the cozy mezzanine
bar, ideal for a rendezvous. The staff and management are attentive
and courteous.

The bedrooms are paneled with a reddish South American
wood. Cleverly compact, the rooms utilize built-in pieces well and
come with air conditioning, TV, and radio. Doubles start at 6,800$
($51); singles, at 5,400$ ($40.50). These prices include a continen-
tal breakfast.

The **Hotel Fenix,** 8 Praça Marquês de Pombal, 1200 Lisboa (tel. 53-51-21), lives in the shadow of the Ritz. From its perch
at the top of the Avenida da Liberdade, it offers a location in
the heart of Lisbon. This eight-story hotel is owned by the Husa
chain. Most of the bedroom windows open onto views of Parque
Eduardo VII. Each of the 112 rooms is air-conditioned and has
a private bath with shower, built-in headboards, pushbutton service, and phone. For double- or twin-bedded rooms the charge is
11,200$ ($84), and for singles, 9,900$ ($74.25) daily. All taxes are
included.

There's a two-level reception lounge, with a hideaway mezzanine nook for drinks. On the ground floor is a rustic-style restaurant, the Bodegón, specializing in international food.

The **Hotel Jorge V,** 3 Rua Mouzinho da Silveira, 1100 Lisboa
(tel. 56-25-25), wraps up comforts and little amenities and ties them
with a ribbon of modest prices. Just off the Avenida da Liberdade, in
the heart of the shopping district, the George V is up-to-date. Built
in 1963, it provides balconies for some of the rooms. Light sleepers
may prefer the quieter chambers in the rear. You enter into a miniature reception lobby and a combination lounge-drinking bar dotted
with chairs and sofas in flashy colors.

Each bedroom is comfortable, and you'll find all the necessities: soft beds, built-in wardrobes, bedside tables and lights, air conditioning, and a small tile bath. Singles rent for 5,000$ ($37.50);
doubles, 7,000$ ($52.50) and up. A continental breakfast, taxes,
and service are included.

The **Hotel Rex,** 169 Rua Castilho, 1000 Lisboa (tel. 68-21-61),
is a fine establishment in a desirable location, a few steps from the

Hotel Ritz and the Hotel Meridien. It offers warmly decorated accommodations and a friendly staff at prices far below those of its prestigious neighbors. Many of the rooms have a spacious balcony, with views over Edward VII Park and the baroque Manueline church on its far side.

The cozy bedrooms have mini-bars, TVs, radios, tile baths, and built-in beds with wide edges covered in lengths of full-grain and well-rubbed Iberian leather. If you take one of the suites, you'll enjoy a sitting room with its own breeze-swept terrace, in addition to the comfortable bedroom. The rent is 10,500$ ($79) in a double, 9,000$ ($67.50) in a single.

From the large front windows of the elegant lobby, an unusual bronze statue of women bearing baskets is visible. The coffered wood-and-plaster ceiling adds the illusion of even greater height to the room. On the ground floor, an intimate restaurant, Cozinha d'El-Rey, has two levels lined with provincial artifacts. Another restaurant on the top floor offers a sweeping view of one of Lisbon's most beautiful parks as well as of the city below.

The **Hotel Presidente,** 13 Rua Alexandre Herculano, 1100 Lisboa (tel. 53-95-01). On a convenient, central corner near the Avenida da Liberdade and Edward VII Park, the Presidente is so clean-cut and modern that the effect is stark. Small enough to avoid staffs that overpower and intimidate, it contains only 59 rooms, each with private bath, central heating, air conditioning, and phone.

The rooms are compact, with chestnut-paneled walls and furniture more functional than stylish. Single rooms rent for 6,400$ ($48); doubles, 7,800$ ($58.50). A continental breakfast, the only meal served, is included.

The **Hotel Príncipe,** 201 Avenida Duque d'Avila, 1000 Lisboa (tel. 53-61-51), an establishment more than a quarter of a century old, is a favorite of visiting Spanish and Portuguese matadors. All of its large rooms have private baths, air conditioning, phones, music, and color TVs, and most have a private balcony. A single room costs 6,000$ ($45); a double, 8,000$ ($60). A continental breakfast is included. Full board is available at 6,900$ ($51.75) to 8,900$ ($66.75) per person, and those matadors do seem to like the Príncipe's dining room and bar.

LISBON'S BUDGET LODGINGS: Built as an apartment house, the **Residência Horizonte,** 42 Avenida António Agusto de Aguiar, 1000 Lisboa (tel. 53-95-26), has an impressively proportioned flight of stone steps leading up from the busy tree-lined boul-

evard outside. As you enter, the lower-level reception area is at the bottom of a short flight of stairs. What used to be the elegant lobby of the building is a bit grim today. Nonetheless, the 52 rooms upstairs are clean, freshly scrubbed, and unpretentiously comfortable. A few have a balcony. The units in the back are a little less sunny than those at the front, but they are also quieter. With breakfast included, singles rent for 3,800$ ($28.50); doubles, 4,500$ ($33.75). Metro: Parque.

The **Residência América,** 47 Rua Tomás Ribeiro, 1000 Lisboa (tel. 53-67-12), was built as a bank about 40 years ago and became a comfortable, simple hotel through later renovation. Each of the 36 bedrooms contains a private bath. The 1950s-style accommodations all differ in floor layout and size. The quiet rooms in back are somewhat smaller and darker than those in the front. Prices quoted by the young staff in the tiny lobby are 4,000$ ($30) for a single, 5,200$ ($39) for a double, and 6,200$ ($46.50) for a triple, all with breakfast included.

No visitor to the América should leave without checking out the seventh-floor bar, whose leatherette furniture has been there so long that by now it's back in style. Having a drink in this eyrie can be a lot of fun, giving a note of nostalgia to a stay here. The América has no restaurant.

The **Residência Imperador,** 55 Avenida 5 de Outubro, 1000 Lisboa (tel. 57-48-84), not far from the center, provides rooms with private baths or showers costing 3,000$ ($22.50) in a single, 3,800$ ($28.50) in a double. The front entryway, designed in Portuguese pinewood, is barely large enough for one's suitcase; however, the bedrooms and upper lounge are adequate in size. Opening onto balconies, the front bedrooms face a tiny private garden. The units are contemporary in concept, neatly planned with built-in beds and simple lines. Muted colors are used on the walls and in the fabrics. On the top floor is an airy public room and terrace with a glass front where breakfast is served. Tram 1 or 21 and the Metro (Saldanha station) can whisk you into the city center.

BELÉM

Now a suburb of Lisbon, Belém once had its own share of greatness. Here the Portuguese built the ships to sail on their voyages of discovery. Today Belém still has its share of charm. It's an attractive little town in its own right, filled with regional restaurants. And since it happens to be the site of the major sightseeing attractions in the Portuguese capital, it is rarely missed by visitors.

A CONVERTED CONVENT: A convent built in the 16th century, **York House**, 32 Rua das Janelas Verdes, 1200 Lisboa (tel. 66-24-35), was skillfully restored by a French lady, Mme Andrée Goldstein —and it has been savored by discerning guests ever since. The location is on one of the tree-shaded streets up from the Tagus, next to the National Art Gallery. A great many professors, painters, and writers from both America and England wouldn't stay anywhere else.

You enter on a lower level, passing through iron gates, ascending steps past trailing vines and pepper trees into the patio where guests relax under fruit trees. The rooms overlook either this courtyard or the river below, with its parade of ships and tugs. Madame has ambitiously installed a private bath in all rooms except the six student accommodations. Each room has its own architectural shape and personality and its own share of antiques.

The cost for two in a room with private bath is 12,000$ ($90). A single with bath is 10,000$ ($75). A luncheon or dinner in the restaurant begins at 1,500$ ($11.25). Those who request half or full board are given preference on the reservation list.

The dining room has coved ceilings and whitewashed walls, enhanced by a touch of gilt wall sconces. There are several living rooms furnished in a personal manner, with old furniture, rare prints, high-backed leather and velvet armchairs, brass-studded chests, and fresh flowers brought in daily from the market. The most popular room is the two-level bar-lounge, with its open fireplace, carved wooden figures, bronze chandeliers, coats-of-armor, and lamps made from hand-carved gilt candelabra.

Good news to York House patrons is the annex across the street. It's a fine old town house, which has been renovated and restored to create a comfortable pension.

The lounge of the annex is predominantly red, chic Victorian, turn-of-the-century Lisbon. Over the fireplace is a grotesque portrait of Alfonso, the former king of Spain, as a child. The bedrooms have a unified color theme and antiques—and tile baths.

A BUDGET CHOICE: The **Hotel da Torre**, 8 Rua dos Jerónimos, 1400 Lisboa (tel. 63-62-62), is in Belém, a suburb of Lisbon, near an estuary of the Tagus, suitable primarily for those who want to be in Lisbon's museum belt. The renovated inn rises three stories and is furnished in a regional style. Doubles, with a continental breakfast included, peak at 5,000$ ($37.50), and singles are charged

ON TOP OF OLD MONTE: The **Albergaria da Senhora do Monte,** 39 Calçada do Monte, 1100 Lisboa (tel. 86-28-46), is perched on a hilltop belvedere in the Graça section, at a spot where knowing Lisboans like to take their guests for a view of their city. Once a small rambling apartment house, the hotel has been converted to provide unique guest bedrooms, each with a sense of style. Multilevel corridors lead to the rooms; a few have a private terrace. Decorator touches abound, as reflected by the grass-cloth walls, the tile baths (one with 18th-century *azulejos* rescued from an old villa), and solid bronze fixtures. A single rents for 5,500$ ($41.25), a double is 6,800$ ($51), with a continental breakfast, taxes, and service included. Suites are also available, costing 8,500$ ($63.75) for two people. The combination reception area and lounge is intimate, containing a few fine antiques—note the monumental rosewood sofa. A bar is on the top floor.

4,000$ ($30). The air conditioning is confined to the public rooms and the wood-paneled bar and restaurant.

The modern lobby contains sunken seating areas, overhead balconies, and an innovative design with many horizontal lines washed with sunlight from the big front windows. The bar serves drinks in air-conditioned comfort and with personalized charm. Regional and international food is offered in the provincial restaurant.

CARCAVELOS

THE UPPER RANGE: The **Hotel Praia-Mar,** 16 Rua do Gurué, Carcavelos, 2775 Parede (tel. 247-31-31), is a modern palace of angular design, with recessed balconies. A private world unfolds behind the plant-bordered walls separating the elliptical swimming pool from the street outside. Unlike some of the other hotels on the coast, the Praia-Mar is in a quiet neighborhood a few blocks from the four-lane highway cutting along the coast. The lobby, fashioned from white marble, is somewhat sparsely furnished with upholstered leather armchairs, many of which face the large windows leading toward the sun-bathed swimming pool. There's a bar near the roof and another blue-and-white version in a secluded corner of the lobby, graced with an imposing statue of an Amazon brandishing a ferocious-looking infant.

Each of the 158 bedrooms has a balcony, usually with a view toward the sea, along with a pleasing combination of contemporary and Iberian-inspired furniture. Singles cost from 8,200$ ($61.50); doubles, from 9,300$ ($69.75). The restaurant on the eighth floor serves well-prepared meals costing from 2,700$ ($20.25).

SINTRA

THE TOP HOTEL: The finest hotel in Sintra is the modern, airy **Hotel Tivoli Sintra,** Praça da República, 2710 Sintra (tel. 923-35-05), opened in 1981. It lies only a few doors to the right of the National Palace mentioned above. The hotel offers an abundance of modern conveniences, including a garage (most important in Sintra). However, the decorator stuck to the *típico* Portuguese style in the décor, and the combination of modern with traditional is successful. In the cavernous lobby, the floors are of marble. Brass lamps are used, and many earth tones are among the colors.

Bedrooms, air-conditioned, are spacious and comfortably furnished, with complete baths, phones, color TVs with video, radios, large beds, and big easychairs for relaxation. The balconies and the public rooms look out onto a wooden hill, with views of some of Sintra's quintas. In high season, two people can stay here for 9,200$ ($69); a single guest, for 7,500$ ($56.25). Prices include a continental breakfast. The hotel has a panoramic restaurant and bar, a beauty parlor, and a travel agency.

ESTORIL

About 15 miles west of Lisbon, Estoril—with its splendid, cabaña-studded beaches—is one of the most fashionable resorts of Europe. Raymond Postgate wrote that it has "everything Cannes has except a film festival."

Much of the history of Estoril is associated with Fausto Figueiredo and his deluxe Hotel Palácio. His vision of a chic seaside resort in Estoril predated World War I. And in the 1930s, with the opening of the hotel, Estoril began attracting a steady stream of international visitors—such as the Crown Prince of Japan and his bride on their honeymoon. During World War II, spies—both Allied and Nazi—thronged through the rooms of the Palácio and the nearby Casino.

Since rebuilt, the Casino remains a potent attraction. In the center of the resort is the Parque Estoril with its sweep of palms and subtropical gardens extending from the Casino to the shore road. But to many the major attraction of Estoril is its golf course.

A DELUXE CHOICE: Receiving guests since 1930, the **Hotel Palácio do Estoril,** Parque Estoril, 2765 Estoril (tel. 268-04-00),

A CONVERTED PALACE IN SETEAIS: The **Palácio de Seteais,** 8 Rua Barbosa do Bocage, 2710 Sintra (tel. 923-32-00), is a small palace converted in 1956 into an elegant hotel. Lodged in the hills adjoining Sintra—it is approached by an encircling avenue of shade trees and a clipped yew hedge—its twin formal buildings are linked by an ornate towering gate. The estate was built at the end of the 18th century by a Dutch gildemeister, then restored by the fifth Marquis de Marialva, who used it for lavish parties and receptions. Even its gardens are appropriate for its regal interior.

A lightness, a sense of joy, pervades the interior—there's nothing stuffy about this palace. You enter a long galleried hallway, with white columns and a balustraded staircase leading to the lower-level drinking salon and the L-shaped dining room. Along the corridors are several tapestries, groupings of antiques, and hand-woven Portuguese carpets.

Unfolding before you are a music salon, a sedate library, and a main drawing room overlooking the countryside so beloved by Byron. There are only 18 rooms, so reservations are imperative. But even the simplest chamber has antiques or reproductions. In high season, the tariffs, including breakfast, range from 20,000$ ($150) in a single, from 21,000$ ($158) in a double, service and tax included.

Meals are events here; many Portuguese travel for miles just to dine here (see the restaurant chapter immediately following). Full-board rates are quoted, but you may order your meals separately.

won its fame as a haven for royalty, a "court away from home," so to speak. The longtime dream of one man, Fausto Figueiredo, the hotel has been known as one of the finest in all Europe since it opened its doors. At the height of World War II it was a hub of espionage and intrigue with international spies and counterspies everywhere. One night the swastika might be hoisted for a Nazi cocktail party; the next night the Stars and Stripes would hang in the lounge as the Allies took command of the drinks.

The two-story entrance hall is grand indeed, with handsome furnishings, hand-woven carpets, and fine paintings. You walk along a series of intimate salons, with Wedgwood paneling, large chandeliers glittering with sparkling prisms, fluted pilasters, and arched windows opening onto the large garden and lawn. The main drawing room, with its classic columns and black-and-white marble floors, is a stately place for after-dinner coffee accompanied by soft piano music. The dining room is a proper backdrop for impeccable service and good-tasting food. There is also the Grill Four Seasons, an outstanding à la carte restaurant, where both Portuguese and French cuisine are served in an atmosphere of class and distinction. The center of pre-dinner life is the bar, also in neoclassic décor. On the pool terrace, under a border of shaped bougainvillea, guests gather for breakfast or a buffet lunch.

The bedrooms are traditional in style, some with brass beds, a dressing table, and a double wardrobe. Many of the rooms have a sun balcony with a view of the pool. In high season (mid-March through October), bed-and-breakfast rates for singles are 16,000$ ($120) to 18,500$ ($139), and for doubles, 18,500$ ($139) to 20,500$ ($154), service and taxes included. Of course, the air-conditioned duplex suites overlooking the pool cost more. Off-season, all tariffs are lowered. Everything is run expertly, supervised by the general manager, Manuel Quintas.

The bonus—for golfers—is the 9- and 18-hole course in the foothills of Sintra, bordered by pine woods, about a three-minute drive from the hotel. Guests of the Palácio are granted a temporary membership. A further attraction is the seven tennis courts, three floodlighted for night games, located immediately next door to the hotel.

Fronting Estoril Park, the hotel is but a short walk from either the water or the Casino.

THE MIDDLE BRACKET: The tastefully modern little **Hotel Alvorada,** 3 Rua de Lisboa, 2765 Estoril (tel. 268-00-70), is directly opposite the grand entrance to the Estoril Casino. What makes staying here so special is the attractiveness of the rooms, plus such facilities as a solarium and a private garage. The décor combines modern with provincial: carved country pieces, simple wall colors, wooden screens used as dividers, lounge chairs, and coffee tables. For all this you pay 4,300$ ($32.25) to 7,500$ ($56.25) for a double, depending on the season. The Alvorada is as well a pleasant place at which to entertain.

MONTE ESTORIL

Monte Estoril, with its many hotels, is a satellite of Estoril, sprawling across the slope of a hill, offering vistas of the Bay of Cascais.

A BUDGET CHOICE: Right in the center of this hillside resort, the **Zenith,** 1 Rua Belmonte, 2765 Estoril (tel. 268-11-22), is a modern, six-story hotel, just high enough up from the coast to provide a view of the ocean and of the rooftops of villas, palm trees, sunrises, and sunsets. A drink on the rooftop cocktail lounge at twilight is a treat. The Zenith's small wood-paneled lounges are intimate and comfortable, done with attractive furnishings. There's even a wood-burning fireplace for nippy evenings. Each of the bedrooms contains a private bath, radio, and phone. Those on the seaside have a little balcony; others, a bay window. The furnishings are tasteful and restrained. In high season, singles begin at 6,000$ ($45), and doubles 8,000$ ($60). Rates include a continental breakfast, and from November 1 to April 1 a reduction is granted. English is spoken here. A good-sized swimming pool is a special feature.

LUXURY LIVING IN A FORTRESS: A unique resort hotel, the **Hotel do Guincho,** Praia do Guincho, 2750 Cascais (tel. 285-04-91), is the remake of a 17th-century fortress, standing high on a rocky coast, near Cabo da Roca on the westernmost tip of the European continent. The Portuguese regard it as a honeymooner's hotel, and, as such, it is not recommended for singles. Its stark-white exterior in no way reveals the opulence and high-fashion taste reflected inside. The inner courtyard is encircled by a colonnade of stone arches, with potted subtropical plants and flowers.

Inside, the stone coved ceilings, the Romanesque arches, the curving staircases, the heavy beams, the baronial fireplaces have been preserved. Furnishings and trappings both handsome and harmonious add to the ambience. These include large gilt ecclesiastical sculptures, Portuguese tapestries, oil paintings, and hand-woven rugs.

The bedrooms, all with a private bath and many with a loggia, are equally tasteful, with beautiful fabrics. High-season rates remain in effect from April to the end of October. With breakfast included, doubles cost from 18,200$ ($137) daily, with half board costing an extra 2,750$ ($20.75) per person. The suites cost the same whether occupied by one or two people.

Even if you can't stay here, try to visit for a meal, costing 3,200$ ($24). The spacious ocean-view dining room has a regal touch, with hand-embroidered draperies, high-backed red chairs, and overscale antique armoires. The food is impeccable, the service the same. Watching the maître d'hôtel flambé a peach is worth the trek up from Lisbon, which, incidentally, is 20 miles away.

TAKING FLIGHT IN CASCAIS: The **Hotel Albatroz,** 100 Rua Frederico Arouca, 2750 Cascais (tel. 28-28-21), takes its name from the wandering albatross, a bird noted as a master of gliding flight, capable of staying airborne on motionless wings for hours at a time. Positioned on a ledge of rocks just above the ocean, the hotel seems to float over the water like its namesake. This is the most delectable treasure along the Costa do Sol, a "good luck" choice whether you're seeking rooms or food.

The Albatroz is centered around a neoclassic villa built as a luxurious holiday retreat for the Duke of Loulé and acquired in the 19th century by the Count and Countess de Foz. Sometime in the present century it was converted into an inn, and in time received such guests as Anthony Eden, Cary Grant, the Duke and Duchess of Bedford, Claudette Colbert, William Holden, and the former Queen of Bulgaria. Prince Rainier and Princess Grace visited on more than one occasion.

Today the hotel has benefited from a tastefully elegant refurbishing which incorporates a lavish use of tiles in garlanded patterns of blue and yellow, acres of white latticework, and expanses of panoramic glass, through which you can see dozens of fishing boats bobbing at anchor. The stone-trimmed main structure has been expanded with a terraced series of balconied additions, each containing some of the 40 elegant bedrooms. Depending on the season and the exposure, doubles cost 17,250$ ($129) to 24,000$ ($180); singles, 13,800$ ($104) to 21,900$ ($164). An oval swimming pool nestles alongside the sun terrace between the new and old wings. Dining here is a worthwhile experience.

CASCAIS

THE UPPER RANGE: Facing the ocean on the edge of Cascais, the **Estoril Sol,** Parque Palmela, 2750 Cascais (tel. 28-28-31), is a showcase resort hotel. It is the most elaborate and all-encompassing in the area. Everything here is outsize: the hotel is the largest along the coast with 317 bedrooms. Its dining room is also the largest on the Costa do Sol. Twenty floors of superb and serviceable bedrooms, each with a bath, await the visitor. The chambers open onto balconies with views of ocean or hills. In high season, standard singles cost from 15,700$ ($118); regular doubles, from 18,200$ ($137). Warning: The lower rooms facing the sea reflect the coastal traffic—so ask for a lodging on a higher perch. Facilities abound, including radios, color TV, in-house movies, and mini-bars in the bedrooms, an elegant grill room, a coffeeshop, a health center, squash courts, at least five bars, a boîte, even a swimming pool with a five-level diving board and adjoining café. The management doesn't look askance if you slip away to the Estoril Casino for a late-night supper or show. The Estoril Sol family clan built it and run it too.

The **Cidadela,** Avenida 25 de Abril, 2750 Cascais (tel. 28-29-21), is a gem. It is set on a knoll, with six floors of balcony bedrooms overlooking an enclosed garden and swimming pool. The lounges and dining room have been furnished with both restraint and good taste, plus a sense of the best of Portuguese décor. You may never make it to the beach once you discover the thatched bar and poolside restaurant at one end of the garden. Two blocks from the center of Cascais, the "Citadel" offers rooms, suites, or apartments. From July to September, the highest tariffs are charged—13,000$ ($98) in a single, 15,500$ ($116) in a double. Suites and apartments are more expensive, of course. Full board costs 5,500$ ($41.25) per person.

THE MIDDLE BRACKET: One of the loveliest hotels in the region, the **Estalagem Senhora da Guia,** Strada do Guincho, 2750 Cascais (tel. 28-92-39), is owned and operated by the Ornelas family, who opened it after returning to their native Portugal from a sojourn in Madeira. The Estalagem was a villa built in 1970 by heirs of the Sagres brewery fortune, who fled to Brazil, allowing the house to fall into ruin until it was rescued by the Ornelases. The thick walls, high ceilings, and elaborately crafted moldings give the impression of a much older structure, and the restoration has capitalized on that fact through use of antiques and period reproductions throughout.

Each of the elegant bedrooms is tastefully furnished with copies of 18th-century Portuguese pieces, thick carpets, and louvered shutters, and has a modern, spacious bath. The price of a double is $50 (U.S.) to $107, depending on the season and the view (sea views are higher). Suites for two people are available for $107 to $140, all tariffs include a continental breakfast.

When you arrive at the Estalagem, a polite member of the staff will usher you up a staircase of elegantly crafted wood, wrought iron, and crystal to your immaculately maintained quarters. Even the unvarnished floors of the place are frequently scrubbed with sand, giving them the warm patina that use alone takes years to achieve. The sun-washed bar is one of the more alluring public rooms, filled with some of the family's antiques, many of them English and acquired during their years in Madeira. Plush sofas provide quiet corners, and there's a fireplace for cold weather.

Because of the villa's position on a bluff above the sea, the views are excellent. Breakfast is served buffet style under parasols at the edge of the swimming pool. Lunches and dinners are offered beneath a ceiling of African hardwood in a formal dining room that remains cool even on the hottest days, thanks to its thick walls and terracotta floors. The establishment is named for the patron saint of lighthouses and fishermen, the name also of a nearby lighthouse and the region around it.

The **Estalagem Belvedere,** 8 Rua Dr. António Martins, 2750 Cascais (tel. 268-91-63), built as a private villa during the Edwardian age, was converted into a charming hotel some 25 years ago. This English-owned establishment offers two dozen bedrooms, each with a private bath. Depending on the season, singles cost 3,500$ ($26.25) to 5,700$ ($42.75), and doubles run 4,000$ ($30) to 9,000$ ($67.50), with breakfast included. It sits in a gracious neighborhood of faded 19th-century residences, among century-old trees and pleasant gardens. Inside, the comfortable public rooms contain Iberian furnishings, a cozy bar filled with rustic bric-à-brac, and a dining room serving dinner only from 7:15 to 10 p.m.

CHAPTER IV

RESTAURANTS IN AND AROUND LISBON

□ □ □

Early British visitors spoke contemptuously of the Portuguese diet they encountered. They claimed the Portuguese sustained themselves on cod, but thrived on their dreams. Codfish, in fact, is the national dish, prepared in hundreds of ingenious ways. For instance, there's . . .

Bacalhau (salted codfish). This is most often served boiled, accompanied by potatoes and greens. The true connoisseur tosses in olive oil and vinegar as well, but this is an acquired taste. Appearing commonly on menus—in both upper-grade restaurants as well as low taverns—are such variations as bacalhau à Brás (Brás style); bacalhau no forno (baked in the oven); and bacalhau à gomes de sá (with eggs and onions, flavored with garlic).

When you see the different ways it is cooked and how it's savored by the locals, then you'll know why the Portuguese speak of bacalhau as *o fiel amigo* (faithful friend).

Another Portuguese specialty is **caldeirada,** described to visitors as a "fishermen's stew" or the "Portuguese bouillabaisse" if someone is trying to be fancy. This savory kettle of goodness is made with at least four different types of fish, even in simple establishments, although I know of one Portuguese chef who uses a dozen different kinds of fish. The fish is cooked with onions and tomatoes, but many contain nearly 12 different vegetables.

Portuguese **sardines,** packed in tins with olive oil, are shipped around the world. One publicist for the sardine industry claims that they are "the ideal health, strength, and beauty food." This is not disputed, except to say that one woman reported that after such a *típico* meal she was trailed by half the cats in the Alfama. Sardines are best when you see the menu listing sardinhas assadas (grilled). In the Alfama, housewives cook the sardines over an open brazier in front of the doorways to their houses.

As you've gathered by now, the item to order in Portugal is fish. Even in the simplest tavern, it's likely to be fresh and abundant—that is, all except shellfish. Portuguese **lagosta** (crayfish), for example, is justly famous. Once it was served commonly throughout the land, almost as a side course. But in recent years catches have yielded less and less, and foreign markets in such countries as Italy and France have demanded more and more. Because the price of crayfish varies from day to day and it's quite expensive, it is rarely set forth on the menu, so inquire about the price before ordering or eating it.

Meat tends to be inferior in Portugal, especially beef and veal. However, acorn-fattened porco (pork) is tender and packed with flavor. A real banquet is **porco alentejano** (pork in the style of the province of Alentejo—that is, fried and coated with a savory sauce of clams and mussels, often accompanied by bay-leaf-flavored tomatoes and onions). Another good dish, popular in taverns with beer, is **bife na frigideria** (steak with mustard sauce, but it's suggested that you forgo its usual accompaniment, a fried egg).

Many a peasant has staved off hunger with **tripe** cooked with fat white beans and flavored with bits and pieces of pungent sausage. **Iscas** is also good—calves' liver thinly cut and coated with onions and served (most often in an earthenware dish) along with fried potatoes.

A Portuguese specialty, with infinite regional variations, is **cozido** (a boiled dinner including beef and pork as well as cabbage, bacon, sausages, potatoes, and other greens—almost anything the chef has in abundance). Lamb is poor, but a savory treat is **cabrito** (roast kid), especially when it's prepared in the style of the province of Alentejo.

Portuguese **dining hours** have less in common with the country's Iberian neighbor—and are more related to hours in the United States—that is, between 1 and 2 p.m. for lunch, between 7:30 and 9 p.m. for dinner. Of course, meals are served both earlier and later at most establishments. For example, many visitors dine between 10 p.m. and midnight in the fado cafés of Lisbon.

WHERE TO DINE: Whether you're seeking regional or international fare, the restaurants of Lisbon offer a rich, imaginative banquet of choices. To give you the widest possible sampling, I've selected restaurants that have exceptional appeal, not only because

of their well-prepared cuisines, but often because of their *típico* décor
or atmosphere.

I'll lead off with:

LISBON—DELUXE CHOICES

Restaurante Aviz, 12-8 Rua Serpa Pinto (tel. 32-83-91), for
many years reigned supreme as the most prestigious—and the
finest—restaurant in Portugal. Clement Freud once proclaimed it
"the best restaurant in Europe," which put it in heady company. Today its position has been seriously challenged by other fast-rising establishments, and many readers have complained about the service,
food, and prices. Nevertheless, it should be noted that many re-
spected food critics still consider it the Número Uno choice in Lisbon. The Aviz was once part of Lisbon's special hotel of the same
name, catering to the whims of the greats of Europe. When the hotel was torn down, its restaurant operation was rescued.

Today you encounter an old-world aura as you enter the reception lounge for a before-dinner drink. You plan your meal with de-
liberation while munching from a bowl of roasted slivered almonds
from the Algarve. You look around and find yourself in a private-
club atmosphere of green marble columns, deep, tufted, black leather chairs, crystal chandeliers, and a pair of paintings of respectable
nudes reclining in bed.

As you glance into the glittering dining room, you see three
communicating salons, their walls paneled or covered with grained
silk, gilt sconces, even a life-size statue of an American Indian girl,
with a brief skirt of tobacco leaves (known as "Miss Tobacco Leaf of
1800" by the waiters). The two smaller rooms are more intimate,
the larger one more animated.

To begin your meal, try, if featured, the espadon fumé, razor-
thin slices of smoked swordfish served with half a lemon wrapped in
white gauze to prevent seeds from falling on the fish. Its delicacy is
memorable. My most recent duck had an orange sauce that was bit-
tersweet with shredded orange peel, and the dish was accompanied
by light, crisp potato croquettes. Crêpes Suzette is a popular dessert.
Sipping Portuguese coffee from tiny Vista Alegre cups is an appropriate way to conclude.

Your bill is discreetly presented in a leather folder. That final
charge is likely to be 5,000$ ($37.50) or a whole lot more. The restaurant, serving from 1 to 3 p.m. and 8 to 10:30 p.m., is closed on
Sunday.

Tagide, 18 Largo da Academia Nacional de Belas Artes (tel. 32-
07-20), has had a prestigious past, and now it is a distinguished
place to dine in the Chiado. Its situation is colorful—up from the

docks, on a steep hill on a ledge overlooking the old part of Lisbon and the Tagus. Once the town house of a diplomat, then a leading nightclub, it is now one of Lisbon's leading restaurants. Some gourmets say it serves the finest food in town.

It's very old, with a museum look to it. You go up marble steps with shiny brass balustrades. The dining room has view windows, overlooking moored ships and the port. Set into the white plaster walls are overscale figures made of blue and white tiles, each depicting a famous queen. The chairs are provincial and the tablecloths have hand-crocheted edges. Glittering above are crystal chandeliers.

Both Portuguese dishes of quality as well as selections from the international repertoire are featured and are beautifully served. For an appetizer, try the salmon pâté, cold stuffed crab, or smoked swordfish. Other specialties include suprême of halibut with coriander, pork with clams and coriander, and grilled baby goat with herbs. For dessert, I recommend the stuffed crêpes Tagide. Expect to spend from 3,500$ ($26.25), plus the cost of your wine. Food is served from noon to 2:30 p.m. and 7:30 to 10:30 p.m. The restaurant is closed for Saturday dinner and all day Sunday, and it's important to reserve a table.

António Clara, 38 Avenida da República (tel. 76-63-80), one of the capital's best-rated restaurants, is in an exquisite turn-of-the-century villa which was once the home of one of Portugal's most revered architects, Miguel Ventura Terra. Built in 1890 by and for its designer, the interior has Ventura Terra's photograph hanging amid polished antiques and gilded mirrors. The angled and tiled wings of the villa seem to embrace visitors as they approach the Moorish-influenced façade. Inside, the soaring height of the curved stairwell and the elegant moldings serve as attractive backdrops for the 17th-century wood carvings and Belle Époque porcelain.

Before going to the dining room, one of the loveliest in Lisbon, you can enjoy a drink in the 19th-century salon, where griffins snarl down from their position on the pink-shaded chandelier. Even the service areas of this house, rarely seen by visitors, contain ceiling frescoes. In the dining room, the efficient staff of wine steward, headwaiter, and attendants make wine tasting a ceremony. Full meals, priced from 6,000$ ($45), include such specialties as smoked swordfish, cheese soufflé, paella for two, chateaubriand béarnaise, codfish Clara style, tournedos "symphony," and beef Wellington.

The restaurant is open from noon to 3 p.m. and 7 p.m. to midnight daily except Sunday. Reservations are suggested. There's a ground-floor bar, accessible through its own entrance, where you can have an after-dinner drink.

Restaurante Clara, 49 Campo dos Mártires da Pátria (tel. 57-04-34), is an elegant hideaway in a green tile house on a quiet hillside amid decaying villas and city squares. It was opened a few years ago by a quartet of Portuguese businessmen. You might enjoy a drink under the ornate ceiling of the bar, a room which has served variously over the years as an antiques store, the living room of a private apartment, and the foyer of a palatial house. At lunchtime, you may prefer a seat near the plants and fountain of the garden terrace. At night, an indoor location—perhaps near the large marble fireplace—is more appealing. A piano is played softly during dinner.

Menu specialties include tournedos Clara, stuffed rabbit with red wine sauce, four different kinds of pasta, codfish Clara, lobster crêpes, filet of sole with orange, pheasant with grapes, cheese soufflé, filet Wellington, and Valencian paella. Full meals, costing from 5,500$ ($41.25), are served daily except Sunday throughout the year. Hours are noon to 3:30 p.m. and 7 p.m. to midnight.

LISBON—OTHER TOP RESTAURANTS
Escorial, 47 Rua Portas de S. Antao (tel. 36-44-29), has an exclusive club aura, rich in wood paneling from South America, opera-red carpets and tablecloths, plus sedate, but attentive, service. Near the Rossio, it offers excellent Portuguese cookery, attracting a steady clientele of business people and out-of-towners, even owners of fashionable villas out at Cascais. The English menu helps the foreigner. A good opener is steamed clams in the Cataplana style, followed by sea bass cooked "the Portuguese way." If you want something more festive, you can order a barbecue of lamb or spring chicken on the spit. It's good to finish off with a peach Melba. Expect to pay 2,800$ ($21) to 4,800$ ($36) for a dinner here. Try to reserve a table for this centrally located establishment, right in the heart of the city, serving from noon to midnight daily.

Michel, 5 Largo de Santa Cruz do Castelo (tel. 86-43-38), is the most fashionable restaurant in the Alfama. On a tiny plaza near St. George's Castle, this popular first-class restaurant serves a continental cuisine prepared under the watchful eye of Michel da Costa, the restaurant's Moroccan-born owner and chef. Tempting continental specialties include smoked swordfish, seaweed sea bass, and black bass Don Fernando. A recommendable main dish is green-pepper duck. For dessert, the apple tart Michel is favored. Michel also specializes in his own version of the "new cuisine," as exemplified by a prosciutto-like specialty made from goose with a well-seasoned salad, or blinis with swordfish. The cost of a regular meal ranges from 3,000$ ($22.50) to 4,500$ ($33.75). The restaurant is open daily from noon to midnight. Reservations are necessary.

LISBON'S OLDEST RESTAURANT: A prestigious star, the **Restaurante Tavares,** 37 Rua da Misericórdia (tel. 32-11-12), has been favored since the 18th century by gourmet-minded politicians, diplomats, authors, and exiled royalty drawn to its personalized cooking and service.

The preferred street-level dining room is a salon of mirrors, with panels of ecru and gilt, crystal chandeliers, and sconces. You dine on Louis XV–style armchairs, enjoying a small bouquet of roses (or the flowers of the season) on your finely set table. The Tavares is the oldest restaurant in Lisbon, founded in 1784 by Nicolau Massa (nick-named "O Talão"). In the 19th century it became the property of two Tavares brothers.

For an appetizer, you can choose presunto de Chaves (Chaves ham). Among the main dishes are santola (crab) recheada à Tavares, linguado (sole) Newburg, and the special beef of the house. At the start of your meal, you can ask the chef to whip up an Alp-high soufflé as a finale. Then top it off with a café filtro. Your final bill is likely to run 3,000$ ($22.50) to 5,500$ ($41.25) for a complete meal, available from 1 to 3 p.m. and 8 to 10:30 p.m. Closed Saturday and for Sunday lunch.

LISBON—MODERATELY PRICED RESTAURANTS

What follows is a selection of restaurants in the Portuguese capital that serve good food at moderate prices. Of course, if you order shellfish, such as lobster, you can expect to pay a lot of money.

Sua Excelência, 40-42 Rua do Conde (tel. 60-36-14), is the creation of Francisco Queiroz, who was a travel agent in Angola before he returned to Portugal. In Lisbon he has created his little dream restaurant, with a refined, sedate atmosphere, attracting a discerning clientele. Outside you'll see no sign. There is only a large heavy door with a bell which you ring to announce your arrival. The host will greet you with personalized hospitality. The atmosphere he has created is modish, somewhat like a fashionable drawing room, with round tables in an intimate Portuguese provincial décor, cooled by the terracotta floor and high, painted ceiling.

The host recites the menu-of-the-day specialties, some uncommon to Portugal. These include prawns piri-piri (not unreasonably hot), rollmop sardines, what Senhor Queiroz proclaims as the "best smoked swordfish in Portugal," and clams in at least five different recipes. One unusual specialty is "little jacks," a small fish of which diners eat heads, tails, everything. It's served with a well-flavored paste made from two-day-old bread. You can also order sea bass puffs with "doctored" rice. Meals cost 2,500$ ($18.75) and up. Hours are 1 to 2 p.m. and 8 to 10:30 p.m. The place is closed on Wednesday, on Saturday and Sunday at lunchtime in July and August, and for the entire month of September. The restaurant is just a block up the hill from the entrance to the National Art Gallery, so it could be visited on a tie-in museum/luncheon adventure, although its ambience is more charming in the evening.

Conventual, 45 Praça de Flores (tel. 60-91-96), is in many ways one of my favorite restaurants in Lisbon. This preference is influenced strongly by the taste and sensitivity of its gracious owner, Mrs. Dina Marquês. Her establishment is on one of the loveliest residential squares in town, behind a discreet, plain wood door. Inside, you'll see a display of old panels from baroque churches, religious statues, and bric-a-brac from Mrs. Marquês's private collection. A large, ornate silver incense burner which once scented the interior of a 17th-century church hangs over the bar. The restaurant is kept pleasantly cool by the old, thick stone walls and terracotta floor of the building.

Many of the delectably flavored recipes were invented or developed by the owner, among them a creamy coriander soup, stewed partridge in port, ox tongue in egg sauce, pork filet Portuguese style, steak with onion sauce and fried potatoes, and a tempting grilled monkfish in a herb-flavored cream sauce. Meals begin at 3,000$ ($22.50), and reservations are suggested. Food is served from 12:30 to 3:30 p.m. and 7:30 to 11:30 p.m. As is appropriate in any business even resembling a convent, work stops on Sunday.

Restaurante O Faz Figura, 15-B Rua do Paraíso (tel. 86-89-81), is one of the best and most attractively decorated dining rooms in Lisbon. Part of its atmosphere is a veranda where you can order both lunch and dinner overlooking the Tagus. When reserving a table, ask for one there. The restaurant lies in the heart of the Alfama, and it offers faultless service and typical Portuguese food along with international specialties. A complete meal will cost around 3,000$ ($22.50). You are given a warm reception and then shown to your table, unless you want to stop first for a before-dinner drink in the handsome international cocktail bar. The restaurant serves from 12:30 to 3 p.m. and 8 p.m. to midnight. It is closed on Sunday.

Gambrinus, 25 Rua das Portas de Santo Antão (tel. 32-14-66), is an establishment whose stature among Lisbon's leading restaurants is justified. Intimate dining rooms are clustered around an open blue-tile kitchen, where expert chefs in starched white hats prepare fine meals, using large copper pots and a charcoal grill. The location is ideal for those who want to dine in the heart of the city, off the Rossio, near the railway station, and on a little square near the National Theater.

You can have your meal while sitting on leather chairs in the rear under a cathedral-beamed ceiling, or else select a little table beside a fireplace upon the raised end of the room. All is dominated by an impressionistic tapestry along one wall. There is also an alcove with a stained-glass enclosure. The walls of the backroom are sedate with paneling, not unlike a country lodge. For before-dinner drinks, a front bar beckons.

Although there is a diversified à la carte menu, don't fail to check the *especialidades do dia*. The soups are good, everything from cream of shellfish to onion. Fish dishes range from conha com mariscos à thermidor (conch with shellfish) to tobalo (bass) minhote. A Germanic meat dish is frankfurters with sauerkraut. Another specialty is rumpsteak Gambrinus. The restaurant offers elaborate desserts, including a vanilla soufflé and crêpes Suzette. Coffee with a 30-year-old brandy complements the meal perfectly. Expect to spend from 2,800$ ($21) and up for a meal here. It's open seven days a week from noon to 2 a.m.

Chester, 87 Rua Rodrigo da Fonseca (tel. 65-73-47), near the Ritz Inter-Continental, is an attractive restaurant and bar, with a good cellar. Its specialty is grilled steaks. The pepper steak is tempting, as is the rib steak for two. Entrecôte with whisky sauce is hearty, and the fondue bourguignonne is prepared only for two persons. The tab is likely to range from 2,500$ ($18.75) to 3,800$ ($28.50) for a complete meal. Service is efficient, and reservations are suggested. Open daily except Sunday from 12:30 to 3 p.m. and 8:30 to 10:30 p.m., the restaurant is upstairs, and the cozy little bar lies below.

Pabe, 27A Rua Duque de Palmela (tel. 53-74-84), is the Portuguese name for pub, and that's what this cozy English-style place is. Convenient to the Praça do Pombal, the pub has done its best to emulate English establishments. There's soft carpet on the floor, mugs hanging over the long bar, a beamed ceiling, coats-of-arms, and engravings of hunting scenes around the walls. Two saloon doors lead into a wood-paneled dining room, where you can sup on meat specially imported from the U.S. A chateaubriand for two is about the most expensive dish. If you prefer local fare, start off with a shrimp cocktail, then Portuguese veal liver or chicken breast with mushrooms, and finish with a sherbet, all for a cost of 3,000$ ($22.50). The crowd tends to be a well-groomed Portuguese set as well as resident Yanks and Britons. Open from noon to 1 a.m., Pabe is closed on Sunday.

Casa da Comida, 1 Travessa de Amoreiras (tel. 68-53-76), has steadily gained in popularity. If you're in Lisbon between December and March, when the winters are mild, but gray and rainy, this is among the best choices for dining in the city. A roaring fire will greet you and warm you. Not only is the atmosphere most pleasant (at any time of the year), but the food is impeccably served and good-tasting. You enter by way of a step-down garden. The sole is delectable, and the meat, especially veal, is well prepared. Dinners begin at 3,200$ ($24). Hours are 12:30 to 3:30 p.m. and 7:30 p.m. to 1 a.m. Closed Saturday at lunchtime and all day Sunday.

A PALACE AT SETEAIS (NEAR SINTRA): The **Palácio do Seteais** (tel. 923-32-00) provides a background for one of the finest meals you're likely to be served in Portugal. The exquisite 18th-century palace—reached only by car or taxi—is also recommended highly as a place at which to stay.

Meals are served from 12:30 to 2:30 p.m. and 7:30 to 9:30 p.m. in the lower dining room, overlooking the hillside of villas and orchards. However, you may want to have a before-dinner drink in the loggia or the salon at the bottom of the grand staircase. Once seated, you are apt to have a bouquet of pink hydrangeas placed at your table. Serving stewards are skillful and polite.

For 3,600$ ($27), you can order a four-course meal which begins with your choice of any or all of the 20 different kinds of hors d'oeuvres, such as shrimp, Russian salad, fish mousse, egg in a gelatin pâté. The next course is fish, say, turbot Florentine (creamy with spinach and browned in the oven). Your following meat course will be abundant and tasty, with a wide choice of fresh vegetables. When a cart is brought to your table, you'll be tempted by all of the creamy, fruit-stuffed pastries and cakes. In spring, the fresh strawberries from Sintra are the best in the world.

LISBON—THE BUDGET RESTAURANTS

The restaurants described below are patronized mainly by Portuguese, and one characteristic that these restaurants have in common, other than their low prices, is that the chefs are generous with their helpings. Added economy tip: Look for the chef's *prato do dia* (plate of the day)—invariably inexpensive and fresh. And some Portuguese restaurants save you more by still persisting in offering reductions for double portions which are shared.

O Funil (Funnel), 82-A Avenida Elias Garcia (tel. 76-60-07), is recommendable for its *cozinha Portuguêsa*. You almost never find a free table at mealtimes. It's that popular—and with the Portuguese who know they can get good home-cooking at reasonable prices here. The dining rooms are on two levels, the street-floor one in the tavern style, funnel-like, with the tables leg to leg. Most habitués, however, gravitate to the lower level, with its adjoining tiny bar. This is the kind of place where you ask for the *vinho de casa*, and it comes in two sizes of bottles. Wines of all the regions of Portugal are on the wine list, including green wines, ripe wines, and rosés.

The owners have set down-to-earth prices. They offer fresh fish and several meat dishes daily, with specialties of ameijoas (clams) à Funil, cabrito assado (roast goat), and bacalhau (cod) à Funil. To finish your meal, you can choose almond tart, walnut tart, almond cake, or French pudding, among other delicacies, or perhaps you'd like cheese—creamy or smoked serra, for instance. A complete meal costs from 1,400$ ($10.50). The restaurant is open from noon to 3:30 p.m. and 7 to 10:30 p.m. except for Sunday dinner and all day Monday.

SEAFOOD IN CACILHAS: On the left bank of the Tagus, the **Floresta do Ginjal,** 7 Ginjal (tel. 275-00-87), is reached by frequent ferryboat service. You can board ferries at Cais do Sodré. The two-level restaurant opens onto unobstructed views of ships and the river scene of Lisbon. You ascend to the dining rooms via a staircase that's a veritable tunnel of assorted sea shells imbedded in the wall, a proper introduction to the array of fresh and well-prepared fish that will be set before you.

Family-owned and -run, the restaurant attracts a largely Portuguese trade drawn here to sample such regional dishes as caldeirada —the national dish. Other specialties include grilled sole. For dessert, a good Portuguese cheese is queijos serra (from the hills or farm). Almond cake is another favorite dessert. A complete meal here begins at about 1,800$ ($13.50) and is available from noon to 3 p.m. and 7 to 10:30 p.m. daily.

António Restaurante, 63 Rua Tomás Ribeiro (tel. 53-87-80). Just outside the center of the city, the air-conditioned António lies only a few blocks from Edward VII Park, in back of the Lisboa-Sheraton. Special touches here include pewter service plates, a blue-and-white tile motif, and an English menu. Each day the chef features a different soup, and clams are always a favorite opener. A Portuguese regional dish worth recommending is pork with a savory clam sauce, or try the chicken with clams. I'd also suggest the fresh sole and the swordfish. A very special dessert is António pudding.

IN THE "KITCHEN" AT QUELUZ: To feel like a king or queen, dine in the **Cozinha Velha,** Palácio Nacional, Queluz, Largo do Palácio (tel. 95-02-32), housed in the former kitchen of the 18th-century Queluz Palace. A luncheon here can easily be tied in with a sightseeing jaunt to the palace. You enter through a small patio garden. The high, vaulted ceiling with wide stone arches is intact, as is the tremendous walk-in central fireplace.

The cook's 15-foot marble table is still in use, although it's now laden with ready-to-serve delicacies: hors d'oeuvres, salads, fish mousse, assorted cheeses, along with abundant flower arrangements. The ladderback chairs, torchère lights, 15-foot-high front door, the well-trained waitresses in regional dress, plus the superb food, make it well worth the trip. The restaurant is open from noon to 3 p.m. and 7:30 to 10 p.m. daily.

You must order from an à la carte menu, which includes the house specialty, linguado (sole) Cozinha Velha. Other courses include a filet mignon with a béarnaise sauce, or the more traditional bife à Portuguêsa. A good meal is likely to cost from 3,500$ ($26.25). Reserve a table.

Expect to pay about 2,000$ ($15) for a really filling meal. Hours are noon to 4 p.m. and 7 to 10:30 p.m. daily.

The **Restaurante A Colmela,** 110 Rua da Emenda (tel. 37-05-00), is a center of healthy eating and living. On the top floor of a corner building are two entirely separate kitchens and cuisines, one vegetarian and one macrobiotic. In addition, there is a miniature shop where you can purchase such natural ingredients as nuts, raisins, herbs, even pastries and black breads.

You enter on the street floor through an old hall with a stone floor, then ascend a scrubbed wooden staircase with an old Portuguese tile dado. The top floor has a narrow hallway lined with shelves of books dealing with metaphysics as well as healthful living. At your left is a reception room where you can ask for the dishes of the day and learn the prices. Meals cost from 500$ ($3.75). Through the open doors of the two kitchens, you can see the aromatic pastries. Three dining rooms, each with large windows, are decorated differently. The restaurant is open from noon to 3 p.m. and 7 to 8:30 p.m. On Saturday, it closes after the 3 p.m. lunch hour and remains closed on Sunday. English is spoken here.

Choupal, 9 Rua do Salitre (tel. 54-29-63), is a stylized taverna, one minute from the Avenida da Liberdade, where regional dishes are served family style. Its walls have aqua and olive tiles combined with wood paneling, and the ceiling is a warm brown cork. Chairs are natural wood, the tables have bright cloths, and there is an English menu. The waiter brings a loaf of crusty bread and a little ceramic jar of mildly seasoned pâté with sweet butter to begin your meal. You might start with a shellfish soup or savory Spanish-style clams. Two main-dish specialties are roast chicken and lampreys, those tiny eels from the north of Portugal. The chef also does a special beef dish. A meal here will cost from 1,500$ ($11.25). The restaurant is open every day from 9 a.m. to midnight.

THE FOREIGN CORNER

The sun has now set over much of the Portuguese empire, but the memory lingers on in a handful of its restaurants which brought the cuisines of other lands back for the home folks to sample. A good one is **Velha Goa,** 41-B Rua Tomás de Anunciação (tel. 60-04-46). India forcibly annexed the Portuguese colony of Gôa in 1961. Against a backdrop of Oriental décor, Indian dishes are served at this pleasant restaurant where English is spoken. Typically Goanese dishes include curries—prawns, chicken Madrasta, and other specialties. But pork chops and beef are also served. All dishes are prepared according to the taste of the clients—that is, mild, pungent, and very pungent. Expect to pay 1,400$ ($10.50) to 1,600$ ($11) for a meal in the dining hall. The restaurant is open from noon to midnight daily except Sunday. Final orders are taken at 10:30 p.m. You can also visit the bar, which is open from 6 p.m. to 1 a.m., enjoying a drink in a pleasant atmosphere (you can also order food here). Jazz musicians frequently entertain on weekends.

A Gondola, 64 Avenida de Berna (tel. 77-04-26), is Lisbon's "Little Italy," serving what are perhaps the finest Italian specialties, such as ravioli and cannelloni, in town. The restaurant offers indoor dining as well as al fresco meals in the courtyard. Although the décor isn't inspired, the food makes the restaurant worth the trip out of the center. It's best reached by taxi (the street on which it sits crosses the Avenida da República). A full dinner is offered for about 2,500$ ($18.75) and up. This is quite a buy when you realize what you get. A first-course selection might include Chaves ham with melon and figs or liver pâté. For a second course, you're likely to face a choice—say, filet of sole meunière or grilled sardines with pimientos, even red mullet. This is followed by yet another course, ravioli or cannelloni in the Roman style, perhaps veal cutlet milanese. The banquet is topped off by fruit or dessert. The restaurant is open from 12:45 to 3 p.m. and 7:45 to 10 p.m.; closed Saturday night and Sunday.

DINING IN BELÉM

Restaurant S. Jerónimo, 12 Rua dos Jerónimos (tel. 64-87-97). A visit to this lighthearted and elegant restaurant could be combined with a trip to the famous monastery of the same name. The restaurant sits directly on the east side of the monastery, behind a big-windowed façade which floods the interior with sunlight. You'll be invited to enjoy an apéritif in a spacious cocktail lounge. The dining room is stylishly outfitted with bamboo accents and plants separating the tables. A staff of tweed-vested waiters will see to your needs.

The all-Portuguese menu contains such specialties as trout Hemingway style, two types of codfish, osso buco, grilled tournedos, shrimp with garlic, fish pâté with tartar sauce, grouper with champagne, grilled sole, and (in season) melon with prosciutto. A Sunday buffet, held from 12:30 to 3:30 p.m., is considered an important event in Belém. Full meals range upward from 2,000$ ($15). The restaurant is open for lunch from 12:30 to 3 p.m. and for dinner from 7:30 p.m. to 2 a.m.; closed Sunday night and all day Monday.

Dionysos', 124 Rua Belém (tel. 64-06-32), is a good Greek restaurant out in the suburb of Belém, an ideal place for lunch if you're visiting the Coach Museum or the monastery nearby. Of course, it's also open for dinner. At the latter, while ensconced at a crowded table under a beamed ceiling on the second floor, you can dine by candlelight, enjoying friendly service. You might begin with a Greek salad for two. The popular souvlaki is featured, and you can also select from a varied menu of fish and meat dishes, finishing with a homemade dessert. Meals cost from 1,800$ ($13.50). The restaurant is open daily except Tuesday from 12:30 to 3 p.m. and 7 to 10 p.m.

A SNACKBAR

The Ritz Snackbar, 77-C Rua Castilho (tel. 56-14-44), is in the Ritz compound, but reached by a separate entrance on a street bordering Edward VII Park. The snackbar is a bright and attractive counter dining room. In season, it is so popular that it's hard to find a seat. From the Italian kitchen, you can select a pizza, pasta in a bolognese sauce, or lasagne. A hamburger plate is the most popular feature. On a lengthy dessert menu, you'll find such ice-cream concoctions as an Afrodite and a Himalaya. Count on spending from 1,500$ ($11.25) up. It is open from noon to 1:30 a.m. daily.

CASCAIS

Restaurant Albatroz, 100 Rua Frederico Arouca (tel. 28-28-21), provides one of the finest dining experiences along the

A PORTUGUESE BEER HALL: Now more than 150 years old, the **Cervejaria Trindade,** 20-B Rua Nova de Trindade (tel. 32-35-06), owned by the makers of Sagres beer, is one of the oldest beer halls in Lisbon. Along with those steins of beer, you'll be given quite good small steaks, smothered in a mountain of crisp french fries. Also featured are clams (ameijoas) in a savory sauce. You'll be tempted to have more than one of the accompanying beers. Every day a different typical Portuguese dish is featured, including açorda de marisco (bread, panada, and seafood), carne de porco à Alentejana (pork and clams), and presunto de Chaves (ham from Chaves, a town near the northern border of Portugal). If the day is sunny, then head for the open-air terrace. The cost of a regular lunch or dinner, featuring the typical dishes and including a large-size mug of beer, costs about 1,500$ ($11.25). Hours are noon to 2 a.m. daily. *Note:* This beer hall was once a convent, and it survived the great earthquake of the 18th century.

Costa do Sol. This elegantly decorated restaurant is part of the most famous inn along the coast (see my previous recommendation). It's summer décor is inviting year round.

You can begin with an apéritif on the covered terrace, whose edges are balanced on the rocks high above the sea. Then you'll be ushered into a glistening dining room, where, between walls pierced with large panes of glass under a ceiling with alternating beams and lattice work, you can enjoy some of the finest cuisine in Portugal. Your repast might include poached salmon, partridge stew with applesauce, steak Albatroz, sole or lobster prepared as you like it, paella chef's style, lamb with walnuts, or a savory version of stuffed crab. For dessert, your choice will range from crêpes Suzette to an iced soufflé. Accompanying your meal will be a wide selection of Portuguese and international wines. Full meals, served from 12:30 to 3 p.m. and 7:30 to 10 p.m. daily, cost from 5,500$ ($41.25), and reservations are necessary.

The most preferred "middle bracket" restaurant is **Reijos,** 35 Rua Frederico Arouca (tel. 28-03-11). Your hosts are Portuguese-born Tony Brito and an American, Ray Ettinger, a purser for a transatlantic airline (he often brings in hard-to-get items by air, including curry from India and soy sauce from Hong Kong). The cuisine represents a blending of their two countries. For example, Reijos is the only place in Cascais where you can get baked Virginia ham. Portugal is represented by a codfish casserole à Reijos, which requires a 30-minute wait (and it's worth it). A delightful prelude to any meal is the shrimp pâté. The menu includes such items as an excellent roast beef as well as roast loin of pork served with rice and beans. The chef also is proud of his fresh seafood, featuring a "catch of the day." Usually sea bass, turbot, or red mullet are served. The restaurant has one of the most varied menus in town, right down to the homemade chutney and assorted condiments served with the authentic curries. The cost of a regular meal ranges from 2,000$ ($15) to 2,500$ ($18.75). The recent redecoration has produced an Oriental effect. Be sure to reserve your table, as this one's popular. It's open from 12:30 to 3:30 p.m. and 7 to 9 p.m. daily.

Modest tabs are also rung up at **La Gran Tasca Restaurant and Wine Bar,** 3 Rua Sebastião José de Carvalho e Melo (tel. 28-11-40). If a local person in Cascais were to recommend a restaurant to his visiting Portuguese cousin, it would probably be this one. It has good regional fare, the daily plats du jour announced on a blackboard out front. It's always crowded, and with good reason. The décor is enhanced by wood beams and many antiques. There is a wine bar at the entrance where you can drink by the glass or bottle while enjoying tapas, always available at the bar. Try the clam soup, followed by maracana (clams and squid in a coconut-cream sauce) or maracanissimo (king prawns, angelfish, squid, and clams, also in a coconut-cream sauce). Besides these specialties, you can order steaks, poultry, or fish cooked to order from the à la carte menu. This is the type of place to which you are likely to want to return. You can dine well for about 1,200$ ($9). The establishment is open daily from noon to midnight.

CHAPTER V

SIGHTSEEING IN LISBON

□ □ □

Many visitors think seeing the sights of Lisbon can be accomplished by one quick visit to the Coach Museum in the parish of Belém. Not so, and if you limit yourself to just this one sight you'll be missing quite a lot. Lisbon is chock-full of sights, attractions you'll be glad you took the time to see, and which will give you a greater feeling and knowledge of this very individual country, Portugal.

Those on the strictest of schedules should really try to visit the following at least: (1) the Coach Museum, (2) the Jerónimos Monastery, (3) the Alfama, (4) the Castle of St. George (for the view if nothing else), (5) the National Art Gallery, and (6) the Gulbenkian Center for Arts and Culture.

However, if your time is so tight that you've allowed only one day for sightseeing in Portugal, head for the museum-filled area of Belém in the morning, then spend the afternoon enjoying Sintra.

For our exploration of all the major sights (and many esoteric but worthwhile ones), we'll begin in the old quarter . . .

THE ALFAMA (A WALKING TOUR)

The most *típico* district of Lisbon lies to the east of Black Horse Square. It's the old Moorish quarter of the city, the Alfama, partially spared by the earthquake of 1755, because its foundation was more solid than that of the rest of the capital. Here narrow, cobblestone streets stretch down to the Tagus from St. George Castle, crowning the hill.

Today the Alfama is the traditional home of stevedores, sailors, and fishermen. But in days gone by it was the aristocratic sector. Even today you can see coats-of-arms of noble families imbedded in the façades of some of the houses.

Allow at least two hours for your walking tour of the Alfama. The streets are rarely suitable for a car; at times, you must walk up steep stone stairs.

A good point to begin your tour is the **Largo do Salvador** (a taxi can drop you off there), housing a 16th-century mansion that once belonged to the Count of Arcos. From there, turn down the **Rua da Regueira,** which leads to the **Beco do Carneiro,** the "cul-de-sac of rams." The lane couldn't be narrower. Families live in houses literally four feet (if that much!) apart. "Our lips easily meet high across the narrow street," wrote poet Frederico de Brito.

At the end of the alley, circle back via a flight of steps to your left to the **Largo de Santo Estevão,** named after the church on the site. Round the church and from the back proceed to the **Patio das Flores,** via a flight of steps, where you can see some of the most delightful little houses fronted with characteristic Portuguese tiles (*azulejos*). Walk down the steps to the **Rua dos Remédios,** cutting right to the **Largo do Chafariz de Dentro,** where you're bound to see the Alfama housewives busily gossiping in front of an old fountain and often walking with jugs of fresh water balanced on their heads.

From the square, you connect with the **Rua de São Pedro,** which is perhaps the most animated street in the Alfama. Strolling deep into the street, you'll probably eventually attract a trail of children, and will come upon women squatting on the street, bartering furiously with a rough-faced, barefoot *varina* (fishwife) over slices of giant swordfish.

You'll pass some local taverns, and adventurous sightseers will go inside to sample a glass of *vinho verde* (green wine). Later, your head reeling from several glasses, you'll step onto the narrow street again, where you'll be virtually knocked down by an old fisherman with brown nets draped over his shoulder.

The Rua de São Pedro leads into the **Largo de São Rafael,** which convinces you the 17th century never ended. You pass a *leitaria* (dairy), which now sells milk in the bottle instead of via the old-fashioned method (cows were kept right inside, as the women of Alfama wanted to make sure their milk was fresh).

Right off the square is the **Rua de Judiaria,** so called because of the many Jews who settled there after escaping the Inquisition in Spain.

Go back to the Largo de São Rafael, crossing it to rejoin the Rua de São Pedro. Walk down that street to the intersection, forking left. You enter the **Largo de São Miguel,** with its church richly adorned with baroque trappings. From there, walk up the **Rua da São Miguel,** cutting left onto the **Beco de Cardosa,** where from some flower-draped balcony overhead, a *varina* is bound to scream down hell and damnation to her street-urchin son if he doesn't come inside immediately.

As you pass the doorways, you'll see black-shawled old women grilling Setúbal sardines on braziers. The armies of cats who reside in the Alfama will easily devour any bones or heads left over. At the end of the alley, you connect with the **Beco Sta. Helena,** a continuation, which leads up several flights of steps to the **Largo das Portas do Sol.**

On this square is the **Museum of Decorative Art,** handsomely ensconced in one of the many mansions that used to grace the Alfama.

One of the most favored belvederes in the city opens onto the square. Called the **Santa Luzia Belvedere,** it's really a balcony to view the sea, overlooking the houses of the Alfama, as they sweep down in a jumbled pile to the Tagus.

Although best explored by day, the Alfama takes on a different spirit at night, when street lanterns cast ghostly patterns against medieval walls and the plaintive sound of the *fadista* is heard until the early morning hours in the traditional cafés.

CASTLE OF ST. GEORGE

Known as the "cradle" of Lisbon, the present castle is of Visigoth origin; before that, the site was most likely used for a Roman fortress. The castle is named after St. George in honor of the Portuguese and English alliance of 1386. Around the periphery of the fortress is a district of much interest, looking as if it were removed intact from the Middle Ages.

Before entering the grounds, pause at the **Castle Belvedere,** known as the "ancient window" looking over the city below. In the distance, you can see the best view of the "Bay of Straw," the hills of Monsanto and of Sintra, the Ponte 25 de Abril, the rusty-red rooftops of Lisbon, and the Praça do Comércio. The statue is of Afonso Henriques, the first king of Portugal, who is said to have lived here after he liberated the city from the Moors.

Inside the grounds, you can walk along in cool shade or in sunlight, watching the swans gliding by in the moat, peacocks craning their long necks, olive and cork trees fluttering in the wind. Pink flamingos, weeping willows, and oleander create a dreamy feeling until you stumble upon a cannon, reminding you of the castle's bloody history, the lives lost in battles on this hill.

In the only room left of the ancient Royal Palace, the Alcáçova, you can wander in, and study the details of Roman and Islamic tombstones.

The admission-free castle is open daily from 9 a.m. till sunset.

THE CATHEDRAL (Sé)

As European cathedrals go, this one is not wealthy with great art, but it does remain an enduring landmark. Its twin towers give it a fortress-like look and the present structure is a mixture of architectural styles ranging from Romanesque to Gothic to baroque. Actually, the cathedral is a little bit of everything, having been changed and modified considerably after it suffered damage from two different earthquakes—one in 1344, the other in 1755.

It is said to have been built on the foundation of a mosque. After King Afonso Henriques liberated the city in the 12th century, the church was built as a triumphant gesture, the establishment of a Christian bastion. Lisboans speak of it as their mother church, the oldest one in the city.

Inside, the most interesting features are a rose window; the Gothic chapel of Bartolomeu Joanes dating from the 14th century; a "crib" by Machado de Castro, the leading Portuguese sculptor of the 18th century; the original nave and aisles; and the 14th-century tomb of Lopo Fernandes Pacheco. The church, at the Largo da Sé, within walking distance of the Praça do Comércio, may be visited from 9 a.m. to 5 p.m.

BELÉM

This western parish of Lisbon is forever linked to the glory of the Age of Exploration. Here, at the mouth of the Tagus, Vasco da Gama set out to blaze a new trail to India, Ferdinand Magellan to circumnavigate the globe, and Días to round the Cape of Good Hope, even if he didn't know it at the time.

At the point where the caravels, inspired by Henry the Navigator, were launched on their historic missions, Manuel the Fortunate erected:

THE TOWER OF BELÉM: Built between 1515 and 1521, the quadrangular tower is the most distinctive landmark in Portugal. It was designed by Francisco de Arruda in a Manueline style that incorporates Gothic and Romanesque features, also betraying the debt the architect owed to the Moors during his years of work in Morocco. One historian claimed that the tower "seems to epitomize the hybrid yet highly original character of Portugal's people."

If you climb the stairs to the ramparts, you'll have a panoramic view of the Tagus, as well as the handsome villas in the hills. To reach the entrance door, you walk across a drawbridge. Inside, the rooms are sparsely furnished, except for a few antiques that include a circa-1500 throne-armchair with carved finials and an inset paneled

LISBON: SIGHTS □ 61

with pierced Gothic tracery. Along the balustrade of the loggia are stone crosses symbolizing the Portuguese crusaders. On the tower is the coat-of-arms of Manuel I.

Fronting the Praça do Império is the **Fonte Luminosa** (Luminous Fountain), standing majestically between the Memorial to the Discoveries and the Jerónimos Monastery. Erected in 1940, the fountain attracts motorists from Lisbon who come out at night to watch the floodlit waterworks. To see the entire show takes nearly an hour, as there are about 75 original "liquid designs" from the water jets. On the Avenida Marginal, it is open daily, except Monday and holidays. From April 1 through September 30, hours are 10 a.m. to 6:30 p.m. and during the rest of the year, times are from 10 a.m. to 5 p.m. only. The admission charge is 150$ ($1.15).

THE MEMORIAL TO THE DISCOVERIES: The Portuguese

speak of it with pride as their Padrão dos Descobrimentos. Standing in the river, the monument was designed to simulate the effect of a prow of one of the legendary caravels. Along the ramps of either side you'll see some of the more memorable explorers, such as Vasco da Gama. But occupying the most prominent position, at the meeting point of the ramps, is Henry the Navigator.

This memorial was unveiled in 1960 on the fifth centennial of the prince's death. Symbolized in the frieze are sailors, mapmakers, monks (always taken along on the missions of exploration), a kneeling Philippa of Lancaster (mother of Henry the Navigator), artists, cosmographers, and a man holding a flag with a cross representing the crusaders. At the highest point on the memorial is the 15th-century "arms of Portugal."

Dominating the Praça do Império is:

JERÓNIMOS MONASTERY: The extravagant, flamboyant ar-

chitecture of Renaissance Portugal reached its pinnacle in this monastery, the **Mosteiro dos Jerónimos,** Praça do Império (tel. 61-70-20). Traditionalists assert that it was ordered built by Manuel the Fortunate to celebrate the opening of the route to India by Vasco da Gama. Certainly, it was paid for by the flourishing spice trade with the East.

Gothic elements romp with exotic Manueline motifs. The total effect was summed up by Howard La Fay: "Here, frozen forever in stone, is the blazing noontide of empire. Stylized hawsers writhe in the arches. Shells and coral and fish entwine on every column. Sanctuary lamps glow red above carved African lions."

Originally, a modest chapel founded by Henry the Navigator stood on these grounds; then the monastery was ordered built in

1502. Damaged but not destroyed by the earthquake of 1755, it was subsequently restored—the restoration a subject of controversy among architectural critics.

You enter through a magnificently sculpted doorway. To the right in the abbey are the tombs of Vasco da Gama and Luís Vaz de Camões, Portugal's greatest poet, whose fame rests on his *Os Lusíadas* ("The Portuguese"). In that heroic work, he spoke of the accomplishments of his countrymen and their triumphs over the enemies of Christ. With typical Portuguese individuality, he evoked pagan deities in his tome to Christianity. He also wrote of Vasco da Gama's discovery of the sea route to India. Franz Villier was skeptical of the claims made by the tombs: ". . . instead of Vasco, an unknown Gama was buried here by mistake, and the error had to be discreetly rectified, while for a long time people had quite forgotten where on earth Camões might be, and only tourists and illiterates really believe that this is the grave of the author of the Lusiads."

Also allegedly buried here are the kings of Portugal's Golden Age, such as Manuel the Fortunate and Sebastian. The latter was a mystic and religious fanatic who perished with his army in a mad attempt to lead a crusade against the Muslims in Morocco in 1578. (Actually, even though he was killed, many of his countrymen refused to accept the proof of his death. Thus arose "Sebastianism," a cult religion based on the belief that the king would return to Portugal. Four impersonators were unsuccessful in their attempt to claim the title.)

The cloister is of exceptional style and beauty, and it's the most exciting part of a visit to the abbey. As you head down the corridors —observing that each pillar is sculpted in a different and original style—you'll be walking across the unmarked tombs of long-forgotten people. Later, you can climb to the second tier where monks of old paced in meditation. Opening onto the cloisters are the monks' cells (seven feet long, four feet wide).

Open from 10 a.m. to 6:30 p.m. in summer, to 5 p.m. in winter, the monastery charges no entrance fee to the church. Admission to the adjacent cloisters costs 150$ ($1.15). Hours are the same as for the church. Both are closed on Monday and holidays. Take bus 43 from Praça de Figueira or bus 27 or 49 from Praça Marquês de Pombal.

In a wing of the abbey is the:

NATIONAL MUSEUM OF ARCHEOLOGY AND ETH-NOLOGY: Called the **Museu Nacional de Arqueologia e Ethnologia** in Portuguese, this museum, at Praça do Império, was founded in 1893 by José Leite de Vasconcellos and has been in the

Mosteiro dos Jerónimos since 1903. For many years this institution has been one of the most important in Portugal in the field of archeological and ethnological research.

The collections of ancient jewelry are outstanding, as are the Roman pavements and sculpture and the remains from many archeological sites, mainly Vaiamonte, Torre da Palma, and Tróia. The museum also has a fine nucleus of Portuguese ethnography and archeology and a valuable Egyptian collection. The Roman sculpture exhibition has the most significant objects in the museum's collection, and "Treasures of Portuguese Archeology" traces the history of jewelry and its development in the territory that became Portugal since Chalcolithic times (2000 B.C.) up to the Visigothic period. The museum also has various temporary shows.

It can be visited daily except Monday and holidays from 10 a.m. to 12:30 p.m. and 2 to 5 p.m. Admission is free.

Next door to Jerónimos Monastery is:

THE NAVAL MUSEUM AND PLANETARIUM: At the Museu de Marinha, Praça de Império, the glory of a maritime nation lives on in this remarkable museum that recalls in artifacts, ship models, full-size state barges, and traditional Portuguese fishing and traffic boats Portugal's dependence on the sea. As a historical maritime museum, it has navy, merchant marine, fishing, and pleasure craft sections. There is obvious glamour, of course, such as that in the Royal State Barges Hall, displaying an outstanding collection of magnificent barges built from the early 18th century up to the middle of the 19th century. The largest and most impressive one, displayed with 80 wax dummy oarsmen in gold and red jackets, was put into actual use during a state visit of Queen Elizabeth II of England to Lisbon in 1957. Also displayed are models of ships of Portugal's Golden Age, including the *caravela,* which were the most important ships of the discoveries, and *São Gabriel,* the flagship of Vasco da Gama, the great Portuguese navigator who discovered the sea route to India.

A special hall displays Queen Amélia's lodgings removed from the royal yacht of Carlos I, the king who was assassinated along with his son in the Praça do Comércio in 1908. In another hall is a remarkable display of 16th- and 17th-century Portuguese charts, mostly replicas of originals which were taken out of the country.

There are also exhibits from the Portuguese Fleet Air Arm which was in operation from 1917 until the early 1960s, when an independent Portuguese Air Force was created. On display is the seaplane *Santa Cruz,* and other mementos which recall the feat of naval aviators Sacadura Cabral and Gago Coutinho, who in 1922 made the first crossing of the South Atlantic by air with astronomical navigation made possible by use of a modified sextant invented by Gago Coutinho. The sextant is in the museum. By that flight, the Portuguese were the first Europeans to arrive in Brazil by air, some 400 years after their forebears were the first to arrive by sea in the fleet of Pedro Álvares Cabral.

The museum (tel. 61-01-92) is open daily, except Monday and holidays, from 10 a.m. to 5 p.m. Admission is 100$ (75¢) for adults, 50$ (40¢) for children under 16.

In the same building stands an 82-foot domed **Planetarium,** with a sky theater where astronomical performances can be viewed. The entrance fee for the Planetarium is 100$ (75¢) for adults, 50$ (40¢) for children. Visitors are admitted only on Saturday and Sunday, at 4,5, or 6 p.m. from March 1 to September 30 and at 4 or 5 p.m. from October 1 to February 28.

FOLK ART MUSEUM: Nowhere are the folk arts and customs of the Portuguese displayed more dramatically than here at the **Museu de Arte Popular,** Avenida de Brasília (tel. 61-12-82). The walls of the building, which previously housed the Regional Center during the 1940 Portuguese World's Exhibition, are painted by contemporary artists, some of the best in Portugal, including Carlos Botelho, Eduardo Anahory, Estrela Faria, Manuel Lapa, Paulo Ferreira, and Tomás de Melo (Tom). Their work is supplemented by enlarged photographs of the people of the provinces, with each individual region maintaining a separate personality. The establishment of the Folk Art Museum in 1948 was a result of a campaign for ethnic revival directed by António Ferro. On an ethnic basis, the collections, including ceramics, furniture, wickerwork, clothes, farm implements, and painting, are displayed in rooms which correspond more or less to the provinces.

The room devoted to Entre-Douro and Minho comprises examples of various subjects related to different features of that area. There are flowers, musical instruments, goldsmith pieces, Barcelos painted pottery, and Vila Nova de Gaia painted earthenware dolls. Elaborate harnesses used for oxen are on display, along with farm implements. You can see models of regional boats, fishing tools, embroidered sweaters, Azurara stockings, rugs, a Viana do Castelo weaver's loom, and various items for the preparation of linen, for spinning, and for knitting. Bilros laces and fiancés' handkerchiefs are also on exhibit.

The exhibition from Tras-os-Montes gives a survey of the northeast area, based on its main activities. You'll see straw *escrinhos* (baskets), a Vila Real oxcart and a harrow for threshing corn, kitchen items (*transfogueiro* and a piece of furniture, *escano*), black earthenware, and a collection of rugs and bedspreads. *Chocalheiros* masks, worn by men called by the same name who appear on feast days, are interesting displays.

The Algarve, well known to tourists, is represented by palm mats and baskets, a water cart, horse trappings, fishing nets, and a manually operated millstone, plus line-cut chimneys.

The room devoted to Beiras contains a reproduction of the interior of a Monsanto country house, as well as a variety of wicker and straw baskets, fine Molelos black earthenware items, bedspreads, and rugs. Here, too, is a set of tools used in salt making from Aveiro. Of special interest is a *moliço*-catcher's boat. *Moliço* is seaweed dredged up and used as fertilizer.

The final room, containing displays from Estremadura and Alentejo, holds a variety of objects such as glazed pottery pieces from Leiria and Mafra; Nazaré fishing and clothing items, sculpture, and saints' registries; and a wax dummy modeling the garb of the *campino,* a herdsman who looks after the bulls on the plains. From Alentejo, you'll see a replica of a kitchen, glazed Redondo earthenware, Nisa earthenware, Estremoz polished and striped pottery, and earthenware painted dolls, together with items of shepherds' art and votive paintings.

The museum is open daily, except Monday and holidays, from 10 a.m. to 12:30 p.m. and 2 to 5 p.m. Admission is 100$ (75¢). Buses 12 and 14 go there.

THE COACH MUSEUM: This is Lisbon's number-one sightseeing attraction. In what was once a riding academy attached to the royal residence at Belém, Queen Amélia, seeing many of Portugal's greatest old coaches falling into disrepair, started the nucleus of the collection. But poor Amélia used a yacht—not a coach—when she fled with her son, Manuel II, following the collapse of the monarchy in Portugal.

Gathered here are the magnificent coaches, some royal, ranging from the 17th through the 19th centuries. Far superior in the scope and style of its collection to that of the Palacio Real in Madrid, the **Museu Nacional dos Coches** is acclaimed as the world leader.

At Praça Afonsô de Albuquerque, the museum (tel. 63-80-22) is open daily from 10 a.m. to 6:30 p.m. from June through September. During the rest of the year, hours are 10 a.m. to 5 p.m. The entrance fee is 150$ ($1.15).

Among the more intriguing coaches is a 17th-century vehicle in which the Habsburg monarch, Philip II, rode to Lisbon in the era of Spain's domination. The most lavish trio—a collection of elegant gilded baroque carriages—was built in Rome for the Portuguese ambassador to the Vatican of Pope Clement XI in 1716. Less celebrated—but of much interest—is a *berlinda* belonging to the queen, Maria I. On the second floor, you'll find a collection of harnesses, saddles, armor, stirrups, and portraits from the deposed House of Bragança.

OTHER MUSEUMS OF LISBON

For art lovers, the two most important museums are the National Art Gallery and the newer Calouste Gulbenkian Museum.

NATIONAL MUSEUM OF ANCIENT ART: Although drawing fewer visitors than the Coach Museum, this is actually Portugal's greatest museum. It is the country's major showcase for both Portuguese and foreign paintings, exhibited along with an assemblage of French and Flemish tapestries; Portuguese embroidered carpets; antiques (many from the 15th century); a remarkable collection of gold and silver jewelry; and porcelain, pottery, and Oriental carpets. The museum, at 95 Rua das Janelas Verdes (tel. 66-41-51), is open from 10 a.m. to 1 p.m. and 2:30 to 5 p.m. daily except Monday and holidays. The charge for admission is 150$ ($1.15), except Sunday, when it's free.

The most celebrated painting here is *The Temptations of St. Anthony* by Hieronymus Bosch, which was restored in the early 1970s by the José de Figueiredo Institute for the Examination and Preservation of Works of Art. In the west building, the best-known Portuguese work is the 15th-century polyptych found in the convent of St. Vincent de Fora. These panels were probably the masterpiece of Nuno Gonçalves, Portugal's painter who worked at the court of Afonso V, and are an example of early Renaissance collective portraits.

Notable foreign paintings include a *St. Catherine* and a *Salomé* (with the head of John the Baptist resting on a platter) by Lucas Cranach; plus works by Anthony Van Dyck, Sir Joshua Reynolds, Velázquez, Raphael, Andrea del Sarto (a remarkable self-portrait), Tiepolo, Guardi (a small Venetian scene), Poussin, Zurbarán (a whole room), Murillo, Ribera, Dürer (seek out his *St. Jerome*), Hans Holbein (*Virgin and Saints*), Memling, and Pieter Brueghel (*Charity Work*).

The collection is rich in Portuguese works, including canvases by Frey Carlos, a well-known artist of the Flemish-Portuguese School. The jewelry collection here stuns—everything from a processional cross from the Monastery of Alcobaça to a *custódia* removed from the Monastery of Belém. This latter monstrance was said to have been made in 1506 by Gil Vicente from the first gold brought back from the East by Vasco da Gama.

From the 18th century, a silver plate, the work of the Germain family, is considered the finest in the world. Weighing more than a ton, it was ordered by King Joseph I. The miracle is that this group was never melted down to fill up some later king's sagging treasury.

Among sculptural exhibits are works by Machado de Castro, the leading Portuguese sculptor of the 18th century and a master of terracotta relief.

CALOUSTE GULBENKIAN MUSEUM: Opened in the autumn of 1969, this museum houses what one critic called "one of the world's finest private art collections"—that of Armenian oil tycoon Calouste Gulbenkian, who died in 1955. The multimillion-dollar modern center, at 45 Avenida de Berna (tel. 73-51-31), is in a former private estate which belonged to the Count of Vilalva. It is open on Tuesday, Thursday, Friday, and Sunday from 10 a.m. to 5 p.m.; on Wednesday and Saturday from 2 to 7:30 p.m. (closed Monday and holidays), from June 1 to October 31. During the other months of the year, it's open every day except Monday and holidays from 10 a.m. to 5 p.m. The admission is 40$ (30¢), except on Sunday when it's free.

The collections cover Egyptian, Greek, and Roman antiquities, a remarkable set of Islamic art including ceramics and textiles of Turkey and Persia, Syrian glass, books, bindings, and miniatures, Chinese vases, Japanese prints, and lacquer work. The European displays include medieval illuminated manuscripts and ivories, 15th- to 19th-century paintings and sculpture, Renaissance tapestries and medals, important collections of 18th-century French decorative arts, French impressionist painting, René Lalique jewelry, and glassware.

In a move requiring great skill of negotiation, Gulbenkian managed to make purchases of art from the Hermitage at Leningrad. Among his most notable acquisitions are two Rembrandts: *Pallas Athene* and *Portrait of an Aging Man.* Two other well-known paintings are a portrait of *Helen Fourment* by Peter Paul Rubens and Renoir's *Madame Claude Monet Lounging.* The French sculptor Jean Antoine Houdon is represented by a statue of *Diana.* Much of the collection of 18th-century silver—said to be the finest in the world—came from the sales by the Soviet government during their cash-raising activities of the 1920s. Much of it belonged to Catherine the Great, and many pieces from the French monarchs are also displayed.

As a cultural center, the Gulbenkian Foundation sponsors plays, films, ballet, and musical concerts, as well as a rotating exhibition of works by leading Portuguese and foreign artists.

CENTER FOR MODERN ART: Around the corner from the

central main entrance to the Gulbenkian Museum, the **Centro de Arte Moderna,** Rua Dr. Nicolau de Bettencourt (tel. 73-51-31), is the first major permanent exhibition center of modern Portuguese artists to open in Lisbon. The center shares park-like grounds with the Gulbenkian Foundation, and was, in fact, a gift left from the legacy of the late Armenian oil magnate.

Housed in a British-designed complex of clean lines and dramatically proportioned geometric forms, with a Henry Moore sculpture in front, the museum houses a collection of some 5,000 works of art. It displays the works of many modern Portuguese artists, some of which enjoy world reputations. Some of the paintings on exhibit were considered aggressively iconoclastic at the time of their execution.

Admission is 30$ (25¢). July to November, hours are 10 a.m. to 5 p.m. on Tuesday, Thursday, Friday, and Sunday, and from 2 to 7:30 p.m. on Wednesday and Saturday. November to July, it's open from 10 a.m. to 5 p.m. Tuesday to Sunday. Closed Monday and bank holidays.

MUSEUM OF DECORATIVE ART: The decorative arts school museum, **Fundação Ricardo do Espírito Santo Silva,** 2 Largo da Porta do Sol (tel. 86-21-83), is a foundation established in 1953 through the vision and generosity of Dr. Ricardo do Espírito Santo Silva, who endowed it with items belonging to his private collection and set up workshops of handcrafts in which nearly all activities related to the decorative arts are represented. The handsomely furnished museum is in one of the many mansions of the aristocracy that used to grace the Alfama. The principal aim of the foundation is the preservation and furtherance of the decorative arts by maintaining the traditional character and developing craftsperson's skill and culture. In the workshops, you can see how perfect reproductions of pieces of furniture and other objects are made in the purest styles. The foundation also restores furniture, books, and Arraiolos rugs.

The museum has been given the character of an inhabited palace through placement in the mansion, in order to enhance the esthetic value of the objects on display by setting them in appropriate surroundings. Visitors can have a fairly accurate picture of what the interior of a posh Lisbon home in the 18th and 19th centuries might have been like. There are particularly outstanding displays of furniture of the 17th through the 19th centuries; Portuguese silver of the 17th through the 19th centuries; and Arraiolos rugs of the 17th, 18th, and 19th centuries.

The museum is open daily except Sunday and Monday from 10 a.m. to 1 p.m. and 2:30 to 5 p.m. Admission is free. Visitors must wait downstairs in the entrance hall, where an old coach sits, for a guide to show them through the three floors of rooms. To reach the museum and the foundation, take tram 28 or bus 37.

LISBON'S CHURCHES

Lisbon, past and present, lives on in its churches. The earthquake of 1755 destroyed many of them completely. Others were reconstructed, more or less well according to the times.

CHURCH OF MADRE DE DEUS: The most intriguing one is
the Church of Madre de Deus. Queen Leonor founded this *convento* in 1509; today it contains some of the most precious *azulejos* (glazed tiles)—virtually a museum of them—of any church in Lisbon. The Manueline façade hardly reveals the lush decorations inside. At 4 Rua Madre de Deus, the church may be visited from 10 a.m. to 1 p.m. and 2:30 to 5 p.m. daily except Monday. There is no admission charge, but you should tip the guide who shows you around.

Leonor was the queen of João II. To her meager chapel were added a church and cloisters by King João III, a 16th-century monarch. João V further embellished the church, but his reign ended five years before the great earthquake of 1755, which left much of the church in ruins. The task of rebuilding fell to the lieutenants of José I in the 18th century.

As you enter the church, you see walls lined with glazed tiles in clear blues and whites, the effect crowned by oils framed in lavish baroque gilt.

The guide will show you through the two-tiered cloisters. The rooms opening off the cloisters are lined with remarkable 16th- and 17th-century tiles, many from Delft (why anyone wanted to import tiles from Holland to *azulejo*-rich Portugal remains a mystery). Seek out the chapel dedicated to St. Anthony and don't miss the choir, with its delicately carved stalls from the 18th century.

PANTHEON CHURCH OF ST. ENGRÁCIA: When a builder
starts to work on a Portuguese house, the owner often chides him, "Don't take as long as St. Engrácia." Construction on this Portuguese baroque church began in the 17th century and it resisted the earthquake. Nevertheless, it was only completed in 1966. The church is so well planned and built that relief and architectural idiosyncrasies would have been welcomed. It is graced with a quartet of square towers. The completed product appears pristine and cold, and the state has fittingly turned it into a neoclassic Pantheon, containing memorial tombs to Portuguese greats as well as heads of state.

Memorials honor Henry the Navigator; Luís Vaz de Camões,

the country's greatest poet, author of *Os Lusíadas,* an epic poem of Portugal's world history; Pedro Álvares Cabral, discoverer of Brazil; Afonso de Albuquerque, viceroy of India; Nuno Álvares Pereira, warrior and saint; and Vasco da Gama, of course.

Also entombed in the National Pantheon are presidents of Portugal: Sidónio Pais, assassinated in 1918; Marshal António Óscar de Fragoso Carmona, under whose government António de Oliveira Salazar began his climb to power; and Téofilo Braga, first president of the provisional government after settling of the Republic. Several Portuguese writers are also interred here, including Almeida Garrett, the country's most outstanding writer of the 19th century; João de Deus, lyric poet; and Guerra Junqueiro, also a poet.

The National Pantheon, Campo de Santa Clara (tel. 87-15-29), is closed on Monday and holidays. Otherwise, it is open to the public from 10 a.m. to 5 p.m. Admission is 50$ (40¢). Ask the guards to take you to the terrace for a beautiful view over the river.

A visit to the Pantheon can be combined with a shopping trip to the Flea Market (walk down the Campo de Santa Clara, heading toward the river).

ST. ROQUE CHURCH AND MUSEUM: The St. Roque Church (tel. 36-03-61) was founded in the closing years of the 16th century by the Jesuits. To reach it, head for the Largo Trindade Coelho any day between 10 a.m. and 5 p.m., except on Monday when it closes at 4 p.m. The museum is open daily from 10 a.m. to 5 p.m. (to 4 p.m. on Monday) and charges 25$ (20¢) for admission (free on Sunday). Take bus 37 from the Rossio.

The St. Roque Museum is visited chiefly for its collection of baroque jewelry. A pair of gold and silver torch-holders, weighing about 840 pounds, are considered among the most elaborate in Europe. The gold embroidery from the 18th century is a rare treasure, as are the vestments. The paintings are mainly from the 16th century, including one of a double-chinned Catherine of Austria, another of the wedding ceremony of King Manuel. Look for a remarkable 16th-century *Virgin (with Child) of the Plague,* and a polished conch shell from the 18th century that served as a baptismal font.

The church, with its painted wood ceiling, contains a chapel honoring John the Baptist by Luigi Vanvitelli. The chapel was assembled in Rome in the 18th century with such precious materials as alabaster and lapis lazuli, then dismantled and shipped to Lisbon, where it was reassembled. It was ordered by the Bragança king, João V, nine years before the end of his reign in 1750. The marble mosaics look like a painting.

You can also visit the Sacristy, rich in paintings illustrating scenes from the lives of the Society of Jesus saints. The Jesuits held great power in Portugal, at one time virtually governing the country for the king.

ST. VINCENT OUTSIDE THE WALLS:
This outstanding Renaissance church houses the Pantheon of the House of Bragança, the dynasty that ruled Portugal beginning with the collapse of Spanish domination in 1640 and lasting until 1910. A former convent, the church contains an estimated one million *azulejos* (glazed earthenware tiles). The Sacristy is graced with Portuguese marble, jacaranda woodwork from Brazil, and an 18th-century ivory Christ from Goa.

When St. Vincent was first built between 1582 and 1627, it was outside the walls of Lisbon—hence, its name. The earthquake of 1755 caused its cupola to collapse. At Largo de S. Vincente, it is open daily from 10 a.m. to 1 p.m. and 3 to 6 p.m., charging 50$ (40¢) for admission. It is closed on Monday.

In the burial chamber is entombed the twice-married Maria II, who ascended to the Portuguese throne at the age of 15. Dom Carlos I is buried near his son, Luís Felipe, the latter only 19 when both were assassinated at the Praça do Comércio in 1908. Manuel II, who ruled for only two years, lived a life of exile in England, dying there in 1932, at which time his body was returned home to Lisbon.

The House of Bragança also ruled Brazil from 1822 to 1889. The coffin of Dom Pedro, the first emperor of that country (he abdicated in 1831), rests in this Pantheon. Finally, because there was no native burial ground for him, Michael, the last king of Rumania, was placed here in a handsome sarcophagus. King Michael of Rumania was forced to abandon his throne in the closing hours of 1947, and he lived in exile in Portugal until his death in 1953.

QUELUZ PALACE
For most visitors, the **Palácio Queluz** is the first stop of their venture into the suburbs of Lisbon. And what a fortunate choice. One writer called it "the prettiest pink palace in the world, as well as the most important and charming example of rococo architecture in Portugal." The Portuguese government is so proud of the little 18th-century nugget that it houses foreign dignitaries in its Pavilion of Dona Maria I (former guests have included General Eisenhower and Elizabeth II).

Queluz is most often described as Portugal's Versailles, but so lofty a comparison detracts from its true character. Essentially, it's a palace of faded pink walls that stands quietly in the bright sunshine, looking out over beds and beds of mauve-colored petunias. Its character has always been that of a summer residence, whose façade is rather simple and classic, although the interior is rich and ornate, overlooking beautiful gardens and ponds.

The palace was an adaptation of an old hunting pavilion of the Marquis Castelo Rodrigo, which came into the possession of the royal family in 1654. King Pedro III, husband of Maria I, liked it so much he decided to turn it into a summer residence, enlarging it and having it decorated with lavish interiors. What you see now is not the way it was, as the palace suffered greatly during the French invasions. Almost all the belongings were sent to Brazil with the royal family at the beginning of the 19th century.

Maria I was a well-educated princess who became queen at a troubled time. She had so many problems and suffered so much during her life that near the end she became insane. Before going mad, she was a bright, intelligent, and brave woman who did a fine job as ruler of her country. Her husband was her uncle, who became king by marrying her. A fire swept over the palace in 1934, but it has subsequently been restored. The glassy Throne Room intrigues visitors the most. You can stroll under the watchful eye of a guard through the dressing room of the queen, through the Don Quixote Chamber, and into the Music Salon, with its grand French piano and 19th-century harp.

The furnishings and general accoutrements are eclectic: Venetian chandeliers, Empire antiques, Florentine marbles, Delft plates, Macao screens, Austrian porcelain, Portuguese Chippendale and tapestries, and pieces made of jacaranda wood from Brazil.

After a royal tour, you can wind down by strolling through the handsomely laid out gardens, with their lily-studded fountains, earthenware tiles, beds of flowers, and 18th-century statuary.

The palace is open daily except Tuesday from 10 a.m. to 1 p.m. and 2 to 5 p.m. (On the grounds is the Cozinha Velha, or old kitchen, described in the preceding restaurant chapter.) Admission to the palace is 150$ ($1.15), only 50$ (40¢) if you wish just to visit the gardens.

Queluz lies on the road to Sintra, about 9½ miles from Lisbon. To reach it by public transportation, take a train at Rossio Station in Lisbon; a one-way fare costs 55$ (40¢).

SINTRA

Ancient Sintra, on the rugged slope of the Serra de Sintra, is the town Byron dubbed "glorious Eden." John Cam Hobhouse and Byron came this way in 1809 on their grand tour, and later Byron was to write his autobiographical poem, *Childe Harold,* in which he included his praise of the beauty of Sintra. Thus Sintra became a focus for a host of English visitors.

Byron and Robert Southey, another English poet, didn't discover the wonders of this remarkable oasis. Its praises were sung centuries before by the Luís Vaz de Camões poem, *Os Lusíadas.*

Even before Portugal's Golden Age, Sintra was favored by the Moors, who selected it as a site of one of their greatest castles, which stands in ruins today crowning a hilltop. The castle fell to the Christian crusaders in 1147.

Today Sintra is virtually a suburb of Lisbon, favored by the aristocracy, even exiled royalty, who inhabit the elaborate villas—often compared to birthday cakes—studding the hills.

Sintra lies about 17½ miles northwest of Lisbon, and is reached by private car, on an organized tour, or else by frequent train service, about a 45-minute ride from the main railway station at Rossio in Lisbon. But connections are possible from such Costa do Sol resorts as Estoril and Cascais.

Much of Sintra's charm comes from its luxurious vegetation—camellias, ferns, mimosa, eucalyptus, lemon trees, strawberry beds, pink bougainvillea, red geraniums, pine trees (and more lizards crawling up more damp tile walls than in any other place in Portugal).

One publicist summed up the charm of the town quite well by saying, "It is indeed a fairytale setting and gives one the feeling that this is where Sleeping Beauty must have rested all those years."

When you arrive in the central square, your main destination will be:

THE NATIONAL PALACE: This royal palace (tel. 923-00-85) was constructed primarily during the reign of two Portuguese kings: João I (1385–1433) and Manuel I (1469–1521, known as "the Fortunate"). Subsequent additions were made in later centuries, and the palace continued to function as a royal palace until 1910 when Manuel II fled to exile in England.

Portuguese kings and queens summered here. Although the original Moorish palace that stood on this spot was torn down, the Muslim influence lived on when it was reconstructed. The introduction of the Gothic or Manueline style makes for a bizarre effect. Be sure to note the painted *azulejos* (tiles) that line many of the rooms, as these are considered the finest in Portugal. This is one of the most important Portuguese monuments.

The palace has been intimately linked to the lives and legends of many members of the Portuguese royal family. For example, Afonso V, king of Portugal from 1438 to 1481, was born at Sintra. He was named king only six years later. But to a later king, Afonso VI, the palace was a gloomy prison. Imprisoned by his brother (later Pedro II), he lost not only his throne but his wife. The ill-fated Afonso endlessly paced his cell until his death in 1683.

The Room of the Swans was favored by João I, part of its window decoration coming from what is now Spanish Morocco (Ceuta). One of the most interesting legends of the palace revolves around João I, who married Philippa of Lancaster (they were the parents of Henry the Navigator). As the oft-repeated tale goes, Philippa discovered her husband making love to one of her fair ladies-in-waiting. Although the English queen forgave her errant spouse, gossips speculated at length. Enraged, the king ordered that the room be redecorated, its ceiling adorned with magpies, these noisy birds symbolizing the chattering court. Hence, the nickname Room of the Magpies.

For many visitors, the Stag Room—also called the Heraldic Room—is the most expressive, with its coats-of-arms of the noble families of Portugal and scenes from the hunt. The Room of the Mermaids (sometimes known as Sirens) is also graceful. In the old kitchen there are two enormous original chimneys.

From many of the salons there are excellent vistas opening onto the hills surrounding Sintra. Tapestries, paintings, sheltered patios, softly falling water, potted plants, and long, dark corridors evoke the faded life of another era.

Tickets to the palace cost 150$ ($1.15). Purchase your ticket downstairs at a counter on the left, then walk up the stairway to the right and ring the bell to be let in. The palace is open daily, except Wednesday and holidays, from 10 a.m. to 4:45 p.m.

THE PALACE OF PENA: Some have called this the most romantic scenic spot in all of Portugal. The palace was built on a peak about 1,500 feet high, overlooking the Moorish castle on the opposite hill. Pena Palace (tel. 923-02-27) majestically looks down on Sintra from its regal throne. (Some actually walk to it from the town square, but others take a taxi or drive their own car.)

The *National Geographic* labeled Pena Palace a "soaring agglomeration of towers, cupolas, and battlemented walls." A fantasy in the sky it truly is, constructed to the specifications of Ferdinand of Saxe-Coburg-Gotha, the consort of Queen Maria II. When she died in 1853 at the age of 34, leaving 11 royal offspring, one of her sons, the ill-fated Pedro V, was named king. But the German consort served as regent until Pedro was of age.

Helping Ferdinand achieve his dream was Baron Eschwedge, a German architect. The baron attempted to re-create the aura of the Middle Ages; in some respects he succeeded, but it's "merely the mock." The present castle was built on the grounds of a monastery ordered erected in the early 16th century for Jerónimos monks by Manuel the Fortunate. What remains of the monastery is a cloister and a tiny ogival chapel (see its alabaster panel and stained-glass window).

Most critics satirize the interior of the palace, suggesting that it is Wagnerian or lacking in taste. Actually, it's quite fascinating, as it's been left almost intact since it was last occupied by the royal family in 1910. It was from this palace that the mother of Manuel II gathered her jewelry and most valuable possessions on a long-ago autumn day and was driven on a wild ride to Mafra, where she collected her son, the king, to flee with him into exile. Around the top of the hill is the **Parque de Pena,** mapped out between 1846 and 1850 under the direction of Ferdinand. It's acclaimed as one of the most majestic landscapes in Europe. Climb to the **Cruz Alta** for a panoramic view.

Tickets cost 200$ ($1.50). The hours are 10 a.m. to 5 p.m.; closed Monday.

A BULLFIGHT SPECTACLE

Portuguese bullfights, of course, differ from the Spanish in that the matador doesn't kill the bull. This tradition dates from the 18th century when the son of the Duke of Arcos (bullfighting was then a nobleman's sport) lost his life in the arena. His father jumped into the ring and personally killed the bull. The dictator prime minister, Marquês de Pombal—worried about manpower needed to rebuild Lisbon after the earthquake—decreed that that was the last life to be sacrificed in the ring. From that day forth, the horns of the bull were bound with leather bandages known as *emboladas.*

The prohibition against killing the bull is always under fire from certain critics. For example, Jaime Saraiva, a commentator in Lisbon, was once quoted in the press as saying, "a bullfight without a kill is a great lie; it is not serious." But don't let his words keep you from attending a spectacle. The fight may not be "serious," but it is what Marvine Howe termed "one of the most beautiful equestrian displays in the world."

Warning: Even though the bull isn't killed in Portugal, it must be pointed out, in fairness, that many readers still find this spectacle nauseating and take strong exception to Howe's comment that it is "beautiful." The spears jabbed into the neck of the bull produce blood, of course, making the unfortunate animal visibly weaker. The so-called fight has been labeled no contest! One reader wrote, "The animals are frightened, confused, and badgered before they are mercifully allowed to exit. What sport!"

Bullfighting in Portugal doesn't enjoy the number of fans it has in Spain. It's estimated that only one-quarter of the populace attend the *corridas,* as opposed to three times that number in neighboring Spain.

Opening the corrida, the matadors parade in wearing their colorful suits, many unchanged in design for 200 years. They are followed by *cavaleiros,* the horseback-riding men who place darts in the bull, and the *forcados,* the troupe of men who tackle the bull. Traditionally, the latter wear jaunty green caps with red bands on their heads. They are attired in gold jackets and olive trousers, with a red sash around their waists, white stockings covering their calves.

At the sound of a trumpet, the gates open and out comes the cavaleiro on a horse he's most likely trained from its birth. The trick is to lead the galloping horse into the pathway of a rampaging bull —only to get the steed to swerve in time to prevent a head-on collision (which has happened). Darts are thrust into the bull's neck at this point to weaken him.

In Portugal, the bull is tackled by hand, the action known as a *pega.* A phalanx of eight forcados advances on the bull. One takes the angry animal by the horns; another may latch onto his tail; still another may grab the flesh hanging from the bull's chest, and so forth until the matador enters and finishes up the show.

The "season of the corridas" runs from Easter until early autumn, and in Lisbon, bullfighters are presented at the Moorish **Campo Pequeno,** reached by the subway. Alternatively, you can attend the **Monumental de Cascais** (tel. 28-31-03) at one of the leading resorts on the Costa do Sol. Fights are usually scheduled for Thursday night and Sunday afternoon.

Seats are sold in three different categories: *sombra* (shade), *sombra y sol* (a seat in the sun for part of the fight, in the shade for the rest), and *sol* (a seat in the sun during the entire fight). Naturally, the shady seats are the most expensive.

ORGANIZED TOURS

Many travel agents in Lisbon offer organized tours for those who want to have all the arrangements, including transportation, made for them. One of the largest agencies is **STAR Travel Service,** the representative for American Express at 4-A Sidónio Pais (tel. 53-98-71). In high season, from March 1 to October 31, tours are operated daily, departing from the Praça Marquês de Pombal.

Lisbon is broken into several different sections, each one highlighting a particular cultural, historic, or scenic sight, such as St. George Castle or the Jerónimos Monastery at Belém. Most of the city tours last three hours. The **Cityrama Tour** by sightseeing bus, for example, lasts three hours, departing at 9:45 a.m. and again at 2:15 p.m. However, another tour departs at 5 p.m. from April 1 to September 30 only.

The most heavily booked excursion to the environs is to **Queluz, Sintra,** and **Estoril,** with a luncheon stopover at Sintra.

CHAPTER VI

SHOPPING IN LISBON

□ □ □

All the major Portuguese handcrafts get their best showing in Lisbon. Shopkeepers or their agents scan the country, as well as Madeira and the Azores, ferreting out the best work from the most skillful artisans and craftspeople. Owing to the versatility of the Portuguese and their ability to absorb other styles, handcrafts often betray exotic influences.

Although frowned upon in prestigious shops, bargaining is still a respectable custom throughout Lisbon. You'll have to let your intuition be your guide. A good rule of thumb to follow is to determine if the shop is small enough to be owner managed. If it is, you might possibly work out a deal.

Shops are spread throughout the city, but the major area for browsing is the **Baixa,** the district forming downtown Lisbon. Its three principal streets are the Rua do Ouro (Street of Gold, with major jewelry shops), Rua da Prata (Street of Silver), and Rua Augusta. To the west is the more fashionable **Chiado,** the second major shopping district, whose main street is the Rua Garrett.

You'll find especially good buys in Portugal in handmade embroideries (blouses, tablecloths, napkins, and handkerchiefs) from the Madeira Islands and the Azores; cork products in every size, shape, and description, everything from placemats to cigarette boxes; decorative *azulejos* (glazed tiles); porcelain and china from Vista Alegre; Nazaré fishermen's sweaters; gold and silver filigree jewelry; Arraiolos carpets; local pottery; and fado records, of course.

Most stores open at 9 a.m., closing at noon for lunch. They generally reopen at 2 p.m., shutting down at 7 p.m. However, many proprietors prefer to shut down for lunch from 1 to 3 p.m., so keep a watch out. Most stores in Lisbon and elsewhere in Portugal remain open a full day on Saturday.

MADEIRA EMBROIDERIES: A good place to shop, **Madeira Superbia,** 75-A Avenida Duque de Loulé (tel. 53-79-68), is an outlet for one of the finest embroidery factories on the Madeira Islands. This showcase of the exquisite craft offers excellent—although not inexpensive—linens, tapestries, and women's apparel, such as embroidered blouses, and petit-point handbags. High-quality fabrics are often imported from Ireland and Switzerland, then embroidered in the islands. The collection of hand-embroidered pillowcases, tea cloths, napkins, and table centers is exceptional. Placemats often come in organdy with a linen appliqué (some double-edged with shadow work embroidery). Another popular item is monogrammed linen handkerchiefs. There are branches at the Hotel Ritz in Lisbon and the Hotel Estoril Sol in Cascais.

EMBROIDERIES FROM THE AZORES: In the Chiado district, the **Casa Regional da Ilha Verde,** 4 Rua Paiva de Andrade (tel. 32-59-74), is the "Regional House of the Green Island." As such, it specializes in handmade items—especially embroideries—from the Azores. Every piece of merchandise is guaranteed to have been made by hand. Good buys are found in linen placemats with napkins. Some of the designs have been in use for centuries. Other gift items include products made of sperm whale teeth, such as cigarette holders, letter openers, and rings.

PORCELAIN AND CHINA: Unparalleled for china and glassware, **Vista Alegre,** 18 Largo do Chiado (tel. 36-14-01), numbers diplomats and royalty, or whoever demands the very best, among its regular clientele. Of special interest to the casual shopper is the colorful porcelain from Ilhavo, with many of the figurines depicting regional costumes.

Decorators, both professionals and do-it-yourselfers, are fond of the porcelain birds and figures. Amazingly lifelike, they are also expensive. However, you'll do better ordering a set of dishes or porcelain fruit bowls.

SILVER AND GOLD: The most distinguished silver- and goldsmith in Portugal is **W. A. Sarmento,** 251 Rua Aurea (tel. 32-67-74). The shop at the foot of the Santa Justa elevator provides Lisboans with treasured confirmation and graduation gifts, and is favored by diplomats, movie stars, and the Costa do Sol aristocracy. In 1970 Sarmento celebrated its 100th anniversary—it's remained in the hands of the same owners all the while.

Gold is considered a good buy in Portugal, as the government strictly regulates its sale, requiring jewelers to put a minimum of 19¼ karats in articles made of the precious metal. Sarmento specializes in lacy filigree jewelry in gold or silver. Just hold an earring or brooch up to the light and enjoy its intricacy and delicacy. Especially popular are small gold filigree caravels, which come in many prices. Less expensive filigree jewelry is made of silver and plated with gold. In this category earrings and cufflinks predominate. For the charm collector, Sarmento is a Roman holiday. Literally dozens of choices are offered.

FILIGREE: Filigree items are all the rage not only in Lisbon but all over Portugal. This art of ornamental open work made of fine gold or silver wire dates back to ancient times. The most expensive items, often objets d'art, are fashioned from 19¼-karat gold. Depictions of caravels are one of the forms this art expression takes. However, less expensive trinkets are often made of sterling silver, perhaps sterling silver which has been dipped in 24-karat gold. Well on its way to being a century old, **Joalharia do Carmo,** 87-B Rua do Carmo (tel. 32-30-50), is the best place in Lisbon to shop for filigree work. Some of the gold pieces here have been further adorned with either precious or semiprecious stones.

AZULEJOS: Founded in 1741, **Sant'Anna,** 95-97 Rua do Alecrim (tel. 32-25-37), is Portugal's leading ceramic center. In the Chiado section, Sant'Anna is known for its *azulejos* (glazed tiles). The Rua do Alecrim location is the showroom outlet; however, you can also visit the factory at 96 Calçada da Boa Hora, but you must call ahead and make an appointment. The craftspeople who create and decorate the tiles are among the finest in Europe, many of them following designs in use since the Middle Ages.

Fábrica Cerâmica Viúva Lamengo, 25 Largo do Intendente (tel. 57-59-29), sells reproductions of old Portuguese pottery and tiles, including an interesting selection of planters and umbrella stands. When you reach the address, you'll know you're at the right place: its façade is decorated with these colorful *azulejos* with figures in their rich plumage and dress.

SUEDE: A "one-couple" show is **Caprice,** 67-B Rua Joaquim António de Aguiar (tel. 53-86-28), diagonally across from the Ritz Hotel. M and Mme Gaulier sell a fine line of washable suede items, such as long coats, skirts, and suits. Philippe L. Gaulier's mother was a Lanvin stylist, and apparently he inherited a great deal of her taste.

He and Mme Gaulier (English-speaking) will present you with an assortment of Ultraqua-suede garments, particularly dresses and coats, that are wrinkle free and machine washable. The suede comes in an interesting assortment of colors, including dark chocolate, pink, aqua, navy, and caramel. In addition, the Gauliers offer a selection of hand-crocheted suits and dresses, but, regrettably, the high cost of producing these items has made them suitable only for the carriage trade.

CORK PRODUCTS: For something typically Portuguese, try the **Casa das Cortiças,** 4 Rua Escola Politécnica (tel. 32-58-58). "Mr. Cork" became somewhat of a legend in Lisbon for offering "everything conceivable" that could be made of cork, of which Portugal controls a hefty part of the world market. Mr. Cork is gone now, but the store carries on. You'll be surprised at the number of items that can be made from cork, including a chess set or a checkerboard. Perhaps a set of six placemats in a two-toned checkerboard style will interest you. For souvenirs, the cork caravels are immensely popular. Other items include a natural cutting board and an ice bucket.

ROSSIO RAILWAY STATION SHOPPING MALL: There are some 150 boutiques, shops, and snackbars installed in four of the five floors of the Rossio Railway Station, in the heart of downtown Lisbon. The fifth floor is where the trains arrive and depart. Banks of escalators whisk you from floor to floor, and shopping in the maze of small shops is easier than walking on the congested streets. Conveniently, the shops are open every day of the year from 9 a.m. to midnight. The street floor is deceivingly shabby—ignore it and take the escalator to the boutiques. You'll find apparel for men, women, and children, shops specializing in jewelry, fado records, whatever. There's a pharmacy for "naturalists," beauty parlors, hairdressers, bookstores, leather goods, sweaters, and Portuguese handcrafts.

ANTIQUE ALLEY: Along both sides of the narrow **Rua de São José** are treasure troves—shops packed with antiques from all over the world. Antique dealers from America come here to pick up bargains. You'll find ornate carvings or time-seasoned woods, brass, plaques, copper pans, silver candelabra, crystal sconces, and chandeliers, plus a wide selection of old wooden figures, silver boxes, porcelain plates, and bowls.

Rua Dom Pedro V is another street of antique shops, of which my personal favorite is **Solar,** 68-70 Rua Dom Pedro (tel. 36-55-22). It is stocked with antique tiles salvaged from some of Portugal's historic buildings and manor houses. The condition of the tiles varies, of course. Many go back as far as the 16th century. The store also sells antique furniture and pewterware.

ARRAIOLOS CARPETS: In the little town of Arraiolos, the fine woolen rugs made here have earned the place an international reputation. Legend says these rugs were first made by Moorish craftspeople expelled from Lisbon in the early 16th century. Those designs were said to be in imitation of those from Persia. Some of these carpets eventually found their way into museums.

In Lisbon, the showcase for the Arraiolos carpet is **Casa Quintão,** 30-34 Rua Ivens (tel. 36-58-37). Rugs here are priced by the square foot, according to the density of the stitching. Casa Quintão can also reproduce intricate Oriental or medieval designs in rugs or tapestries, and create any custom pattern specified by a client. The shop also sells materials and gives instructions on how to make your own carpets and tapestry-covered pillows. The staff seems genuinely willing to help.

THE THIEVES' MARKET: This open-air street market—called the **Feira da Ladra**—is similar in character to the flea markets of Paris and Madrid. Almost every conceivable article is offered for sale in the street stalls. Vendors peddle their wares on Tuesday and Saturday (it's best to go in the morning when the pickings are riper).

In the Alfama district, about a five-minute walk from the waterfront, the market lies in back of the Military Museum, adjoining the Pantheon of São Vicente. Begin your shopping expedition at the Campo de Santa Clara. The hilly street with its tree-lined center is lined with portable stalls with individual displays.

You may pick up a valuable object here, but you'll have to search through an abundance of cheap clothing and useless junk to find it. The following types of merchandise are displayed: old brass door knockers with clasped hands, brass scales, brass beds, oil lamps, portable bidets, cowbells, old coins, Macao china, Angola wood-carvings, antique watches, meat grinders, broken torchiers, ships' lanterns, and gas lamps.

Yes, you not only can bargain, you *should* bargain. After the stallkeeper quotes you the first price, assume a not-interested stance. Then the fun commences, the price (usually) sliding downhill like a toboggan ride.

MODERN SHOPPING COMPLEXES: The most spectacular shopping complex in Lisbon is the **Amoreiras Shopping Center de Lisboa,** the largest in Iberia and fourth largest in Europe. You can wander through this Oriental fantasy, exploring the contents of more than 300 shops and boutiques. A huge array of merchandise is offered for sale, including Portuguese fashions, leather goods, crystal, and souvenirs. In addition to several restaurants and snackbars, there is also a health center. The location is on a hill at the entrance to Lisbon, lying in back of the old reservoir called Aguas Livres. The blue-and-pink towers rise 19 stories and have already changed the skyline of Lisbon. The mall is open daily from 10 a.m. to midnight.

CHAPTER VII

LISBON AFTER DARK

□ □ □

Fado singing is Portugal's most popular and important art form, originating as it does in the hearts and experiences of every Portuguese, whether a fisherman from Nazaré, a cork grower from the plains of Alentejo, or a metropolitan Lisboan. Every Portuguese has a point of view about fado: either he or she sings it, or else has a favorite artist whose particular style speaks to him or her directly.

Fado ("fate" in Portuguese) is the true folk song of the people, not superimposed on them in the name of art or culture. It's in their blood. The songs are poignant, from the core of the heart—sometimes tragic, sometimes wistful, even joyful at times, but usually melancholic, filled with nostalgia. The sound originates in Portugal, combining the Arabic "wail" with the throaty, almost guttural voice of the peasant.

Even if you don't understand the Portuguese language, fado speaks vibrantly for itself. Translations aren't really necessary, as the word images are lyrical and powerful. Traditionally, fado is sung to the accompaniment of one or two guitars. These songs of sorrow have been heard for more than a century. The most famous singer of the 19th century was a beautiful gypsy, Maria Severa. Originally from the province of Ovar, she migrated to Lisbon, where her electric and dynamic style won the attention of all the city, especially the Count of Vimioso, who loved her, defiantly making her "the toast of Lisbon."

Her style of singing stimulated others and sparked a host of imitators. Upon her death, the reverence for her was so great, the respect so lasting, that every female *fadista* to this day drapes herself in a black shawl in memory of Severa. This story is legendary, of course, and many knowledgeable fans of fado tend to discount it as "fanciful."

North Americans first heard fado in New York City in a chic club, La Vie en Rose, when Portugal's best known *fadista*, Amalia Rodrigues, appeared. She rose from a lowly beginning—a barefoot urchin of the streets of Lisbon selling fruit to Alfama housewives—to fame and fortune, and an international reputation.

There are more than 20 restaurants or cafés where fado is sung in Lisbon. Fado long ago became popularized, and purists scorn the songs that have been given a newer and slicker beat. There are two major areas in Lisbon where the wailing cry of fado can be heard nightly: the **Alfama** and the **Bairro Alto** (upper quarter). Both of these are the old sections of the city, spared in part from the ravages of the 1755 earthquake.

You can spend an entire evening—till dawn if you wish—"fado hopping" in Lisbon. You can begin with a meal around 9:30 p.m. and continue throughout the night, sipping the heady Portuguese wine and sinking deeper and deeper into a sweet melancholia. To begin your hop in the Alfama, go to the **Largo do Chafariz**, a little plaza about a block from the harbor. Three of Lisbon's top-ranking clubs are within a one- to five-minute walk from this point. The Bairro Alto fado district is found just off the **Largo de San Roque**.

While fado is without question the major attraction of Lisbon nightlife, there are other divertissements as well: discos for agile bodies, hotels, and nightclubs for conventional dancing, vaudeville and opera, theater and ballet. Motion pictures are shown in their original languages, with Portuguese subtitles. Local newspapers contain listings of what's on after dark. Or refer to a weekly copy of *What's On In Lisbon*, usually obtainable from your hotel concierge.

THE FADO CAFÉS

Lisboa à Noite, 69 Rua das Gáveas (tel. 36-85-57), is a recreation of a 17th-century tavern, complete with several open rooms separated by thick stone arches. Near the kitchen is a stone well, yielding fresh water since the 17th century. The décor consists of leather and brass-studded chairs, blue tile walls, and old engravings and prints. At one time the club was a stable, but now glamour prevails, a proper backdrop for some of the best fado in Lisbon.

In winter, eucalyptus logs burn in an open fireplace. *Típico* touches are added by the collection of pewter candlesticks on a mantel, the hanging hams and strings of garlic in the open kitchen, and the old leather bottles. Waitresses wear white lace on black, the waiters black on brown.

All of this forms a setting for the great *fadista*, Fernanda Maria, the owner of the café. When it comes time for Fernanda to perform, the air becomes charged with intensity.

Lisboa à Noite is not the cheapest place to drink or dine, but worth every escudo. You can order from an à la carte menu in English, enjoying a "flambé evening" by selecting either dry codfish Fernanda Maria or steak Lisboa à Noite. Expect to spend 3,500$ ($26.25) to 4,600$ ($34.50). The club is open from 8 p.m. to 2:30 a.m. daily except Sunday.

The **Cota D'Armas,** 7 Beco de São Miguel (tel. 86-86-82). Nightclub cookery isn't always the best in Lisbon (is it anywhere?), but one restaurant would rank among the top ten in the capital even if it didn't present a nightly program of "fado and folklore." The elegantly decorated Cota D'Armas is one of the leading attractions on the nighttime circuit for those wishing to venture into the Alfama at night. You can arrive early for dinner, enjoying drinks in the bar decorated in the style of a regional stable without the smells. The dining room is upstairs, and it's graced with a hand-painted ceiling. The coat-of-arms (the English translation of the restaurant's name) is depicted on the export china of the East India Company. In winter, this setting is made even more inviting by an open fireplace. During dinner, well-seasoned fadistas and guitar players entertain you with Portuguese songs and music. You can also go for unch except on Sunday, when it's closed all day. Dinner is served Monday to Saturday. Hours are 12:30 to 3 p.m. and 7 to 11 p.m. Meals begin at 3,500$ ($26.25).

Parreirinha da Alfama, 1 Beco do Espérito (tel. 86-82-09). Seemingly, every *fadista* worth her shawl has sung at this oldtime café, just a one-minute walk from the docksite of the Alfama. It's fado and fado only that enthralls here, not folk dancing. You can order a good regional dinner beginning early, but it's suggested that you go toward the shank of the evening . . . and stay late. It's open from 8 p.m. to 3 a.m. In the first part of the program, the *fadistas* get all their popular songs out of the way, then settle in to their own more classic favorites. You can order a filling dinner for 2,500$ ($18.75), and the menu often includes specialties from nearly every region of Portugal. The atmosphere is self-consciously taverna, with all sorts of Portuguese provincial oddments. The singers selected by management are first-rate.

A Severa, 49-61 Rua das Gáveas (tel. 36-40-06), is one of the oldest and most consistently successful fado houses in the Bairro Alto. Many *fadistas* who went on to greater fame got their start here. It's bistro-style, and you can have either drinks or order a complete Portuguese dinner with all the trimmings. The house specialty is chicken cooked and served in a clay pot. A typical dinner, including wine, costs from 3,500$ ($26.25). Hours are 8 p.m. to 3 a.m.; closed Thursday.

THE CASINO IN ESTORIL

The magnet for international society along the Costa do Sol, the **Casino Estoril,** Praça José Teodoro dos Santos (tel. 268-45-21), is a contemporary structure, with walls of glass opening onto a wide formal garden stretching to the shore road. The magnetic attraction, of course, is the gaming room of the casino, which is open from 3 p.m. to 3 a.m. On Friday and Saturday, a private room for baccarat chemin de fer is open from 3 to 8 a.m. You can clear the official barrier by presenting your passport and purchasing a tourist card for 440$ ($3.30) valid for one day, or a one-week card for 1,190$ ($9). A monthly card is also available. Once upstairs, you can play American and French roulette, French banc, blackjack, baccarat punto banca, chemin de fer, craps, and cussec (a Chinese game). The casino also has a Bingo room and a slot machines room. You're likely to rub elbows with deposed royalty. Men are required to wear jackets and ties in the gaming room.

In the **Grand Salon Restaurant,** you can sample a standard international dinner, where a three-course meal costs from around 4,000$ ($30), not including wines or coffees. However, you can dine either in Estoril or Cascais, then drop in for drinks only, paying a minimum of 1,500$ ($11.25) from Sunday to Thursday, although the minimum tab goes up to 2,000$ ($15) on Friday, Saturday, and the eves of national holidays. The floor show, which starts at 11:15 p.m., is usually a lavish production in the tradition of Paris or Las Vegas. You can count on lots of show girls in glittery gauze— most often crowned with billowing feather headgear—strutting and demonstrating their curves.

Movies from around the world—with their original sound tracks—are shown at the **Casino Cinema,** and you can attend matinees or nighttime showings for 225$ ($1.75).

THE DISCOS OF LISBON

Banana Power, 53 Rua Cascais (tel. 63-18-15), generates a lot of youthful enthusiasm among disco devotees in Lisbon. An old warehouse was converted into a stylish disco in the Alcantara section, lying between the heart of the city and the suburb of Belém. Hundreds of Lisboans, all young, can pour in here to enjoy the bands, paying a minimum of 1,000$ ($7.50) per person. Go late, as it usually doesn't open until 11 p.m. and rarely gets jumping until midnight. Once the action begins, it often lasts till dawn. You can take tram 17 from Praça do Comércio, but since taxis are inexpensive, it's best to take one to the entrance, which has only a small sign announcing itself.

Ad Lib, 28 Rua Barata Salgueiro (tel. 56-17-17), is one of the

THE VALOR OF PORT WINE: Portuguese port wine is known in every country of the world. The English were the first foreigners to discover rich, blended port, which they've enjoyed since the 17th century. The wine comes from grapes grown in the mountainous Douro River Valley in the north of Portugal. After port is fortified with brandy, it is shipped out to the "ports" of the world from Porto, Portugal's second-largest city.

The soil and climate of the Douro are said to be unique in the world, hence the special taste of the wine. Vintage port is the best wine produced from an especially good year. Crusted port, another vintage-like wine, takes its name from the fact that its "crust" must be decanted before it can be drunk.

"Wood ports," matured in wooden casks, fall into three major types: ruby, white, and tawny, made from the blending of the grape yield over a period of many years, assuring a consistent quality. The ruby-colored port is the young wine, but as it ages it becomes tawny.

Owned and sponsored by the Port Wine Institute, the **Solar do Vinho do Porto,** 45 Rua São Pedro de Alcântara (tel. 32-33-07), contains many relics related to the history of port wine. You can stop here at any time of the day, ordering from its *lista de vinhos*. If you want a glass (*cálice*) you can get it, costing 50$ (40¢) to 500$ ($3.75), or even a vintage bottle, should you prefer to make an afternoon of it. The place is open every day except Sunday from 10 a.m. to midnight.

chicest discos in Lisbon, created by a coterie of society lads who wanted to have an elegant and discreet place for young people to meet and dance. Just a few minutes from the Ritz Hotel compound, it operates on the seventh floor of a modern apartment house. Downstairs there isn't a sign or a clue as to what is going on upstairs. A uniformed doorman screens guests, escorting them to the elevator. Readers are advised to telephone first.

Inside, the penthouse club offers a shimmering sky view—a world of black mirrors with two levels of tables opening onto a plant-filled terrace. The décor is sophisticated, with stone Buddhas from Macao and many mirrors and flickering candles. The latest records imported from America, England, Italy, and France are played. Most of the cocktails, including a "kiss in the dark," go for 600$ ($4.50). The minimum entrance fee is 6,000$ ($45), which can be applied to drinks. Hours are 11 p.m. to 4:30 a.m.

O Porão da Nau, 1-D Rua Pinheiro Chagas (tel. 57-15-01), is a central boîte/disco which is about the best place in the capital if you want to dance to a live combo. Popular with the under-25 set, it is a reproduced hold of a 15th-century Portuguese man-of-war. Upon entering, you feel at any moment that the gangplank will be lifted, and you'll be embarked upon a voyage of discovery. The décor consists of carved wooden figures, stained glass, an early map of Portuguese possessions, a rope railing, lanterns, and a gun collection. The minimum consumption is 1,000$ ($7.50). It is open only on Friday, Saturday, and Sunday from 11:30 p.m. to 4:30 a.m.

Whispers, Edifício Aviz, 35 Avenida Fontes Pereira de Melo, next to the Sheraton Hotel (tel. 57-54-89), is a chic disco. The minimum is 1,500$ ($11.25) to 2,500$ ($18.75). It is open nightly from 11 p.m. to 4 a.m.

BARS IN AND AROUND LISBON

Bachus, 9 Largo da Trindade (tel. 32-18-18), offers one of the capital's most convivial watering spots, in addition to its role as a restaurant. In an environment of Oriental carpets, fine hardwoods, bronze statues, intimate lighting, and polite uniformed waiters, you can hobnob with some of the most glamorous names in Lisbon. An organist provides live music from a cubbyhole beneath a winding staircase. Late-night suppers are served in the bar by candlelight. The array of drinks, costing from 400$ ($3), is international, and the place is a good one in which to unwind in privileged circumstances. Open from noon to 4 p.m. and 7:30 p.m. to midnight.

Metro e Meio, 174 Avenida 5 de Outubro (tel. 77-59-97), has as its façade a giant yellow ruler, with the entrance cut into it. The management rented a certain amount of space, but carpenters renovating the bar discovered many more rooms hidden for decades. The overall effect is grotto-like, with stone and brick arches, a maze of salons, and a central fireplace. The unusual décor is a mélange of artifacts—hand-loomed wool wall hangings, gilt mirrors, statues, hanging lamps, and Victorian fringed shades. Recordings are piped in. Whiskies begin at 450$ ($3.40). Hours are 6 p.m. to 2 a.m. Near the Gulbenkian Museum, the bar is a taxi ride from the center of town.

Ray's Cocktail Bar and Lounge, 25 Avenida Saboia, Monte Estoril (tel. 268-01-06), is popular with American expatriates, many of whom make it their private club. It's a souped-up decorator extravaganza. Inside, you're likely to find an eclectic assortment of elements—a Fátima hand from Tangier, a ruby-colored glass newel post finial, chandeliers dripping with crystal, an ostrich fan (in black, no less), antique benches, provincial chairs, and a heterogene-

THE CAFÉ OF THE LITERATI: In the Chiado district behind an art nouveau façade, **A Brasileira,** 102-A Rua Garrett (tel. 36-87-92), is one of the oldest coffeehouses in Lisbon. It's a 19th-century holdover, once a favorite gathering place of the literati. Today, like much of the world, the atmosphere has grown somewhat tatty, but the place remains a favorite with some diehard devotees. A demitasse of coffee, called a *bica,* costs about 50$ (40¢), as does a simple glass of beer. It's open daily except Sunday from noon to 2 p.m. and 7 to 9 p.m. Guests sit at small tables on chairs made of tooled leather, while taking in the mirrored walls and marble pilasters. Aside from the architectural adornments, there is also a collection of paintings to admire. Old men go around offering to shine your shoes just as they did in the 19th century.

Outside, the street speaks of its past associations with men of letters. Garrett, a romantic dandy of the last century, was one of Portugal's leading poets (the street is named after him). The district itself, the Chiado, was named for another poet. On the square near the café, a statue honors António Ribeiro, a 16th-century poet. Yet another poet, Bocage of Setúbal, used to frequent this coffeehouse. When once accosted by a bandit, he is said to have replied, "I am going to the Brasileira, but if you shoot me, I am going to another world."

ous mixture of modern art. Everyone seems to enjoy the drinks (many enjoying quite a few). Most strong libations cost 350$ ($2.65) to 475$ ($3.50). The bar is open from 4 p.m. to 2:30 a.m.

Spirits Piano Bar, 3 Rua Alexandre Herculano, Cascais (tel. 28-38-64). When you ring the doorbell of this chic rendezvous, a tuxedoed employee will open the speakeasy portal if you look appropriate. Once inside, you descend a flight of stairs into a slightly cramped but intimate hideaway accented with ceiling beams, black mosaic floors, and thick stucco walls. Live music is presented on weekends, and the bar is open from 5 p.m. to 2:30 a.m. every night. Somewhat difficult to find, the bar is on a terrace a few feet above the street running into one of the corners of the triangle-shaped Jardim Visconde da Luz. A whisky here costs 450$ ($3.50).

Estalagem Muchaxo, Praia do Guincho, in Guincho (tel. 28-50-221), has stark drama, a unique and ideal place for a drink, with whiskies costing around 500$ ($3.75). Of course, you can come here for lobster (very expensive), even a room; but many prefer to drive out from Lisbon just to enjoy the jagged coastal rock, the Cabo da Roca, marking the westernmost point of Europe. The inn has a rustic atmosphere, with a rugged stone fireplace, Madeira wicker stools and rows of waterside tables. Open from 7 p.m. to midnight.

CHAPTER VIII

PORTUGAL IN A NUTSHELL

□ □ □

For years, guides have told their clients: "If you want the sun, go to the Algarve. If you want history and monuments, head for the north of Portugal." With some exceptions, this is good advice.

Portugal is still a relatively undiscovered country. A travel agent in Lisbon—in the business for more than 30 years—said that only two of his clients had ever asked to see every province. Most visitors, assuming that Portugal is so small it can't offer *that* much, never allow enough time for adequate exploration.

Before winging out of the Portuguese capital, why not take the extra days and pleasurable effort at least to skim the surface of some of the most rewarding spots on the Iberian peninsula?

While still based in Lisbon, you can day-trip it to the **Costa do Sol** (Estoril and Cascais) for fun at the beach; or go to the medieval fortress city of **Óbidos**; or the 12th-century Cistercian monastery of **Alcobaça**; the "battle abbey" of **Batalha**; the famous fishing village of **Nazaré**; or the world-renowned pilgrimage site of **Fátima.**

On a second day, you can head south across the Tagus to the fishing port and resort of **Sesimbra,** or take in the spectacular scenery of **Portinho da Arrábida,** or the ancient city of **Setúbal.** On yet a third day, while still based in Lisbon, you can drive to **Évora,** the ancient Roman city of Alentejo.

Take your pick of the following: fun in the sun, or history, monuments, and a bit of culture.

THE COSTA DO SOL: The strip of beach on the north bank of the mouth of the Tagus is also called the "Coast of Kings" because of all the exiled royalty who live in and around its shoreline.

Don Juan, the Count of Barcelona, was the son of the last king of Spain, Alfonso XIII, who went into exile in 1931. Ever since his father's death in 1941, he has claimed the throne of Spain. However, in the summer of 1969, Generalissimo Franco named the pretender's son, Don Juan Carlos, a young man trained and educated in Spain, as his successor and King of Spain, a position he assumed following the death of the Spanish dictator.

The "Coast of Kings" is sometimes known as the Portuguese Riviera, as it does evoke the Mediterranean. Even if you arrive in January, you should take the electric train from the Cais do Sodré station in Lisbon. The scenery is that intriguing. It's been called "a microcosm of Portugal."

You'll pass *azulejo*-fronted houses, red-tile roofs, and in summer, cabaña after cabaña of bronzed Portuguese bodies. Try to avoid the Sunday rush, however, as what appears to be every family in Lisbon heads to the sun strip. While the folks fight it out for a place in the sun, the aristocrats are languishing in their *quintas* (farms) in the hills around Cascais and Sintra.

Already previewed in the hotel chapter, the fashionable resort of **Estoril** lies about 15 miles west of Lisbon and is your first stopover. However, you can continue along the coast to the following two most rewarding targets.

Cascais

Over the years, returning travelers have waxed rhapsodic about the "fashion and chicness" of Estoril, while praising the so-called fishing village of Cascais for its picturesque quality and quaintness. But Cascais today is no longer a fishing village (many are calling it a city), and it rivals Estoril for supremacy along the Costa do Sol.

Once the monarchy of Portugal summered at Cascais, thus creating its reputation as a royal village. In time, its 17th-century citadel was occupied by Gen. António de Fragoso Carmona, the military dictator who named Dr. Salazar minister of finance in 1928.

Before the advent of a string of deluxe and first-class hotels, life in Cascais centered around its fish market, where auctions are still held. In the harbor, fishing boats and nets bob up and down in the water alongside luxury yachts.

The fish market, overlooking the Hotel Baía, continues to delight those searching for local charm—and many of the denizens of Cascais like it too. They're earning their livelihood, and not just putting on a show for foreign visitors. Nevertheless, they are photographed indiscriminately, as if they were tourist attractions and not a people of staunch pride and vigor. In fact, the fishermen claim that one of their own, Afonso Sanches, discovered America (quite by accident) in 1482, a decade before Columbus got all the attention.

On Sunday in summer, half of Lisbon seemingly drives out to attend the bullfights at the **Monumental de Cascais.** If you are among them—and especially if you're driving yourself—don't get caught in the impossible serpentine trek back to Lisbon after the *corrida* is over. Wait about two hours, idling away your time walking the cobbled streets of the resort, or else sipping port in a sidewalk café.

Better yet, take an excursion outside of town (on the road to Guincho) to the **Boca do Inferno.** The Mouth of Hell was so named because of its ferocious roar when the sea is rough. It's worth seeing.

Cascais, four miles west of Estoril, is easily reached by taxi, bus, or electric train from Lisbon.

The reputation of Cascais as a place in the sun dates back for centuries. Writing in 1620, Fr. Nicolau de Oliveira called it "one of the most pleasant and healthy resorts within Portugal." It still is.

Guincho

The open Atlantic surges in against the shore. The undertow is dangerous, but the site is ruggedly inspiring. Four miles west of Cascais (reached by bus or car), Guincho is at a point the Portuguese call **Cabo da Roca,** the most westerly site on the continent of Europe. In the background, beyond the hearty pines beaten by the Atlantic wind, looms the Serra de Sintra, sometimes covered with a misty spray on wintry days.

In summer the dunes of the **Praia do Guincho** draw beach devotees who like to flirt with danger. For those who defy the sea, Jennings Parrott wrote this advice: "If you are caught by the current, don't fight it. Don't panic. The wind forces it to circle, so you will be brought back to shore. A local fisherman, however, advises that you take a box lunch along. Sometimes it takes several days to make the circle."

After listening to the sea on a rough day, you'll know why the beach is called "Guincho," which means "screech, shriek, or scream" in Portuguese.

SESIMBRA: This village is "rich in fish"—or so wrote Luís Vaz de Camões, author of the 16th-century *The Lusiads,* the national epic of Portugal. That statement is still true in the 20th century. In addition to the action at the fish market, anglers are also attracted to Sesimbra.

With the opening of a gem of a hotel scaling a hillside, the **Hotel do Mar,** 10 Rua Combatentes do Ultramar, 2970 Sesimbra (tel. 01/223-33-26), many visitors are finding that they can not only enjoy the individual quality of the port, but they can do so in comparative luxury. Full board costs 12,200$ ($92) to 22,600$ ($170) in a single, 20,900$ ($157) to 27,600$ ($207) in a double.

Overlooking the town and sea is the **Castle of Sesimbra,** rebuilt after the earthquake of 1755, but now in ruins. Originally, it was a Moorish stronghold.

Sesimbra lies only 15 miles from Lisbon, across the Ponte 25 de Abril, the spectacular expansion bridge, the largest in Europe.

For another day trip, we strike out to the east for:

ÉVORA:
Dubbed a "living museum," Évora was once an ancient Roman town known as *Liberalitas Julia*. Nowadays it's the district capital of Alto Alentejo province, that region of cork trees, wheatfields, and olive branches. The city of whitewashed houses and ancient monuments lies 96 miles east of Lisbon, and can be reached by train.

The city is especially noted for its Corinthian-style **Temple of Diana,** dating from the 2nd century A.D. Among its curiosities is the macabre **Chapel of Bones** in the Royal Church of St. Francis, built in the Gothic-Manueline style in the 15th century.

The government-owned **Pousada dos Lóios,** Largo Conde de Vila Flor, 7000 Évora (tel. 066/240-51), is acclaimed as the most spectacular inn in Portugal. Installed in what was a former convent, it makes for an ideal luncheon stopover, as it features regional specialties from Alentejo. Meals cost 2,700$ ($20.25). Rooms rent for 13,000$ ($98) to 15,000$ ($113) in a double, 10,000$ ($75) to 12,000$ ($90) in a single.

ÓBIDOS:
This fortress town is almost too perfect a gem of the Middle Ages. No wonder King Denis once offered the town to his saintly wife as a wedding gift. The turreted towers and ramparts of what was a 12th-century castle dominate the hilltop.

The government has installed a honey of an inn, the **Pousada do Castelo,** 2510 Óbidos (tel. 062/950-15), in a former wing. The *pousada* is in good taste, its bedroom windows opening onto views of Estremadura. Doubles cost from 14,400$ ($101). If you're touring, you can visit for a lunch or dinner at a cost of 2,200$ ($16.50) to 3,000$ ($22.50). Food is served from 12:30 to 3 p.m. and 7:30 to 9:30 p.m. daily.

The village is accurately considered one of the most unspoiled in Europe, and is cared for by the state as a national monument. Seek out the baroque **Church of Santa Maria,** where Afonso V, at the age of 10, is said to have married his 8-year-old cousin.

Óbidos lies 59 miles north of Lisbon. Trains leave from the Rossio Station in Lisbon.

ALCOBAÇA:
People come here today to see Alcobaça's 12th-century Cistercian monastery. In it, the "Romeo and Juliet" of Por-

tuguese history, Dom Pedro and his murdered mistress, Inez de Castro, lie in tombs facing each other. Pedro wanted it that way—so that when he was "resurrected," the first person he'd face would be his beloved Inez. The tragedy: Pedro's father, the king, secretly had Inez murdered (by slitting her throat). After learning of the murder, Pedro kept his cool, but when he became king, he sought revenge—rounding up the killers of his fair Inez and ripping their hearts out. He then exhumed Inez's body, placed it by him on a throne, and forced his court to pay homage to her as his queen by kissing her hand.

Ahem. After that gloomy tale, you're best off slipping away from the tombs and walking down to the lower level to see the monastic kitchen, through which a brook was directed. The monastery dates from the 12th century, having been founded by Portugal's first king, Afonso Henriques. It lies about 67 miles north of Lisbon. If you're driving, you can stop here following a visit to Óbidos. If you go by train from Lisbon, you must go to Valado. From the train station at Valado, buses connect to Alcobaça.

BATALHA: The "battle abbey" of Portugal rises from the plain, in stark contrast to the flat countryside. It's called the Monastery of Our Lady of Victory. King John I (João I) had a monastery and church built about a mile from the battlefield of Aljubarrota in 1385, in which the Portuguese defeated the Castilians. This battle had far-reaching consequences, not only for Portugal by preserving her independence, but also for the world in that it enabled the Portuguese to carry out their maritime discoveries.

In the shadow of the abbey, a village bearing the same name has sprung up. Begun at the end of the 14th century, and continued through the 15th and 16th centuries, the monastery is in the Gothic and Manueline style. The monastery shows much originality in its features. For example, it has a degree of austerity, in spite of the florid type of Gothic style adopted in its architecture. The color of stone used is especially interesting, a golden and pinkish limestone from the Serra de Aire. It gives off a warm, coral-like hue. Many English and French architectural influences are seen as well.

The visitor will want to explore the naves in their ethereal elegance. In an octagonal chapel are the tombs of the founder, King João I, and his wife, Philippa of Lancaster, daughter of John of Gaunt of England. Their tombs are surrounded by those of the princes, their sons. The bathroom in the royal cloister is also of interest.

The *Capalas Imperfeitas,* the so-called unfinished chapels, have a lushness of style, showing their potential decorative beauty. They make one regret that the artisans abandoned their work to join the task force building Jerónimos Monastery at Belém.

Batalha lies about 73 miles north of Lisbon. To reach it by train, you must go first to Valado where you can make bus connections bound for Batalha.

NAZARÉ: The fishermen of this "village turned summer resort" are unique. Seymour Pearlman once wrote about these sailors who "appear different from other Portuguese and who remain seemingly unchanged in a rapidly changing world."

Their dress—the plaid trousers and shirts—evoke the Highlands. Legend has it that these plaid and tartan designs were copied from seafaring Scots shipwrecked centuries ago in Nazaré. However, others attribute the origin to the troops of Wellington, who camped near Nazaré during the wars with Napoleon. The young girls of Nazaré are said to wear seven petticoats, but it's illegal to count them! Also, note the fishermen's distinctive high-prowed boats. The style is said to date from the time of Nazaré's Phoenician settlers.

The lower part of the village is known as the Praia, the upper part—a promontory towering over the bay—is called Sítio. At the latter, reached by a funicular, the view is spectacular.

A train (three hours) from Lisbon arrives at Valado, where it's possible to make bus connections to Nazaré.

FÁTIMA: On May 13, 1917, three shepherd children claimed that a vision of a young girl appeared before them and that she made a sacred vow to reappear every month on the same day until October. Word of the vision gradually spread across the world, stirring enthusiasm and bitter controversy.

The final vision on October 13 drew an estimated 70,000 who watched the phenomenon of "The Miracle of the Sun." Although no one except the three children claimed they saw the Virgin Mary that day, hundreds upon hundreds reported seeing the sun hurtling toward the earth. Many screamed and panicked, fearing the Last Judgment.

Eventually, in 1930 the church finally accepted the story that the three children had indeed been "visited" by the Virgin Mary. By then, two of the children had died of fever. The third became a nun in a convent at Coimbra. Even today Fátima draws thousands upon thousands of pilgrims on the 13th of every month from May through October.

Reached on the Northern Line, it lies about 36 miles east of Nazaré, some 88 miles north of Lisbon.

Those who want to continue on the northward trip can visit the two following cities.

COIMBRA: This is the university city of Portugal, lying on the banks of the Mondego River, the capital of Beira Litoral province. Its university is reputed to be the second oldest in the world, dating from 1290. In its stunning baroque library, built in the 18th century, are about one million volumes, including a rare first edition of Camões' *Os Lusíadas,* the Portuguese national epic.

PORTO: Portugal's "second city" is the home of port, the world-famous Portuguese wine. Near the mouth of the Douro River, Porto is an industrial city, although it has many worthy attractions. Once a Roman encampment, it is one of the oldest cities in Europe. In particular, seek out its Romanesque **Sé** (cathedral); the **Clérigos Church,** with its landmark tower; and the **Church of the Carmelites,** a fine example of Portuguese Baroque.

Opposite Porto is the thriving center of the port business, **Vila Nova da Gaia.** Visit one of its wine cellars. You'll not only learn something about port, you'll get to drink it.

From the city, you can travel through the **Douro Valley,** known as "port wine country." The best time to visit is when the grapes are harvested in September.

Porto lies about 175 miles north of Lisbon.

THE ALGARVE: For fun in the sun, the Portuguese, along with increasing hordes of bikini-clad foreigners, head south to the Algarve, where the scenery strikes many as similar to that of North Africa. It's a delight even in late January and early February, when the almond blossoms dot the landscape like snow.

Stretching along a hundred-mile coastline, the Algarve begins at **Cape St. Vincent** in the west (the most southerly point of Europe), running to **Vila Real de Santo António** near the Spanish frontier. For five centuries the province was ruled by the Moors, and much of their influence remains.

To the east of Cape St. Vincent is **Sagres.** It was from here that Prince Henry the Navigator directed his caravels on their world exploration.

Continuing east, you come across **Lagos,** overlooking a bay of the same name. Henry once lived here. To the east of it is **Praia da Rocha,** with its grottoes—and some of the finest beaches in the country. The capital of the province is **Faro,** a terminal point for trains from Lisbon. In addition, the local jet airport reduces travel time from Lisbon to less than an hour.

AFTER LISBON—WHERE TO? Every first-time visitor who comes to Portugal usually visits Lisbon, Estoril, and Sintra, and this small guide is aimed at those travelers. However, there are those who will want a deeper look at this most fascinating little country, particularly its beachfront, the Algarve, or such old cities of the north as Porto and Viana do Castelo. Nazaré is considered the country's most intriguing fishing village, and the old Roman city of Évora draws visitors west across the plains of Alentejo. Others will want to fly to the popular tourist island of Madeira off the coast of Africa, and perhaps as an offbeat adventure, the Azores, said to be the peaks of volcanoes on the lost continent of Atlantis. These islands are part of Portugal.

With that in mind, we publish a large guide devoted to Portugal, Madeira, and the Azores, documenting their many sightseeing attractions, along with hotels and restaurants in all price ranges, from budget to deluxe. Its philosophy is to help you get the best value for your dollar: *Frommer's Dollarwise Portugal.*

CHAPTER IX

GETTING ACQUAINTED WITH MADRID

□ □ □

Madrid is the Mother Superior of Spain, more to be venerated than loved.

In *The Sun Also Rises,* Hemingway described her as "a white sky-line on the top of a little cliff away off across the sun-hardened country."

Papa would not know her today. The little pueblo that was Madrid continues to grow at a dramatic rate, expanding rapidly in land area and industrial development, sprouting suburbs of apartment houses for the burgeoning population.

On a plateau of the Sierra de Guadarrama, the capital of Spain is the highest in Europe, reaching a peak of 2,373 feet above sea level at its loftiest point.

The sierra air is dry, almost crystal pure, the sky cerulean as painted by Velázquez.

As Spanish cities go, Madrid is still young. *Don Quixote* was known throughout the world when Philip II made Madrid the capital of Spain in 1606. The location was apt: geographically it was the heart of the Iberian peninsula.

On your way into Madrid from Barajas Airport, you're likely to see an aging *dueña* shrouded in black—perhaps mourning for her husband who died in the Spanish Civil War in the late '30s. Or your eyes will fall on a weather-hardened old man riding a heavily laden donkey, a scene undisturbed by the centuries in Spain. These are *tableaux vivants,* frozen in time and space.

As you near the center of the city, however, skyscrapers herald tomorrow's world. Flashy billboards implore everybody to "*bebe* Coca-Cola," or to wear Yankee-style Levi's for greater sex appeal.

Spain is in metamorphosis. Now that the country is justifiably called "the playground of Europe," authorities are forced to grant concessions to the hordes of invaders pouring across its borders or winging in from the skies. For example, ever-increasing numbers of visitors now stroll the streets of Madrid in summer shorts. In the not-too-distant past, such apparel would have given a skimpily clad visitor firsthand experience for an autobiography, "My Life in a Spanish Jail."

It is impossible to separate Madrid or Castile from the saga of the nation as a whole. It was from the barren, undulating plains of the country's heartland that the proud, sometimes arrogant, Castilians emerged. They were destined not only to unify the country, but to dominate it—and to go even further, carving out an empire that was to embrace the Aztecs and Incas, even the far-away Philippines.

In Castile you'll meet a survival-sharpened people. One scholar put it this way: "The Spaniards are a fierce, idealistic, generous people, capable of great sacrifice and heroism when driven by their proud and burning passions, but they are also intolerant, dogmatic, and individualistic."

Regardless, know that the Spaniard—whatever his or her background—is generally friendly, especially to the well-behaved *gringo*. As hosts, they have great style and graciousness, and Spain today is among the most hospitable nations in Europe.

FLYING TO MADRID: The capital of Spain is without parallel the busiest and most convenient airport in the country. It is well known to many travelers who make Spain a return destination year after year. Until the recent entry of **American Airlines** into the busy transatlantic routes into Madrid, the major airlines servicing Madrid from North America were **Iberia** and **Trans World Airlines.**

Iberia Airlines, the national carrier of Spain, offers more routes into and within Spain than any other carrier. These routes include daily nonstop service from New York, Chicago, and Los Angeles to Madrid, with ongoing service to Málaga, Barcelona, the Canary Islands, and Galicia. Since it was founded in 1927, Iberia has proven itself a solid and reliable choice. Based on the number of passengers transported annually, Iberia is the third-largest airline in Europe, carrying more than 13 million passengers in one recent two-year period.

More recent news, especially for Spain-bound passengers living in America's southwestern and western states, is a service into Madrid introduced in 1988 by what might be America's premier airline, American. This carrier has daily flights from Dallas to Madrid, offering the safety and style for which American Airlines is known.

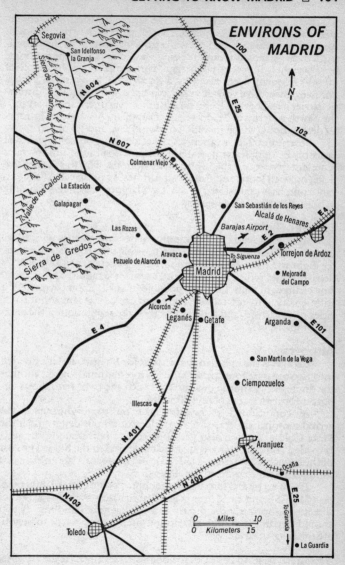

ENVIRONS OF MADRID

Segovia
San Idelfonso la Granja
Sierra de Guadarrama
N 604
N 607
Colmenar Viejo
Valle de los Caídos
La Estación
Galapagar
Las Rozas
Sierra de Gredos
Aravaca
Pozuelo de Alarcón
Madrid
Alcorcón
Leganés
Getafe
San Sebastián de los Reyes
Alcalá de Henares
Barajas Airport
To Sigüenza
Torrejón de Ardoz
Mejorada del Campo
Arganda
E 4
E 25
100
102
E 2
E 4
E 101
San Martín de la Vega
Ciempozuelos
Illescas
N 401
Aranjuez
Ocaña
E 25
To Granada
N 400
N 403
Toledo
La Guardia

Miles 10
Kilometers 15

Because Dallas is considered the airline's busiest hub, convenient connections can be made from all parts of North and South America. Although American is a relative newcomer to the transatlantic sweepstakes, it is rapidly being viewed as one of the routings' heavyweights. It recently emerged as the top carrier in a poll of 30,000 frequent flyers taken by a Swiss-based consumers' group. For five consecutive years it was also judged as the best U.S. domestic carrier by a London-based travel authority. American's entry into the North America to Madrid market supplements its other European destinations, which include London, Paris, and Frankfurt.

American offers a variety of ticket options, one of which will probably be right for you. A travel agent or one of the airline's sales representatives can explain the many options. The least expensive ticket on both Iberia and American Airlines is a midweek APEX (advance purchase excursion), which is available to passengers traveling in both directions on a weekday.

Charter Flights

Strictly for reasons of economy, some travelers may wish to accept the numerous restrictions and possible uncertainties of a charter flight to Spain. Charters require that passengers strictly specify departure and return dates, and full payment is required in advance. Any changes in flight dates are possible (if at all) upon payment of a stiff penalty. Any reputable travel agent can advise you about fares, cities of departure, and most important, the reputation of the charter company.

Airports

Barajas is the international airport for Madrid, and it's divided into two separate terminals—one for international flights, another for domestic. A shuttle bus runs between the two. For Barajas airport information, telephone 205-40-90.

Air-conditioned yellow buses take you from right outside the arrival terminal at Barajas to the underground bus depot under the Plaza Colón. You can also get off at several points along the way, provided you don't have your suitcases stored in the hold. The cost of the service is 190 pesetas ($1.75), and buses leave about every 20 minutes, either to or from the airport.

If you go by taxi into town, the approximate cost is 1,800 pesetas ($16.25), and the driver is entitled to assess a surcharge (either direction), not only for the tip but for baggage handling. If you should step into a nonmetered limousine, it is important to negotiate the price in advance.

TRAINS: Madrid has three major railway stations. At the **Atocha,**

Glorieta de Carlos V, you can book passage for Lisbon, Toledo, Andalusia, and Extremadura. The nearest Metro is Atocha. For trains to Barcelona, Asturias, Cantabria, Castilla-León, Pais Vasco, Aragon, Cataluña, Levante, Murcia, and the French frontier, go to **Charmartín** in the northern suburbs, at Agustín de Foxa. The third is **La Estación del Norte** (Príncipe Pío), which is the main gateway for trains to Northwest Spain (Salamanca and Galicia). For railway information, telephone 552-05-18.

Warning: In Madrid, don't wait to buy your rail ticket or make a reservation at the train station. By this time there may be no tickets left—or at least no desirable tickets remaining. For most tickets, go to the principal RENFE office at 44 Alcalá (tel. 247-74-00).

ORIENTATION

NAVIGATING YOUR WAY: No one ever claimed that knowing or getting around Madrid was easy. Surprisingly, many of the Madrileño taxi drivers are often unfamiliar with their own city, once they branch off the main boulevards.

Everything in the Spanish capital is spread out, and this may cause you initial difficulty until you get the feel of it. For example, on one typical night, you may want to sample the *tapas* (hors d'oeuvres) at a *tasca* on the Ventura de la Vega; dine at a restaurant opening onto the fairly far-off Plaza Mayor, witness an evening of flamenco near the Ritz Hotel, then head for your hotel, at—say, the gateway to Toledo. The easiest, most sensible and practical means of getting around to all the above mentioned, widely scattered places is by:

Taxi

Fortunately, the cabs are cheap—among the least expensive in Western Europe, in fact. At the start of a ride, the meter registers 90 pesetas (80¢), and that fare will surely have gone up by the time of your visit. An average ride costs about 400 pesetas ($3.60) to 500 pesetas ($4.50). There are extras as well. Trips to the railway station or to the bullring carry a supplement, plus an additional fee tacked on to the fare on Sunday and holidays. A ride to Barajas Airport carries a 150-peseta ($1.35) surcharge, plus 20 pesetas (20¢) per bag. It's customary to tip at least 10% or more of the fare.

A ride is usually tantamount to an adventure, as Madrileño drivers go fast and furiously, occasionally (but not always!) stopping at a red light.

Although inexpensive, taxi-riding is fraught with some minor traps that a visitor will do well to avoid. There are two types of taxis:

black with horizontal red bands and white with diagonal red bands. Their rates are usually the same.

Many *unmetered,* unbanded taxis also abound in Madrid, their drivers renting their services as guides for the day or half day. But when business is slow, these guides sometimes operate as "gypsy" cabs, picking up unsuspecting passengers, taking them to their destinations, and charging them whatever they think the market will bear.

Beyond that pitfall, you must be careful to require that your driver turns down the meter when you enter his cab. Otherwise, he may "assess" the cost of the ride to your disadvantage.

Another means of transportation in Madrid is the:

Subway (Metro)

The system, first installed in 1919, is quite easy to learn, and you can travel in the underground if not comfortably, at least without any congestion or crushing, as in former years.

Line No. 7 is completely different from the rest, and as modern as some of Europe's newest underground systems. The future lines under construction will be the same type as No. 7.

The central converging point of the metro is at the **Puerta del Sol.** The subways begin their runs at 6 a.m., shutting down at 1:30 a.m. It's best to try to avoid traveling on the subways during the rush hours, of course. The metro fare is 50 pesetas (45¢). For information, call 435-22-66.

Bus

A network of buses also traverses the city, fanning out to the suburbs. The route of each bus is clearly marked at each stop on a schematic diagram. Buses are fast and efficient, traveling down special lanes made for them all over the city. Red buses charge 55 pesetas (50¢) per ride; yellow microbuses, 65 pesetas (60¢) per ride. For information on buses from the airport into Madrid, refer to the "Airports" section, above.

BUS TERMINALS. Madrid has two principal ones: **Auto Res,** 6 Glorieta Conde de Casals (tel. 251-66-44), and the large **Estación Sur de Autobuses,** 17 Canarias (tel. 468-42-00). Buses to the environs of Madrid, such as Toledo and Segovia, leave from numerous other stations; it's best to telephone 401-99-00 for the latest information about departures.

Car Rentals

If you're planning to tour Spain, a car will ease the burdens considerably. Even if you're limited to extensive touring in the environs of Madrid, you'll find that a rented automobile will come in hand, allowing you to stop off at that *típico* roadside tavern for *tapas* or to make that side detour to a medieval village. You'll be your own master, exploring at your leisure places not covered—or covered too hurriedly—on the organized tour.

On my most recent trip to Spain, I tried the services of **Budget Rent-A-Car,** whose offices are scattered strategically throughout Spain. My report on their facilities should give you an idea of the prices and procedures of the other major firms, which include ATESA, Hertz, and Avis.

The smallest—and least expensive car—in Budget's inventory is a Fiat Panda or its equivalent. Suitable for up to two passengers, including their luggage, the car is available for an unlimited-mileage rate of around $161 per week. To qualify for this rate, clients must reserve through a Budget reservations office at least 48 business hours in advance. An additional 12% VAT is added to these figures, and all gasoline, of course, is the responsibility of the renter. For short rentals, it's possible to hire a car on a per-day basis, with a fee for each kilometer driven, but most visitors usually prefer the longer period.

An attractive medium-size car available through Budget would be a Ford Escort. With manual transmission, it costs $268 per week and offers the sometimes much-needed extra benefit of air conditioning. If you are comfortable driving it, a car with manual transmission is much cheaper. (Some companies consider automatic transmission such a costly expense that they don't even offer it.) However, if an automatic transmission is important to you, Budget's least expensive car with automatic transmission is a four-door Ford Orion, renting with unlimited mileage for around $415 a week. Likewise, if you're cutting costs, don't request air conditioning.

More information about the discounted rates available through Budget can be obtained by calling their toll-free U.S. number: 800/472-3325.

Other rental companies include the government-owned **ATESA,** whose offices are at 59 Gran Vía in Madrid (tel. 247-730-001). **Avis** is also well represented in Spain, with 96 depots and kiosks on the Spanish mainland, including ones at all the major airports (call toll free in the U.S. 800/331-1084). Finally, **Hertz** will accept your reservation before you leave America. Their toll-free number is 800/654-3001.

GAS. Gas is easily obtainable and is the normal fuel used in rented cars in Spain. The average Spanish vehicle—predominantly Seats or Fiats—gets close to 45 miles a gallon.

Hitchhiking

This is no longer smiled upon as much as it used to be. It may be technically illegal. However, people still do it, tourists tending to pick up tourists. I don't recommend you stick out your thumb in the presence of the Civil Guard.

THE DIFFERENT MADRIDS:

The Spanish capital, as mentioned, is a fast-growing city, its development sporadic and largely haphazard. It can be described in many ways and from many points of view.

If you're interested in "Royal Madrid," you'll think of the **Palacio Real,** fronting the handsome **Plaza de Oriente,** with its Velázquez-inspired equestrian statue of Philip IV. The gardens and parks, the wide avenues appropriate for state receptions and parades took new significance with the restoration of the Spanish monarchy.

If you're a romanticist nostalgic for the 19th century, you'll watch in sadness as the mansions along the **Paseo de la Castellana** and its satellite streets are torn down to make way for modern offices and shops, deluxe hotels, apartment buildings. Thankfully, a few are still preserved and used today by foreign embassies.

If you're an artist or devotee of art, you'll spend most of your time at the great old **Prado,** treasure house of Spanish masterpieces, sheltering a once-royal collection of European art. If you're on a shopping spree, you'll gravitate to the **Gran Vía,** called the Avenida José Antonio during the long dictatorship of Franco, the main street of Madrid, with its stores, cinemas, and hotels, the latter both luxury and budget. The wide avenue—flanked with sidewalk cafés —ends at the **Plaza de España** with its Edificio España, one of the tallest skyscrapers in Europe. Or you'll wander past the multitude of shops, boutiques, coffeehouses, and couturiers' salons of the more prestigious **Calle de Serrano.**

If medieval Madrid intrigues you, you'll seek out the Moorish towers of the old quarter, looking for the *mudéjar* style of architecture. You'll photograph (in your mind, if not with your instant-shot camera) the **Plaza de la Villa,** and focus especially on the **Torre de los Lujanes.** According to tradition, Francis I of France was held captive at the tower after he was taken prisoner in Pavia, Italy.

The colonnaded and rectangular **Plaza Mayor,** one of the most harmoniously designed squares in Europe, recalls the Madrid of the 17th century. The scene of many an *auto-de-fé,* bullfight, or execution of a traitor, it is today one of the best spots in the city for a *paseo,* especially if you take time out from your walking to explore the adjoining shops, some of which sell sombreros. Later you can select a restaurant, perhaps one with a table opening right on the square.

If you walk through one of the vaulted porticoes of the Plaza Mayor to the south, down the street of *típico* restaurants and taverns—the **Calle de Cuchilleros**—you'll reach the **Calle de Toledo.** Then you'll be entering a special world of Old Madrid, still preserved. Known as the *barrios bajos,* it is home to the Madrileño lowest on the economic scale. In some cities it would be called a ghetto or slum. But in Madrid the area abounds with such style—screaming gypsy *niños,* arcaded markets stuffed with meats and vegetables, shops, *tascas, cuevas,* that it retains great punch.

The real center of the city is the **Puerta del Sol** (the "Doorway" or "Gateway to the Sun"). Despite its grand appellation, it is a dull terminus of considerable traffic congestion and crime. Beginning at the Puerta del Sol, the **Calle de Alcalá** is the most traffic-choked artery in Madrid, a street that runs for more than 2½ miles. It is the avenue of Spanish bankers, and houses the Escuela y Museo de la Real Academia de Bellas Artes de San Fernando.

Madrid's greatest boulevard, its Champs-Élysées, begins at Atocha Railway Station. Heading north, it's called the **Paseo del Prado,** passing on its right the Botanical Gardens and the Prado Museum. It doesn't end, but changes its name at the **Plaza de la Cibeles,** dominated by the "cathedral of post offices" and a fountain honoring Cybele, "the great mother of the gods."

At Cibeles, the boulevard is henceforth the **Paseo de Carvo Sotelo,** and leads into the **Plaza de Colón.** At Colón, the **Paseo de la Castellana** begins. Seemingly endless, the Paseo de la Castellana stretches through a posh area spreading out on both sides and featuring apartment houses, restaurants, department stores, and hotels; it continues past the public ministries, up to the flourishing **Plaza de Castilla,** and then on to the huge **La Paz** hospital complex.

THE ABCs OF MADRID

Whatever your needs or travel problems, you'll find that Madrid has the answer to them. The single question is: How do you find what you are seeking quickly and conveniently? In an emergency, of course, your hotel is your best bet. But some of the smaller hotels aren't staffed with personnel entirely fluent in English; and sometimes—even if they are—the person at the desk can be apathetic about something of vital interest to you.

What follows, then, is an alphabetical listing of important miscellany—the data that can often be crucial to a visitor. Typical queries, answered below, include: How much do I tip a porter?

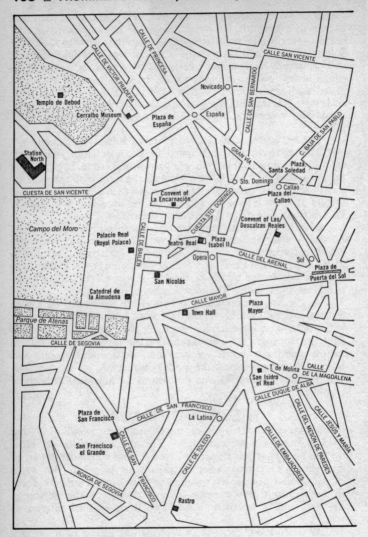

Templo de Debod
Cerralbo Museum
CALLE DE VICTOR PRADERA
CALLE DE PRINCESA
CALLE SAN VICENTE
Novicado
CALLE DE SAN BERNARDO
Plaza de España
España
GRAN VIA
C. BAJA DE SAN PABLO
Station North
CUESTA DE SAN VICENTE
Sto. Domingo
Plaza Santa Soledad
Callao
Plaza del Callao
Convent of La Encarnación
CUESTA STO. DOMINGO
Campo del Moro
Palacio Real (Royal Palace)
CALLE DE BAILEN
Teatro Real
Plaza Isabel II
Convent of Las Descalzas Reales
Opera
CALLE DEL ARENAL
Sol
Plaza de Puerta del Sol
San Nicolás
Catedral de la Almudena
CALLE MAYOR
Plaza Mayor
Town Hall
Parque de Atenas
CALLE DE SEGOVIA
T. de Molina
CALLE DE LA MAGDALENA
San Isidro el Real
CALLE DUQUE DE ALBA
CALLE DEL MESON DE PAREDES
CALLE JESUS Y MARIA
Plaza de San Francisco
CALLE DE SAN FRANCISCO
La Latina
San Francisco el Grande
CALLE DE SAN FRANCISCO
CALLE DE TOLEDO
CALLE DE EMBAJADORES
RONDA DE SEGOVIA
Rastro

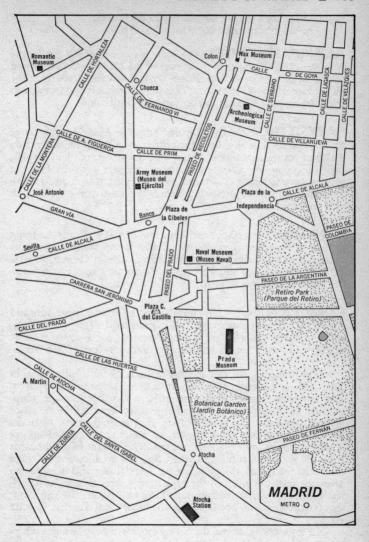

How do I make a telephone call? Find a doctor? etc.

The **telephone area code** for Madrid is 91.

AMERICAN EXPRESS: For your mail or banking needs, the American Express office at the corner of the Marqués de Cubas and the Plaza de las Cortes (tel. 429-57-75), across the street from the Palace Hotel, draws the visiting Yankee. The office is open weekdays from 9 a.m. to 5:30 p.m. and on Saturday until noon.

BABYSITTERS: Nearly all major hotels in Madrid can arrange for babysitters. Usually, the concierge keeps a list of reliable nursemaids or young girls and will get in touch with one of them for you, providing you give adequate notice. Rates vary considerably, but tend to be reasonable. More and more babysitters in Madrid speak English, but don't count on it. Chances are yours won't—although you can request it, of course.

BANKS: You get a better exchange rate here if you're exchanging dollars into pesetas than you do at any of the exchange bureaus around the city. Banks are open at 9:30 a.m. (but it's best to go after 10 a.m.) to 2 p.m. Monday to Friday. Banks are also open on Saturday from 9:30 a.m. to 1 p.m.

CLIMATE: In Madrid, climate is subject to rapid change. July and August are the most uncomfortable months. In fact, the government virtually shuts down in August except for a skeleton crew, going into "exile" at the northeast Atlantic resort of San Sebastián.

The temperature can *average* a high of 91° Fahrenheit in July, 76° in September. In winter, it can plunge to 34° Fahrenheit, although it averages around 46°. In October (average temperature: 56° Fahrenheit), Madrid enjoys its "season." Hotel space is at a premium. Every bullfighter, doll manufacturer, Galician hotelier, Andalusian olive grower, or Santander vineyard keeper having business with the government descends on Madrid at this time. In the same month, wealthy Spanish aristocrats flock here from the secluded ducal palaces in Andalusia and Castile, to savor the sophistication of the capital, its opera, theater, and endless rounds of parties and dinners. The air is clear, the sun kind; the restaurants and *tascas* (bars) overflow with Iberian joie de vivre.

In my view, however, the balmy month of May (average temperature: 61° Fahrenheit) is the best time for making your own descent on the capital.

MADRID: AVERAGE MONTHLY TEMPERATURES

	HIGH	LOW		HIGH	LOW
January	46	34	July	91	65
February	48	34	August	90	66
March	52	39	September	76	65
April	65	45	October	65	52
May	75	52	November	55	48
June	78	58	December	50	41

CLOTHING SIZES: For the most part, Spain uses the same sizes as the continent of Europe. The sizes of women's stockings and men's socks are international.

For Women

Junior Miss		Regular Dresses		Shoes	
U.S.	Spain	U.S.	Spain	U.S.	Spain
5	34	10	40	5	36
7	36	12	42	5½	36½
9	38	14	44	6½	37½
11	40	16	46	7½	38½
		18	48	8	39
		20	50	8½	39½
				9	40

For Men

Shirts		Slacks		Shoes	
U.S.	Spain	U.S.	Spain	U.S.	Spain
14	36	32	42	5	36
14½	37	34	44	6	37
15	38	36	46	7	38
15½	39	38	48	7½	39
15¾	40	40	50	8	40
16	41			9	41
16½	42			10	42
17	43			10½	43
				11	44
				12	45

Warning: This chart should be followed only as a very general outline, as in the same country there are big differences in sizes. If possible, try on all clothing or shoes before making a purchase. You'll be glad you did.

CONSULATES AND EMBASSIES: If you lose your passport or have some other pressing problem, the **United States Embassy** is at 75 Calle de Serrano (tel. 276-36-00), and the **Canadian Consulate** is at 35 Nuñez de Balboa (tel. 431-43-00). The **British Embassy** is at 16 Fernanado el Santo (tel. 419-02-00), and that of Australia is at 143 Paseo de la Castellana (tel. 279-85-01).

CRIME: Increased thefts in Madrid have resulted in a warning by the U.S. Embassy to American visitors, urging that you leave your passport and valuables in a hotel safe or other secure place while you visit sights of the city. Purse-snatching is prevalent, with the criminals working in pairs, grabbing purses from pedestrians, cyclists, and even from cars. If a car is standing still, a thief may open the door or break a window in order to snatch a purse or package, even from under the seat. A popular scam against Americans in Madrid involves one miscreant smearing the back of a jacket or other clothing of the victim, perhaps with mustard or chocolate. An accomplice pretends to help the victim clean off the mess, meanwhile picking all pockets of valuables. The embassy statement advises: Don't carry a purse; keep your valuables in front pockets; carry only enough cash for the day's needs; be aware of who is around you; and keep a separate record of your passport number, traveler's check numbers, and credit card numbers.

Every car can be a target, parked or just stopped at a light. Don't leave anything in sight in your car. Place valuables in the trunk when you park, and always assume that someone is watching you to see whether you're putting something away for safekeeping. Keep the car locked while you're driving and even for a one-minute stop.

CURRENCY: Spain's unit of currency is the **peseta,** worth about $.009 (.9¢) in U.S. terms (as of this writing—subject to change). One U.S. dollar is worth about 110.4 pesetas. Spain also uses **céntimos,** units of currency so low they're almost worthless. It takes 100 céntimos to equal only 1 peseta which is worth slightly less than 1¢ in U.S. coinage.

CUSTOMS: Spain permits you to bring in most personal effects and the following items duty free: two still cameras with ten rolls of film each, one movie camera, tobacco for personal use, one bottle each of wine and liquor per person, a portable radio, a tape recorder and a typewriter, a bicycle, golf clubs, tennis racquets, fishing gear, two hunting weapons with 100 cartridges each, skis and other sports equipment.

Upon leaving Spain, American citizens who have been outside the U.S. for 48 hours or more are allowed to bring in $400 (U.S.)

worth of merchandise duty free—that is, if they have claimed no similar exemption within the past 30 days. Beyond this free allowance, the next $1,000 worth of merchandise is assessed at a flat rate of 10% duty. If you make purchases in Spain, it's important to keep your receipts.

DENTIST: For an English-speaking dentist, get in touch with the **U.S. Embassy,** 75 Calle de Serrano (tel. 276-34-00), which has a list of recommended ones. If you have a dental emergency, you may have to call several before you can get an immediate appointment—hence the need for a comprehensive list.

ELECTRIC CURRENT: Most establishments have either 125 or 220 volts. Carry your voltage adapter with you and always check at your hotel desk before plugging in any electrical equipment. It's best to travel with battery-operated equipment.

EMERGENCIES: If you need the police, call 091. In case of fire, dial 232-32-32, and if in need of an ambulance, as in the case of an accident, telephone 256-02-00.

FILM: As one tourist official put it, film is "expensive as hell in Spain." Take in as much as Customs will allow. I suggest you wait to process it until you return home. However, if you can't wait, and you'll be in Spain long enough to get your pictures back, you can take your undeveloped film to the leading department store, **Galerias Preciados,** 28 Preciados, right off the Gran Vía (tel. 222-47-71). There you'll find a department which will develop your film in two hours.

HAIRDRESSER: A salon offering manicures and hairdressing for women, **Lis,** specializes in styling and dying. It's in the Torre de Madrid (tel. 241-54-39) and is open from 9:30 a.m. to 7:30 p.m. Monday through Saturday.

HOLIDAYS: They include January 1 (New Year's Day), January 6 (Epiphany), March 19 (Day of St. Joseph), Good Friday, Easter Monday, May 1 (May Day), June 10 (Corpus Christi), June 29 (Day of St. Peter and St. Paul), July 25 (Day of St. James), August 15 (Feast of the Assumption), October 12 (Spain's National Day), November 1 (All Saints' Day), December 8 (Immaculate Conception), and December 25 (Christmas). No matter how large or small, every city or town in Spain also celebrates its local saint's days. In Madrid it's on May 15 (Saint Isidro).

LANGUAGE: Spanish is the official language of the land, of course, and French is also widely spoken in parts. In Madrid more and more people, especially the younger ones, are learning English. Nearly all major hotels and top restaurants are staffed with English-speaking persons. However, out in the country it will help a lot if you were a language major in school.

LAUNDRY: In most first-class hotels recommended in this guide, you need only fill out your laundry and dry-cleaning list and present it to your maid or valet. Same-day service usually costs anywhere from 25% to 50% more.

LIQUOR: Almost anyone of any age can order a drink in Spain. I've seen gypsy shoeshine boys who looked no more than 8 years old go into a *tasca* and purchase a glass of wine with their newly acquired tip. Bars, taverns, cafeterias, whatever, generally open at 8 a.m., and many serve alcohol all day until around 1 or 2 a.m. Spain doesn't have many stores devoted entirely to selling liquor and wine. Rather, you can purchase alcoholic beverages in almost any market, along with cheese and other foodstuffs.

METRIC MEASURES: Here's your chance to learn metric measures before going to Europe.

Weights	Measures
1 ounce = 28.3 grams	1 inch = 2.54 centimeters
1 pound = 454 grams	1 foot = 0.3 meters
2.2 pounds = 1 kilo (1000 grams)	1 yard = 0.91 meters
1 pint = 0.47 liter	1.09 yards = 1 meter
1 quart = 0.94 liter	1 mile = 1.61 kilometers
1 gallon = 3.78 liters	0.62 mile = 1 kilometer
	1 acre = 0.40 hectare
	2.47 acres = 1 hectare

NEWSPAPERS: Most newsstands along the Gran Vía or kiosks at the major hotels carry the latest edition of the *International Herald Tribune.* Spain also has an American weekly, a magazine known as the *Guidepost,* packed with information about late-breaking events in the Spanish capital, tips on movies shown in English, musical recitals, whatever. You may also want to become a regular reader of the *Iberian Daily Sun,* an English-language newspaper containing stories and listings of interest to both visitors from North America and Britain as well as expatriates. If you're traveling south, look out for *Lookout* magazine, a quality production in English with stories focused primarily on Spain's Sun Coast, although the staff also runs articles of general interest to the traveler to Spain.

PASSPORTS: A valid one is all an American, British, Australian, or Canadian citizen needs to enter Spain. You don't need an international driver's license if renting a car. Your local one from back home should suffice.

PHARMACIES: Drugstores are scattered all over Madrid. If you're trying to locate one at an odd hour, note a list posted outside the door of any drugstore that's not open. On the list are the names and addresses of pharmacies that are in service. The Spanish government requires drugstores to operate on the rotating system of hours —thereby assuring you that some will be open at all times, even on Sunday at midnight.

POLITICS: In its post-Franco era, Spain now has a constitutional monarchy, and it won't disturb you unless you disturb it.

POST OFFICE: If you don't want to receive your mail at your hotel or the American Express office, you can direct it to *Lista de Correos* at the central post office in Madrid. To pick up such mail, go to the window marked *Lista,* where you'll be asked to show your passport. The central post office in Madrid is housed in what is known as "the cathedral of post offices" at the Plaza de la Cibeles (tel. 221-81-95). An airmail postcard to the United States costs 64 pesetas (60¢) if sent from Spain, and an airmail letter up to 10 grams goes for 69 pesetas (60¢).

Warning: Don't count on being able to buy stamps at the post offices. A tobacco shop is more likely to have them, a peculiarity common to most cities in Spain.

RELIGIOUS SERVICES: Most churches in Madrid are Catholic, and they're found all over the city. Catholic masses in English, however, are given in a church at 165 Alfonso XIII. For more information, call 233-20-32 in the morning. For an Anglican service, the British Embassy Church of St. George is at 43 Nuñez de Balboa (call 274-51-55 for worship hours).

The interdenominational Protestant Community Church is at 34 Padre Damian (tel. 723-04-41), offering weekly services in the Colegio de los Sagrados Corazones, while the Immanuel Baptist Church offers English-speaking services at 4 Hernández de Tejada (tel. 407-43-47).

A Christian Science church is at 63 Alonso Cano (tel. 259-21-35), and a Jewish synagogue is on Calle de Balmes (tel.

445-98-35). It opened in the late 1960s, the first one to do so since the expulsion of the Jews from Spain in 1492. Friday-night services begin at 7:30, while Saturday morning services are at 9:30 a.m.

REST ROOMS: Some are available, including those in Retiro Park in Madrid and on the Plaza del Oriente across from the Royal Palace. Otherwise, you can always go into a bar or *tasca,* but you really should order something—perhaps a small glass of beer or even a bag of peanuts.

The Spanish designations for rest rooms are *aseos* or *servicios. Caballeros* are for men, and *damas,* naturally, are for women.

SMOKING: Temmie and Aubrey Baratz of Briarcliff Manor, New York, write: "Your readers should be forewarned that in Spain virtually everyone smokes. On buses. In the Metro. Everywhere. 'No Fumar' signs are ignored. With all that smoking, combined with inhaling diesel fumes, one wonders about the incidence of lung disease in Spain."

STORE HOURS: Major stores no longer take a siesta, and are open from 9:30 a.m. to 8 p.m. Monday to Saturday. However, smaller stores, such as the "mama and papa" operations, still follow the old custom and do business from 9:30 a.m. to 1:30 p.m. and 4:30 to 8 p.m.

TAXES: Since Spain joined the Common Market (EEC) on January 1, 1986 (which it did simultaneously with Portugal), it committed itself to gradually eliminating most tariff barriers between itself and the rest of Europe. In consequence, internal sales taxes (known in Spain as I.V.A.) were immediately adjusted upward to between 6% and 33%, depending on the commodity being sold. Most of the basic necessities of the Spaniard's life, including food and most wines, are taxed at 6%. The majority of goods and services, as well as rental cars, are taxed at the "ordinary" rate of 12%. Luxury goods such as jewelry, furs, motor yachts, and private airplanes, carry a 33% tax. Luxury hotels are usually subject to the 12% tax, although the increase is almost always quoted as part of the rates. Unfortunately for drinkers and smokers, all imported liquors and all tobaccos (whether Spanish or foreign) are taxed at the 33% rate, making the prices of vices just a little bit higher. Most drinkers solve the problem by switching from scotch to Spanish wines, Spanish beers, or Spanish brandies with soda.

If you buy goods worth more than 47,000 pesetas ($427), you are eligible for a tourist discount which, depending on the VAT, can be 6%, 12%, or 33% of the total value of your purchase. To get this discount you must (a) obtain a completed form (three copies) detailing the value and nature of your purchase (seller retains a copy). Then (b) travelers from non-EEC countries must show the purchase and the form to the Spanish Customs Office. Later on, the shop will refund the amount due. Inquire at the shop about method of refunding.

TELEGRAMS: Cables may be sent at the central post office building in Madrid at the Plaza de las Cibeles (tel. 221-81-95). However, the dialing number for international telegrams is 241-33-00.

TELEPHONES: If you don't speak Spanish, you'll find it easier to telephone from your hotel. Know, however, that this is often a very expensive way of doing it, as hotels impose a surcharge on every operator-assisted call. If you're more adventurous, you'll find street phone booths known as *cabinas,* with dialing instructions in English. Local calls can be made by inserting two coins of 5 pesetas (5¢) each if you don't talk more than three minutes. However, it may be best for long-distance calls—especially transatlantic ones— to go to the main telephone exchange, Locutorio Gran Vía, 30 Gran Vía, or Locutorio Recoletos, 37-41 P° Recoletos. You may not be lucky enough to find an English-speaking operator; however, you will have to fill out a simple form which will facilitate the placement of a call.

TELEX: You can send Telex messages from the central post office building in Madrid, Plaza de las Cibeles (tel. 221-81-95), and from all major hotels.

TIME: Spain is six hours ahead of Eastern Standard Time in the U.S. Daylight Saving Time (one hour ahead of standard time) is in effect from the last Sunday in March to the last Sunday in September.

TIPPING: It is not a problem if you follow certain guidelines, knowing that general rules are to be abandoned in the face of exceptional circumstances, such as someone performing a "lifesaving feat." Tipping is simplified in Spain, since the government requires hotels and restaurants to include their service charges—usually 15% of the bill—in their tariffs or in the price of their food items. However, that doesn't mean you should skip out of a place without dispensing some extra pesetas.

    Hotels: A porter is tipped 50 pesetas (45¢) per piece of luggage he handles, but never less than 100 pesetas (90¢) even if you have only one small suitcase. If the maid has performed some extra task for you, you might give her 50 pesetas (45¢). In front-ranking hotels, the concierge will often submit a separate bill.

Hairdressers: Both barbers and beauticians should be tipped at least 15% of the bill.

Taxis: Add about 12% to the fare as shown on the meter. However, if the driver personally unloads or loads your luggage, increase that to approximately 20%.

Porters: At airports such as Barajas and major terminals, the porter who handles your luggage will present you with a fixed-charge bill.

Restaurants: In both restaurants and nightclubs, 15% is added to the bill. To that, you should add another 3% to 5%, depending on the quality of the service.

Services: The women who guard the washrooms get 10 pesetas (10¢) to 25 pesetas (25¢) and theater ushers—either at the bullfights or in movie houses or legitimate theaters—get from 25 pesetas (25¢) to 50 pesetas (45¢).

TOURIST OFFICE: The headquarters of the main tourist office is at 50 Maria de Molina (tel. 411-40-19) in Madrid. English is spoken.

For information before you go, get in touch with the National Tourist Office of Spain, 665 Fifth Ave., New York, NY (tel. 212/759-8822).

CHAPTER X

THE HOTELS OF MADRID

◻ ◻ ◻

The hotel boom in Madrid has been spectacular: three-quarters of my recommendations have opened their doors since 1964.

What about the relics of yesteryear? Except for those grand old ladies, the Ritz and the Palace (circa 1910–1912), most other older hostelries in Madrid haven't really kept abreast of the times. A handful haven't added improvements or overhauled bedrooms substantially since the 1890s.

Traditionally, hotels in Madrid were clustered around the Atocha Railway Station and the Gran Vía. In my search for the most outstanding hotels in all price brackets, I've almost ignored these two popular, but noisy, districts. The newer hotels have been erected away from the center, especially on residential streets jutting off from the Paseo de la Castellana.

THE STAR SYSTEM: Spain officially rates its hotels by star designation. Riding the crest of the Milky Way are hotels granted a constellation of five stars. That is the highest rating in Spain, signaling a deluxe establishment, complete with all the amenities and high tariffs associated with such accommodations.

Most of the establishments recommended in this guide are three- and four-star hotels falling into that vague "middle bracket" category. Hotels granted one and two stars, as well as pensions (guesthouses), are far less comfortable, although they may be perfectly clean and decent places, but with limited plumbing and other physical facilities. The latter category is strictly for dedicated budgeteers.

REMINDER: The telephone area code for Madrid is 91.

SOME DELUXE HOTELS

The most famous hotel in Madrid is **The Ritz**, Plaza de la Lealtad, 28014 Madrid (tel. 521-28-57), offering all the luxuries and special attentions that world travelers have come to expect of a grand deluxe hotel. The director suggests that guests book very, very early, as rooms are hard to come by at this veritable citadel of gracious and snobbish living. An international rendezvous point, it has been handsomely updated and modernized, although efforts have been made to retain its Belle Époque character, unique in Europe. Acquired by Trusthouse Forte, the Ritz has undergone millions of dollars of "refreshing" to maintain its position as one of the leading hotels in the world.

One of *Les Grand Hôteles Européens,* it was built at the command of King Alfonso XIII, with the aid of none other than Cesar Ritz in 1908. It looks out onto the big circular Plaza de la Lealtad in the center of town, near the 300-acre Retiro Park, facing the Prado Museum and its extension, the Palacio de Villahermosa, and the Stock Exchange. The new hotels going up in Madrid simply can't match its grand-manner elegance. The Ritz was constructed when costs were relatively low, and when spaciousness, luxury, and comfort were the styles of the day. To be coddled in plush comfort, in a setting of beautiful but restrained furnishings, will cost from 44,000 pesetas ($396) in a single room and from 56,000 pesetas ($504) in a double. The marble bathrooms are some of the finest I've seen in more than two decades of inspecting hotels in Europe.

Like the cognoscenti of old, who have long had a liking for the Ritz, today's guest likes its grandeur, comfort, impeccable service, and gracious living, including 24-hour room service. It's not only elegant in the thick-carpeted sense, but it's also quiet. In these days of casual attire, it's important to know that guests at the Ritz dress up, even for breakfast. This is not a "resort" hotel.

Guests are treated to lavish bouquets of fresh flowers in their rooms. The façade of the hotel is classed as a historical monument, or at least it should be. No other hotel, except perhaps for the Palace, has a more varied history.

The five-star Ritz Restaurant is one of the most attractive in Europe, and a Spanish magazine recently called it "the top restaurant of the year." It is decorated in cream, blue, and gold, with paneled mirrors and 16th-century Flemish tapestries. Its chefs present an international menu, and its paella is said to be the best in Madrid. Except for champagne, the wine list is staunchly Spanish.

The **Villa Magna,** 22 Paseo de la Castellana, 28046 Madrid (tel. 261-49-00), on the city's most fashionable boulevard, is one of the finest hotels in all of Spain. And for good reason: a small group of the elite teamed up to create a setting in which their special friends, along with an increasing array of discriminating international visitors, would be pleased to live and dine. They hired an architect, imported a French decorator, and the result is elegant and appropriately expensive.

Separated from the busy boulevard by a park-like garden, its façade has severe contemporary lines. In contrast, its opulent interior recaptures the style of Carlos IV, with its richly paneled walls and marble floors. Through the stunning lobby and elaborate drawing room passes almost every film star shooting on location in Spain. In the Mayfair cocktail lounge, sedate and leathery à la London, the bartender can mix any drink you conjure up.

This luxury palace offers 198 stylized bedrooms—perhaps Louis XVI, Regency, Italian provincial—each, along with its sumptuous marble and tile bath, designed to give you that pampered feeling. And even if you're not one of those "special friends," a bowl of fragrant fresh flowers inevitably awaits you. Single rooms are 28,000 pesetas ($252); a twin-bedded room, 38,000 pesetas ($342).

Next on the deluxe list is the **Eurobuilding,** 23 Calle Padre Damián, 28036 Madrid (tel. 457-17-00). Even while this hotel was on the drawing boards, the rumor was that this five-star sensation of white marble would provide, in the architect's words, "a new concept in deluxe hotels." The Eurobuilding long ago lived up to its advance billing, reflecting a high level in taste and design. It is two hotels linked by a courtyard, the complex away from the city center, but right in the midst of apartment houses, boutiques, nightclubs, first-class restaurants, tree-shaded squares, and the heart of the modern Madrid business world.

The more glamorous of the twin buildings is the main one, with 150 suites recently renovated in luxurious pastel shades and named Las Estancias de Eurobuilding. Drinks await you in the refrigerator. Gold-and-white ornately carved beds, background music, TV, a room-wide terrace for breakfast and cocktail entertaining —all are tastefully coordinated. Across the courtyard, the sister Eurobuilding contains 480 single and double rooms, all compactly designed, and each with a view from its private terrace of the formal garden and swimming pool below. All rooms have security doors and individual safes. Rates for a single are 13,900 pesetas ($125) to 16,600 pesetas ($149), 18,200 pesetas ($164) to 21,000 pesetas ($189) for a double.

Shared by both buildings is the luxury restaurant, Balthasar, on the lower level behind a Turkish spindle screen. La Taberna, also on the premises, offers more rapid dining. Perhaps the ideal way to dine here is al fresco by the pool, enjoying a buffet luncheon.

The **Meliá Madrid,** 27 Princesa, 28008 Madrid (tel. 241-82-00), is one of the most up-to-date, sumptuously modern, yet uniquely Spanish hotels in the country. Its 23-floors' worth of wide picture windows have taken a permanent position in the capital's skyline. It would be difficult to call any of the 265 bedrooms "standard," but all are good-sized, many offer spectacular views of the city, all are air-conditioned, and all have chalk-white walls to dramatize the flamboyant use of color accents. The baths are done in snow-white marble; TV sets are common, and so, too, are refrigerators filled with cold drinks. With service and taxes, singles begin at 15,000 pesetas ($135); doubles, 19,000 pesetas ($171). The Restaurant Princesa is a subdued and restful spot. Equally popular is the Don Pepe Grill, which offers similarly stimulating meals. The cuisine throughout is international, including Japanese and Indian dishes.

The **Miguel Angel,** 31 Miguel Angel (tel. 442-00-22), just off the Paseo de la Castellana, is sleekly modern and has quickly built a reputation for providing some of the finest accommodations in the Spanish capital. It has much going for it—location, contemporary styling, imaginative furnishings and art objects, an efficient staff, and plenty of comfort. Behind its façade is an expansive sun terrace on several levels, with clusters of garden furniture, surrounded by semitropical planting. The Farnesio bar is decorated in a Spanish Victorian style, and piano music is played from 8 in the evening. All the deluxe facilities are provided—an indoor heated swimming pool, sauna baths, hairdressers, and also a drugstore. Best of all, the hotel has style with its luxurious accoutrements. Art exhibitions are sponsored in the arcade of boutiques.

In the large bedrooms, fabrics and carpets are color coordinated, and many of the furnishings are reproductions of classic Spanish styles. The 307 rooms are soundproof and air-conditioned, containing TVs, radios, and mini-bars. Singles rent for 13,850 pesetas ($125); regular doubles go for 26,600 pesetas ($239). A set luncheon or dinner goes for around 4,200 pesetas ($37.75) in either the Florencia or Renacimento restaurant, and the Zacarias restaurant/disco, also on the premises, serves dinner until 3 a.m.

The **Wellington,** 8 Velázquez, 28001 Madrid (tel. 275-44-00), with its impressive antique-tapestried entrance, is one of Madrid's more sedate deluxe hotels, built in the mid-1950s but substantially remodeled since. In the Salamanca residential area near Retiro Park, the Wellington offers redecorated rooms, 325 in all, each air-conditioned and with color TV (with cable and movie channels), music, two phones (one in the bathroom), and a guest-operated combination safe. Units are furnished in English mahogany, and the baths are modern and immaculate, with marble and fixtures newly installed annually. Doubles with private terraces (at no extra charge) are the choice accommodations. Singles cost 13,810 pesetas ($124); doubles, 17,500 pesetas ($158).

In addition to an outdoor swimming pool, the Wellington offers 24-hour room service, a garage, beauty parlor, and same-day dry cleaning and laundry. An added bonus here is the El Fogón grill room, styled like a 19th-century tavern, where many of the provisions for the typically Spanish dishes are shipped in from the hotel's own ranch. The pub-style Bar Ingles is a warm and hospitable rendezvous spot.

OTHER TOP CHOICES

The **Palace,** 7 Plaza de las Cortes, 28014 Madrid (tel. 429-75-51), is the grand *dueña* of Spanish hotels. The establishment had an auspicious beginning, inaugurated by the late King Alfonso XIII in 1912. Covering a city block, it is superbly located, facing the Prado Museum and Neptune Fountain, in the historical and artistic area, within walking distance of the main shopping center and the best antique shops. Some of the city's most intriguing *tascas* and restaurants are only a short stroll away.

Architecturally, it captures the elegant pre–World War I "Grand Hotel" style, with an emphasis on space and comfort. Even though it is one of the largest hotels in Europe—1,000 beds in all—it retains a personal atmosphere. The rooms are conservatively decorated, with plenty of space for leisurely living, color TV, and direct-dial telephones. The bathrooms are large enough to have separate showers and toilets. Single rooms cost from 16,000 pesetas ($144); doubles range from 20,000 pesetas ($180), to 28,000 pesetas ($252).

The hotel is air-conditioned, with a splendid and attractive lobby, restaurant, grill room, and bar. A coffeeshop in the main lobby is open from noon to 3 a.m.

The **Princesa Plaza,** 3 Serrano Jover, 28015 Madrid (tel. 242-21-00), is a sprawling deluxe hotel designed like a series of massive rectangular solids set together. The concrete-and-glass façade looks over a busy series of boulevards in the center of Madrid. The interior contains 406 attractively modern rooms, decorated in springtime colors, as well as a large collection of conference rooms, an underground garage, a hairdressing salon, a restaurant, a bar, and a musical salon. Singles rent for 15,000 pesetas ($135) nightly, and doubles go for 19,000 pesetas ($171).

The **Castellana Hotel,** 49 Paseo de la Castellana, 28046 Madrid (tel. 410-02-00). Now that the Inter-Continental hotel chain is in full charge here, the Castellana has risen fast; today it is one of the finest hotels in the Spanish capital. From the moment you enter, you detect an alert staff, one of the most helpful among the staffs of all the major hotels. Checking in is easy, and soon you're whisked to one of the 311 handsomely furnished and completely air-conditioned bedrooms. The rate in a double is 25,000 pesetas ($225), dropping to 21,000 pesetas ($189) in a single.

The location is ideal, in the center of Madrid on a fashionable and famous tree-lined "paseo." It is convenient to both business offices and banks. The Inter-Continental hotels are always sensitive to the needs of the business traveler, and the Castellana is no exception, as it can arrange secretarial and translation services. But the tourist isn't neglected either. At the concierge's desk, information is willingly dispensed concerning activities from sightseeing to golf or skiing (yes, even skiing). Car rentals can also be easily arranged.

A quick call brings an efficient room service, carrying either a breakfast tray or else summoning someone to pick up your laundry or dry cleaning. Thoughtful facilities include color TV with in-house movies, a mini-bar, and in many cases, a balcony. Many of your needs can be taken care of right at the hotel, as the premises contain an airlines reservation office, a travel agent, and theater ticket desks. You can also go on a shopping expedition in the arcade of the hotel. There are also telex and cable facilities.

At night, the hotel becomes quite romantic, as guests gather to listen to Spanish guitar music in the garden patio. You can also enjoy before-dinner drinks at La Ronda Bar, before having dinner at the hotel's informal restaurant. There is also a coffeeshop for those who want their meals served in a hurry. A host of other facilities include a garage, a health club with a gymnasium, and a massage and sauna room. The Inter-Continental has telephone reservations offices around the world.

The **Hotel Apartamento Escultor,** 3 Miguel Angel, 28010 Madrid (tel. 410-42-03), offers the luxuries of apartment living for the price of a room. Apartments are rented to couples for 12,400 pesetas ($112). The location is supreme, just off the Paseo de la Castellana, in a district of leading hotels and restaurants. The apartments have their own charm and contemporary styling. Each room has a mini-bar, video films system, and color TV. Down a long mirrored corridor with a wash basin and wardrobe area (the bath and toilet are separate), you enter the small bedrooms which open into a terrace. Everything is compact, with "bullet" reading lights. The hotel has a small, comfortable lounge and a bar where a nighttime disco pulsates. In addition, the hotel offers a sophisticated modern restaurant, Vanity, seating 40 to 45 people. The hotel is fully air-conditioned and contains a garage.

The **Plaza Hotel,** 8 Plaza de España, 28013 Madrid (tel. 247-12-00), could be called the Waldorf-Astoria of Spain. A massive rose-and-white structure, it soars upward to a central tower 26 stories high. It is a landmark visible for miles around and one of the tallest skyscrapers in Europe, crowned by a panoramic disco, swimming pool, and sun terrace.

The accommodations are varied, ranging from conventional singles and doubles to luxurious suites, 82 of these with a sitting room. A standard single rents for 11,000 pesetas ($99), and a double goes for 14,000 pesetas ($117). All the rooms are air-conditioned. The furniture in the regular bedrooms is standard modern, with harmonious colors (such as gray and mulberry); there's space for lounging, plus expansive marble bathrooms.

You can order a quick meal and drinks in the coffeeshop in the basement.

The **Meliá Castilla,** 43 Calle Capitán Haya, 28020 Madrid (tel. 270-80-00), is a blockbuster: a mammoth hotel with 1,000 rooms, it qualifies along with the already-mentioned Palace, as one of the largest hotels in Europe. Built primarily for the convention trade, it caters with grace to the needs of the individual traveler. Everything is larger than life here: indeed, you need a floor plan to direct yourself around its precincts. The lounges and corridors of pristine marble are vast. As you wander around, you'll find a swimming pool, a shopping arcade, a coffeeshop, a seafood restaurant, a restaurant specializing in paella and other rice dishes, cocktail lounges, a landscaped garden, saunas, a gymnasium, a parking garage, the Trinidad nightclub, even a showroom full of the latest model cars. In addition to these features, there's the restaurant/show, Scala Meliá Castilla.

As for the accommodations, each of the twin-bedded rooms comes complete with private bath, refrigerator, radio, and color TV. The specific furnishings, all in the modern Spanish idiom, vary from room to room, everything tasteful and luxurious. Double rooms cost from 20,000 pesetas ($180). A standard single room is 17,000 pesetas ($153). The Meliá Castilla is in a section in the north of Madrid.

MODERATELY PRICED HOTELS

The **Hotel Victoria,** 7 Plaza del Angel, 28012 Madrid (tel. 231-45-00), is about as important to the legends of Madrid as Manolete himself. The famous bullfighter used to stay here, giving lavish parties in one of the reception rooms, and attracting mobs in the square below when he went out on his balcony for morning coffee. Other clients have traditionally included historians, writers, and lesser bullfighters, all of whom enjoy the dozens of tapas bars in the neighborhood and the old-world charm of the ornate stone-and-metal façade.

The hotel was built in 1925, and named after the grandmother of the present King of Spain, Juan Carlos. Although the hotel is in a congested area in the center of Madrid, it opens onto its own little plaza, rich in tradition as a meeting place of intellectuals during the 17th century. Today the area is usually filled with flower vendors and older people catching rays of midafternoon sun. Although not lavishly furnished, the rooms are quite comfortable, and a staid but polite atmosphere prevails. The hotel often rents out its banqueting room to middle-class Spanish families for wedding receptions. Doubles here rent for 6,700 pesetas ($60.25), with singles going for 4,500 pesetas ($40.50).

The **Emperatriz,** 4 López de Hoyos, 28006 Madrid (tel. 413-65-11), just off the wide Paseo de la Castellana, is only a minute or so from two of Madrid's leading deluxe hotels. It charges 6,000 pesetas ($54) for a single room, 9,500 pesetas ($85.50) for a double- or twin-bedded room. Each room has a private bath and air conditioning. On the premises are many facilities, including a beauty salon, barbershop, and well-upholstered lounges in which you're likely to meet fellow globe-trotting Americans. If possible, ask for a room on the eighth floor, where you'll get a private terrace. The decor in the bedrooms is a safe mixture of traditional and modern, with the primary emphasis on comfort and cleanliness.

The **Novotel Madrid,** 1 Calle Albacete (at the corner of Avenida Badajoz), 28027 Madrid (tel. 405-46-00), was intended to serve the hotel needs of a cluster of multinational corporations with headquarters 2½ miles east of the center of Madrid, but its rooms are so comfortable and its prices so reasonable that tourists have begun using it as well. It opened in 1986, with an enthusiastic staff. Its position on the highway away from the maze of sometimes confusing streets makes it attractive to motorists.

Each of the comfortably furnished bedrooms offers a well-designed bathroom, color TV with in-house movies, mini-bar, radio, phone, and access to an English-speaking deck staff well-versed in local sightseeing attractions. The 240 bedrooms cost 8,900 pesetas ($80) in a single, 11,200 pesetas ($101) in a double. Children under 16 stay free in their parents' room.

Motorists should exit from the M-30 at Barrio de la Concepción/Parque de las Avenidas, just before reaching the city limits of central Madrid.

The **Hotel Chamartín,** Estación de Chamartín, 28036 Madrid (tel. 733-90-11), is a 378-room hotel rising nine stories, part of the major transportation and shopping complex in this modern train station. The owner of the hotel is RENFE, the government's railroad system, and it's operated by Entursa Hotels. The hotel lies a 15-minute ride from the airport and a five-minute jaunt from the city's major business and sightseeing areas. All guest rooms are air-conditioned, featuring TV, radio, a refrigerator/bar, a private safe, and insulated windows for maximum quiet and privacy. Eighteen one-bedroom suites, some with a balcony, are also available. Rates in the standard rooms are 7,200 pesetas ($65) in a single, 9,900 pesetas ($89) in a double.

Especially oriented to the business traveler, the Chamartín offers a currency exchange, travel agency, bank, car rental, and complete communication services. A screen in the lobby posting the arrival and departure of all trains affords special convenience to the traveler.

A coffee bar serves a buffet breakfast daily, and room service is also available. A choice of drinks is featured at the hotel's bar off the main lobby. Guests can dine at a variety of restaurants and snackbars in the Chamartín complex. Among the extensive facilities and services available to hotel guests are 13 shops, four movie theaters, a roller-skating rink, a disco, and ample parking.

The **Gran Hotel Colón,** 11 Pez Volador, 28007 Madrid (tel. 273-59-00), stands west of Retiro Park, a few minutes by subway from the center. It offers comfortable yet moderately priced accommodations in one of the city's modern hotel structures. More than half of its bedrooms have an individual balcony. To literally top everything off, there is a swimming pool on the roof, 11 stories up, where you can sunbathe with the skyline of Madrid before you. Other assets of the hotel include two dining rooms, a covered garage, and Bingo.

One of the Colón's founders was an accomplished designer, which accounts for the unusual stained-glass windows and murals in the public rooms and the paintings by Spanish artists in the lounge. The furnishings in the rooms are all built-in; each comes with private bath and sitting area. They rent for 7,300 pesetas ($65.75) for a double, 5,100 pesetas ($46) for a single.

The **Hotel El Prado,** 11 Calle del Prado, 28014 Madrid (tel. 425-35-68), doesn't compete with its more famous namesake, the museum, although its lobby is decorated with full-size copies of many of the art treasures that are the Spanish national heritage. While you sip a drink in the lobby, you can gaze upon the serene calm of a series of mannerist paintings whose size almost engulfs the otherwise simple room. The hotel has a cafeteria on the premises, an underground parking garage (a rarity in this neighborhood), and some 54 clean bedrooms. Each has air conditioning, a mini-bar, and a private bath. Singles cost 6,500 pesetas ($58.50); doubles, 9,000 pesetas ($81). The hotel, with its angular modern façade, is near the Teatro Español and the American Express office.

The **Residencia Bretón,** 29 Bretón de los Herreros, 28003 Madrid (tel. 442-83-00), is an ingratiating little modern 56-room hotel on a side street several blocks from the Paseo de la Castellana. It is well furnished with excellent reproductions of Iberian pieces. As a *residencia,* it doesn't offer a major dining room, but it does possess a little bar and breakfast room adjoining the reception lounge. Single rooms, all with bath, go for 5,800 pesetas ($52.25). All doubles have twin beds, a complete bath, and toilet, and rent for 8,600 pesetas ($77.50). All rooms have a bar-refrigerator and four channels of music. Highlighting the living areas are attractive wooden beds, black wrought-iron electric fixtures, ornately designed tile floors and baths, wall-to-wall curtains, and sitting areas. The Bretón is air-conditioned and steam-heated.

The **Grand Hotel Tryp Velázquez,** 62 Calle de Velázquez, 28001 Madrid (tel. 275-28-00), faces an affluent residential street near the center of town. The art deco façade conceals an interior so filled with well-upholstered furniture and richly grained paneling that it shows more of its 1947 origin than any 1930s kinship. Several public rooms lead off a central oval area lined with marble and 19th-century bronzes. One of them includes a warm bar area capped with a reproduction of a 17th-century hunting scene. A cove-ceilinged feeder hallway is adorned with astrological symbols in cerulean blue and gold. Farther on, there's a salon with parquet floors, statues, and russet upholstery.

As in many hotels of its era, the bedrooms vary, some large enough for entertaining but all containing air conditioning. A double used for single occupancy costs 8,300 pesetas ($74.75), 10,750 pesetas ($96.75) for two persons. This is one of the most attractive medium-size hotels in Madrid, with great comfort and convenience. Breakfast is included in the tariffs, and parking is available on the premises.

The **Cuzco,** 133 Paseo de la Castellana, 28046 Madrid (tel. 456-06-00), popular with business people and American tour groups, lies in a business area of big buildings, government ministries, spacious avenues, and the main Congress Hall, only 500 yards away. The Station Madrid–Paris is 1,000 yards away from the Cuzco, so it's a popular, convenient address.

It has been redecorated and modernized since it was completed in 1967, a 15-floor structure set back from Madrid's longest boulevard. The architect of the Cuzco allowed for spacious bedrooms, each big enough to have a sitting area. The decorator provided modern furnishings and patterned rugs, and left the feeling of spaciousness intact. The management supplies direct-dial phones, air conditioning, color TV, and an electronic wake-up call. A twin-bedded room with bath rents for 12,000 pesetas ($108); a single, 9,400 pesetas ($84.50).

There is a bi-level snackbar and cafeteria. The lounge is a forest of marble pillars and leather armchairs, the ambience enhanced by contemporary oil paintings and tapestries. Facilities include a free parking lot, covered garage, a beauty parlor, sauna, massage, gymnasium, and a cocktail bar with a warm atmosphere.

The **Hotel Claridge,** 6 Plaza Conde de Casal, 28007 Madrid (tel. 551-94-00), is a contemporary building beyond the Retiro Park, about five minutes from the Prado by taxi. The air-conditioned bedrooms are well organized and styled: small, compact, with coordinated furnishings and colors. The bathrooms are bright, and the tile setter was given carte blanche to make them lavish. All 150 rooms have a private bath. A single rents for 4,000 pesetas ($36), and a double goes for 7,000 pesetas ($63). You can take your meals in the cafeteria or just relax in the modern lounge.

The **Alcalá,** 66 Alcalá (just off Retiro Park), 28009 Madrid (tel. 435-10-60), offers 153 rooms with private bath and air conditioning. Good news for the lone vacationer: about half the rooms are singles, priced from 7,000 pesetas ($63). The rate for a double is 10,500 pesetas ($94.50). The room décor is tasteful. Wall-to-wall draperies, wide-striped bedcovers, tile-and-wood headboards, all are harmoniously coordinated. The two-level public lounge has a circular fireplace, black hood, hearth, and surrounding black leather armchairs. Other facilities include the ornate Restaurant Basque, a lower-level coffeeshop, a bright Toledo-red American bar opening off the lounge, and an underground garage.

The **Residência Liabeny,** 3 Salud, 28013 Madrid (tel. 232-53-06), is yet another demonstration of Spain's almost instinctive talent for creating comfortable 20th-century hotels that please fastidious travelers. It's in a prime location between the Gran Vía and the Puerta del Sol. Distributed among seven floors are well-maintained, air-conditioned bedrooms. In a single, the rate is 5,600 pesetas ($50.50), 9,000 pesetas ($81) in a double, including a continental breakfast. The bedrooms have an English touch, with mahogany furniture, wall-to-wall draperies, lounge chairs, and desks, as well as private entryways.

THE BUDGET RANGE

The **Hostal Residencia Don Diego,** 45 Calle de Velázquez, 28001 Madrid (tel. 435-07-60), lies in a combination residential/commercial neighborhood that is relatively convenient to many of the monuments of the city. The hostal is on the fifth floor of a building with an elevator. The vestibule contains an elegant winding staircase accented with iron griffin heads supporting its balustrade. The hotel is warmly inviting, filled with leather couches and a kind of comfortable, no-nonsense style of angular but attractive furniture. A bar stands at the far end of the main sitting room. Singles cost from 4,100 pesetas ($37); doubles, from 5,820 pesetas ($52.50).

The **Anaco,** 3 Tres Cruces, 28013 Madrid (tel. 522-46-04), is a modestly modern 37-bedroom hotel, just off the shopping thoroughfare, Gran Vía. Opening onto a tree-shaded plaza, it attracts those seeking a resting place featuring contemporary appurtenances and cleanliness. The bedrooms are charmingly compact, with built-in headboards, reading lamps, and lounge chairs. Each room is individually air-conditioned and contains a private bath (some with a shower). The maximum rate for a single with bath is 4,000 pesetas ($36). In a double room, the rate is 6,500 pesetas ($58.50). Useful tip: Ask for one of the five terraced double rooms on the top floor renting at no extra charge. English is spoken. Nearby is a municipally operated garage.

The **Aristos,** 34 Avenida Pío XII, 28016 Madrid (tel. 457-04-50), is a 24-room, three-star hotel in an up-and-coming residential area of Madrid, not far from the Eurobuilding. Its main advantage is a pleasant garden in front, where you can lounge, have a drink, or order a complete meal. The hotel's restaurant, El Chaflán, is frequented by residents of the neighborhood in addition to hotel visitors. There's a small swimming pool in back for those torrid days. The rooms come with terraces and are decorated with modern decor. Singles cost 5,200 pesetas ($46.75); doubles, 8,300 pesetas ($74.75).

The **Tirol,** 4 Marqués de Urquijo, 28008 Madrid (tel. 248-19-00), a short walk from the Plaza de España and the swank Meliá Madrid, is a good choice. A three-star hotel, it offers singles for 4,000 pesetas ($36) and doubles for 5,700 pesetas ($51.25). Eight of the 93 rooms contain a terrace. Furnishings are simple and functional, somewhat characterless and old-fashioned, but adequate. In the cafeteria downstairs you can order a snack or light meal. There's also a garage in the building.

The **Casón del Tormes,** 7 Río, 28013 Madrid (tel. 241-97-46), is an attractive three-star hotel around the corner from the Royal Palace and Plaza de España. It's a red-brick, four-story structure with stone-trimmed modern windows overlooking a quiet one-way street. The long lobby filling most of the ground floor of the building is graced with glass display cases containing displays of silver and copper serving dishes, lots of grained vertical paneling, and a Spanish refectory table. Breakfast tables are set up on the marble floor, and a bar opens onto a separate room. All the rooms are air-conditioned. Well-furnished doubles with bath cost 6,270 pesetas ($56.50), and singles with bath go for 4,140 pesetas ($37.25), with a continental breakfast included. Public parking is available in nearby Plaza de España.

The **Hostal Embajada,** 5 Calle Santa Engracía, 28010 Madrid (tel. 447-33-00), is a clean, pleasant three-star hotel about one block from the Plaza Alonso Martínez, a rather distinguished residential area. Still standing across the street is a great 19th-century palace. The Embajada has 65 rooms, and doubles with bath cost 7,900 pesetas ($71). Singles go for 5,500 pesetas ($49.50). You'll find the bedrooms tastefully decorated and the bathrooms modern. There's a modest lounge but no bar.

The **Residencia Mercátor,** 123 Atocha, 28012 Madrid (tel. 429-05-00), only about a three-minute stroll from the Prado, draws a clientele seeking a good, modern hotel—orderly, well run, and clean, with enough comforts and conveniences to please the weary traveler. Some of the rooms are more inviting than others, especially those with desks and armchairs. Color is often utilized effectively. The best twin-bedded rooms with private bath rent for 6,500 pesetas ($58.50). Singles peak at 4,275 pesetas ($38.50). The Mercátor is a *residencia*—that is, it offers breakfast only. However, it has a bar and cafeteria serving light meals such as *platos combinados* (combination plates). Happily, the hotel has a garage, and is within walking distance of the Iberia air terminal and American Express.

NOSTALGIA ALONG OLD GRAN VÍA: Despite its commerical location between shops on the main street of Madrid, the **Lope de Vega,** 59 Gran Vía 28013 Madrid (tel. 247-70-00), is a charmer of enduring appeal to traditionalists in pursuit of fast-fading, old-world atmosphere in the city. A small elevator lifts you to this three-star hotel owned and managed by Mrs. Christina Belderrain Garin and named after the great Spanish dramatist. Wood paneling, red velvet, and antiques evoke the ambience of a city clubroom. The bedrooms, each one different, are well maintained and comfortable, although slightly dated. Each has a private bath. The most expensive single costs 2,700 pesetas ($24.25), 4,400 pesetas ($39.50) in a double. You can sit in the lobby of the hotel, looking out onto a view of the royal palace.

The **Hotel Francisco I,** 15 Arenal, 28013 Madrid (tel.

248-43-14), offers 57 modern, clean rooms. Doubles with a shower-bath (sit-down tub) range from 4,500 pesetas ($40.50). Singles—only four in this category—with a similar bath go for 3,200 pesetas ($28.75). There's a pleasant, if aseptic, lounge, a bar, Muzak, and on the sixth floor you'll find a comfortable, rustic-style restaurant where a set meal costs 1,400 pesetas ($12.50).

The **Hotel Nuria,** 52 Fuencarral, 28004 Madrid (tel. 231-92-08), just three blocks from the Gran Vía, has some bedrooms with especially interesting views of the capital. Renovated in the late '60s, the 58-room hotel offers double rooms with private bath or shower for 3,980 pesetas ($35.75), breakfast included. The most expensive singles, with breakfast, rent for 2,250 pesetas ($20.25). The food is highly praised by those who have sampled it. The price of a complete luncheon or dinner is 1,200 pesetas ($10.75).

CHAPTER XI

LATE DINING IN MADRID

□ □ □

At best, the cuisine of Spain is controversial. It inspires some to unqualified praise, others to fulmination.

The kitchens of Spain turn out a pungent, varied, and imaginative fare, ranging from squid cooked in its own ink to Valencian paella to Andalusian gazpacho to grilled pink prawns to garlic soup (said to bestow longevity) to the tail of a bull.

For the versatile, adventurous diner, there is no problem. If you fall into that category, you're in luck, with loads of temptation —such as **anguillas** (baby eels)—waiting to lure you. Still, if you grow faint at the mention of creatures from the deep, never fear. The chefs of Spain, now more than ever, are prepared to accommodate you with what has come to be known as an "international" cuisine.

Whether you're an epicurean of the caliber of Lucullus or the possessor of a Milquetoast palate, you should not rush too rapidly into the Spanish cuisine. If you overindulge in the dishes cooked in olive oil and the wines called "noble" but strong, chances are you'll come down with that traditional tourist malady euphemistically known as "Toledo tummy."

If you don't like garlic, instruct your waiter (*camarero*). If he or she doesn't speak English, say: *"Sin ajo"* (pronounced ah-ho). The word for butter is *mantequilla*. Of course, many dishes of combined ingredients such as paella or gazpacho depend on garlic for their basic flavor.

LIQUID SALAD AND AROMATIC PAELLA: All the major
Spanish cuisines, ranging from Galician and Asturian to Basque (the Basques are said to be the best cooks) to Andalusian and Levantine, are represented in Madrid, along with the traditional Castilian cuisine, which predominates.

Two of the best-known specialties, the **paella** of Valencia and the "liquid salad" or **gazpacho** of Andalusia, need little introduction, as they are served in North America and throughout continental Europe. Both items vary greatly, depending on the skill of the chef and the quality of ingredients used.

At its worst, paella—the Spanish rice dish—is made with whatever leftovers the chef has salvaged from the night before. At its finest, it is cooked with such well-chosen items as tender chicken, artichoke hearts, prawns, clams, bits of sausage, peas, garlic, pimientos—all aromatically seasoned and served on saffron rice. Traditionally, the paella is then presented to you in a piping-hot black iron skillet.

Gazpacho is especially good in summer. Ideally, it should be chilled thoroughly, in the tradition of vichyssoise. Basically, it is a soup of olive oil, vinegar, garlic, fresh tomatoes, with cucumber, peppers, croutons, and raw onions. Another soup in which the Spaniards excel is **sopa de pescado,** literally "soup of fish," again made in infinite varieties from province to province, but usually a taste treat worthy of featuring on any menu.

SUCKLING PIG AND A ZARZUELA: One of the most exciting taste treats of Spain originates in the province of Segovia. It is the roast suckling pig, so beloved by Hemingway at his Casa Botín in Madrid. Called **cochinillo asado,** it is a rich-tasting banquet—and so is the price. At its finest, the suckling pig is tender enough to be carved with china. Roast lamb (**cordero asado**) also draws many admirers. Otherwise, meat dishes, especially beef, sometimes disappoint North Americans used to finer cuts.

In their fish dishes, the Spaniards are quite remarkable and most inventive. Thanks to speedy transportation facilities, inland cities such as Madrid receive daily supplies of fresh fish. Mountain river trout (**trucha**) is superb, as is the paralyzingly priced lobster (**langosta**). A great fish dish is **zarzuela de mariscos,** with hunks of prawn, lobster, and other shellfish.

MEET THE "MENÚ DEL DÍA": The fixed-price *menú turistico* is no longer enforced. However, many restaurants feature a *menú del día*. The principle behind this set meal is to give a tourist (or a Spaniard, if he or she so desires) a complete meal, including soup or hors d'oeuvres, a meat or fish dish, plus dessert, a small carafe of the house wine, service, and taxes—all for one standard charge.

Now for my specific restaurant recommendations:

THE LEADING RESTAURANTS

Fortuny, 34 Fortuny (tel. 410-77-07), is the most elegant restaurant in Madrid, and also one of the best. Lying off the Paseo de la Castellana, the restaurant opened in 1986 in a 19th-century villa, originally the home of the Marqués Cuevas de Vera. Guests, who include expense-account gourmets and foreign visitors, often arrive by limousine. They are ushered across the courtyard and into the beautifully decorated, luxurious restaurant. Diners can choose to eat in the garden in fair weather. Otherwise, they will be seated in a Louis XVI chair at a table in one of the main dining rooms. Individual service is the keynote here.

Imaginative appetizers include codfish ravioli Fortuny, and the menu is likely to feature grilled suckling lamb in its own juice (prepared for two diners), roast duck with fig ravioli, sea bass with shrimp tartare, and grilled pork trotters in a hot sauce. The wine list is among the finest in Madrid. Meals cost 5,000 pesetas ($45) to 8,000 pesetas ($72). The restaurant is closed at lunch Saturday and all day Sunday, but open otherwise from 1:15 p.m. to as late as 5 or 6 p.m. (top bankers and business people in Madrid often lunch quite late). Dinner is from 9 p.m. to midnight, and reservations are essential.

Las Cuatro Estaciones, 5 Général Ibáñez Ibero (tel. 253-63-05), is placed by gastronomes and horticulturists alike among their favorite dining spots of Madrid. In addition to superb food, the establishment prides itself on the masses of flowers which change with the season, plus a modern and softly inviting décor which has delighted some of the most glamorous diners in Spain. Depending on the time of year, the mirrors surrounding the multilevel bar near the entrance reflect thousands of hydrangeas, chrysanthemums, or poinsettias. Even the napery matches whichever colors the resident botanist has chosen as the seasonal motif. Each person involved in food preparation spends a prolonged apprenticeship at restaurants in France before returning home to try their freshly sharpened talents on the tastebuds of aristocratic Madrid.

A fixed-price meal is available for 3,500 pesetas ($31.50), while à la carte meals, as well as an elaborate *menú degustatión,* cost 6,500 pesetas ($58.50) each. Representative specialties include crab bisque, fresh oysters, a petite marmite of fish and shellfish, imaginative preparations of salmon, a salad of eels, fresh asparagus with mushrooms in puff pastry with a parsley-butter sauce, a three-fish platter with fines herbes, brochette of filet of beef in pecadillo, and a nouvelle cuisine version of blanquette of monkfish so tender it melts in your mouth. A "festival of desserts" includes whichever specials the chef has concocted that day, a selection of which is placed temptingly on your table.

Reservations are recommended for meals, which are served from 1 to 4 p.m. and 9 p.m. to midnight every day except Saturday, Sunday, and in August.

The **Jockey,** 6 Amador de los Ríos (tel. 419-24-35), is considered by many to be the finest restaurant in Spain. At any rate, it is the favorite of international celebrities, diplomats, and heads of state, and some of the more faithful patrons look upon it as their own private club.

The restaurant, with tables on two levels, isn't overly large. Wood-paneled walls and colored linen provide autumnal warmth. Against the paneling are a dozen prints of horses mounted by jockeys—hence the name of the place. Reservations are necessary. Hours are 1 to 2:30 p.m. and 9 to 11:30 p.m. If you go early—1:30 p.m. or 9:30 p.m.—you'll stand a better chance of getting a table. You'll also have the dining room virtually to yourself.

If you'd like your decisions made for you, two or more persons can order a "Special Menu," which is changed monthly. My most recent sampling of this menu began with sweetbreads in a puff pastry (perfumed with truffles) and went on to partridge and ended with a cold mandarin soufflé, among other courses.

The chef is always coming up with new dishes, including smoked Asturias salmon, sea bass in papillote, smoked eel mousse with sardines, Aranjuez pheasant in grape sauce, and deboned duck with figs in wine. The cost of a meal here will begin at 7,000 pesetas ($63), going up. The restaurant is open daily, except Sunday, although it closes during the entire month of August.

El Cabo Mayor, 13 Juan Hurtado de Mendoza (tel. 250-87-76), in the prosperous northern edges of Madrid, is not far from the city-within-a-city of Chamartín Station. This is one of the best, most popular, and most stylish restaurants in Spain. The open-air staircase leading to the entranceway descends from a manicured garden on a quiet side street. You'll know you're here by the battalion of uniformed doormen who greet arriving taxis. The restaurant's décor is a nautically inspired mass of hardwood panels, brass trim, old-fashioned pulleys and ropes, a tile floor custom-painted into sea-green and blue replicas of the waves, and hand-carved models of fishing boats. In brass replicas of portholes, some dozen bronze statues honoring fishermen and their craft are displayed in illuminated positions of honor.

Full meals, costing 5,000 pesetas ($45) to 7,000 pesetas ($63), are served from 1:30 to 4 p.m. and 9 p.m. to midnight daily except Sunday. Menu choices include a superb version of paprika-laden peppers stuffed with fish, fish soup from Cantabria (a province between the Basque country and Asturias), stewed sea bream with thyme, asparagus mousse, salmon in sherry sauce, and a loin of veal in cassis sauce. Desserts are appropriately sophisticated, among them a mousse of rice with pine-nut sauce. Because of the restaurant's popularity, reservations are recommended.

Horcher, 6 Alfonso XII (tel. 522-07-31). A so-called global gourmet once wrote of this restaurant, "Dishes that enchanted the Kronprinzes of another period, now captivate the cosmopolitan bons vivants of the Jet Age." Herr Horcher created the restaurant in Berlin in 1904, winning the Grand Prix in Paris in 1937. In a sudden move, Horcher went to Madrid in 1943, and has continued in the same grand tradition. Many Germans make the pilgrimage to Madrid just to sample some of the classic dishes.

A jacket and tie are imperative—as is a reservation. Your best chance of getting a seat is to go early. The restaurant is open from noon to 4 p.m. and 8:30 p.m. till midnight (closed Sunday). The service is excellent indeed.

Where to start? You might try the seafood mousse. Wild duck salad also attains distinction. Both the venison stew in green pepper with orange peel and the crayfish with parsley and cucumber are excellent. Other main courses include veal scaloppine in tarragon. For dessert, the house specialty is crêpes Sir Holden, prepared at your table, with fresh raspberries, cream, and nuts, or you may prefer a Sachertorte. Expect to spend from 5,500 pesetas ($49.50).

Valentin, 3 San Alberto (tel. 521-16-38), founded in 1892, has drawn a clientele from such widely varied categories as bullfighters, artists, high society, and movie stars, many of whose pictures can be seen on the walls. The restaurant's two rooms have a welcoming atmosphere, and its staff provides excellent service. Especially popular at lunchtime, Valentin's serves traditional Spanish food, with a special regional dish offered daily. You might have callos a la madrileña or fabada on a weekday, but on Saturday, if you're there for lunch, I recommend the paella. Main dishes also include grilled veal, fresh baked sea bass, and roast milk-fed lamb. A good dessert list and some fine wines add to the pleasure of dining here. Meals begin at 3,000 pesetas ($27). The restaurant is open from 1 to 4 p.m. and 8:30 p.m. to midnight; closed Sunday and in August.

Zalacaín, 4 Álvarez de Baena (tel. 261-48-40), is outstanding both in food and décor. It's reached by an illuminated walk from the Paseo de la Castellana, housed at the garden end of a modern apartment complex. In fact, it's within an easy walk of such deluxe hotels as the Luz Palacio, the Castellana, and the Miguel Angel. It's small, exclusive, and expensive. In an atmosphere of quiet refinement, you can peruse the menu, perhaps at the rust-toned bar. Walls are covered with textiles, and some are decorated with Audubon-type paintings. The menu is interesting and varied, often with nouvelle cuisine touches, along with many Basque and French specialties. It might offer sole in a green sauce, a superb dish, but it also knows the glory of grilled pigs' feet. Among the most recommendable main dishes are steak with a béarnaise sauce, veal escalopes in orange sauce, and guinea fowl. Appetizers are tempting as well—oxtail soup, chef's pâté, and smoked fish crêpes. For dessert, I'd suggest a sorbet or crêpes Zalacaín style. Depending on what you order, many tabs climb as high as 6,800 pesetas ($61.25) to 10,000 pesetas ($90). The management runs the restaurant with a velvet hand. The Zalacaín, open from 1:15 to 4 p.m. and 9 p.m. to midnight, is closed Saturday afternoon, all day Sunday, and in August.

La Gamella, 4 Alfonso XII (tel. 532-45-09), established its gastronomic reputation shortly after it opened several years ago in less imposing quarters in another part of town. In 1988 its Illinois-born owner, former choreographer Dick Stephens, moved into the 19th-century building where the Spanish novelist Ortega y Gasset was born. Horcher's, one of the capital's legendary restaurants, lies just across the street. The design and décor of La Gamella invite customers to relax in russet-colored, high-ceilinged warmth. Mr. Stephens has prepared his delicate and light-textured specialties for the King and Queen of Spain as well as for many of Madrid's most talked-about artists and merchants, many of whom he knows and greets personally between sessions in his kitchens.

Typical menu items include a ceviche of Mediterranean fish, sliced duck liver in a truffle sauce, caesar salad with strips of marinated anchovies, rolled and truffled capon in a strawberry sauce with mushrooms, a ragoût of fish and shellfish with Pernod, and an array of sophisticated desserts, among which is an "all-American cheesecake." Full meals cost from 5,000 pesetas ($45) and are served from 1:30 to 4 p.m. and 9 p.m. to midnight daily except Saturday at lunchtime and all day Sunday. Annual closing is in August. Because of the intimacy and the small dimensions of the restaurant, reservations are important.

El Cenador del Prado, 4 Calle de Prado (tel. 429-15-49). It's difficult to get a sense of how elegant this place is from the simple anteroom. There, an attendant will check your coat and packages in an elaborately carved armoire, and you'll be graciously ushered into one of a trio of rooms. Two of the rooms, done in rich tones of peach and sepia, have thick cove moldings and English furniture, in addition to baroque touches of floor-to-ceiling gilded mirrors. A third room, perhaps the most popular, is ringed with lattices and floods of sunlight from a skylight.

You can enjoy such well-flavored specialties as house-style crêpes with salmon and Iranian caviar and many succulent fish dishes, including steamed hake, a ragoût of sole with shrimp, a platter of grilled fish of the day, salmon marinated with green peppercorns, and delectable salads of such combinations as fresh asparagus, julienne of mushrooms, and shrimp—all served on elegant china. A *menú degustatión,* as well as most à la carte meals, cost from 3,500 pesetas ($31.50) to 5,000 pesetas ($45). Reservations are recommended. Meals are served from 1:15 to 3:45 p.m. and 8:45 to 11:45 p.m. every day except Saturday at lunchtime, all day Sunday, on Catholic holidays, and in August.

OTHER TOP RESTAURANTS

Armstrong's, 5 Jovellanos (tel. 522-42-30), one of my favorite restaurants in Madrid, combines excellent cuisine with a sense of lighthearted charm and big-city style. It is a pink-and-white labyrinth of street-level rooms which, until they were altered in 1986 by savvy English entrepreneur Ken Armstrong, served as a furniture showroom owned by a former cohort of Franco. Amid rich planting, Chinese Chippendale furniture, and the kind of hidden lighting and deep cove molding sometimes shown in *Architectural Digest,* you can enjoy a sophisticated array of international dishes. The clientele that has preceded you here has included the King and Queen of Spain and the Prince and Princess of Wales.

Brunch is offered every Saturday and Sunday, along with the usual assortment of lunchtime dishes. A full brunch, which might feature a dish such as eggs Casanova, costs from 2,500 pesetas ($22.50). Other menu offerings may include an elegant array of salmon and hake dishes, perhaps a luscious version of caviar-topped crêpes concocted from both fresh and smoked salmon, Waldorf salad, grilled breast of duck, beef Wellington, steak-and-kidney pie, a collection of stuffed baked potatoes (some containing caviar), and a full complement of wines, champagnes, and sherries. Other than brunches, full meals cost from 4,000 pesetas ($36) and are served daily from 1 to 4:30 p.m. and 8:30 p.m. to 2 a.m.

El Bodegón, 15 Calle Pinar (tel. 262-88-44), is imbued with the atmosphere of a gentleman's club for hunting enthusiasts—in the country-inn style. Many of its discriminating clientele number it among the top four or five restaurants in Madrid. International globe-trotters are attracted here, especially in the evening, as the restaurant is near three deluxe hotels: the Castellana, the Miguel Angel, and the Luz Palacio. At lunch you're likely to find men only. King Juan Carlos and Queen Sofia have dined here.

Waiters in black and white, with gold braid and buttons, bring dignity to the food service. Even bottled water is served champagne style, chilled in a silver floor stand. There are two main dining rooms—conservative, oak-beamed.

The following à la carte suggestions are recommended to launch your meal: cream of crayfish bisque or a cold, velvety vichyssoise. Main-course selections include grilled filet mignon with classic béarnaise sauce or venison à la bourguignonne. Other main-course selections include shellfish au gratin Escoffier, quails Fernand Point, and salmon smoked by the chef. For dessert, try homemade apple pie. A complete meal here, served daily from 1:30 to 4 p.m. and 9 p.m. daily to midnight, is likely to cost 3,800 pesetas ($34.25) to 5,200 pesetas ($46.75).

El Amparo, 8 Puigcerda, at the corner of Jorge Juan (tel. 431-64-56), behind the cascading vines of its façade, is one of the most elegant gastronomic enclaves of Madrid. It sits beside a quiet alleyway close to a bustling commercial section of the center of the city. Inside, three tiers of roughly hewn wooden beams surround elegantly appointed tables where pink napery and glistening silver add cosmopolitan touches of glamour. A sloping skylight floods the interior with sunlight by day, and at night pinpoints of light from the hi-tech hanging lanterns create intimate shadows. A battalion of uniformed and polite waiters serves well-prepared nouvelle cuisine versions of cold marinated salmon with a tomato sorbet, cold cream of vegetable and shrimp soup, bisque of shellfish with Armagnac, ravioli stuffed with seafood, roast lamb chops with garlic purée, breast of duck, ragoût of sole, a platter of steamed fish of the day, and steamed hake with pepper sauce.

Full meals, which are priced from 5,500 pesetas ($49.50), are served from 1:30 to 3:30 p.m. and 9 to 11:45 p.m. daily except Saturday at lunch, all day Sunday, during the week before Easter, and in August. Reservations are essential.

Los Porches, 1 Paseo Pintor Rosales (tel. 247-70-53), is open all year in a garden setting next to an Egyptian temple, the Templo de Debod, which once stood in the Nile Valley. Because of the Aswan Dam project, it was dismantled and shipped stone by stone as a gift to Madrid, where it was reassembled. The menu at Los Porches is typically and elaborately gourmet, in the tradition of many of Madrid's finest restaurants, including such savory viands as roast quail with grapes, or duck with pears and prunes. The roast baby lamb is also recommendable. The lobster soup is the best; the lemon tart, the perfect finish. Expect to pay 3,500 pesetas ($31.50) to 4,500 pesetas ($40.50) for a complete meal, available from 1 to 4 p.m. and 9 p.m. to midnight daily.

La Bola, 5 Bola (tel. 247-69-30), is just north of the Te Teatro Real. If you'd like to savor the Madrid of the 19th century, then this *taberna* is an inspired choice. It's one of the few restaurants (if not the only one) left in Madrid that's painted with a blood-red façade. Once, nearly all fashionable restaurants were so coated. La Bola hangs on to tradition like a tenacious bull. Time has galloped forward, but not inside this restaurant, where the soft, traditional atmosphere, the gentle and polite waiters, and the Venetian crystal, the Carmen-red draperies, and the aging velvet preserve the 1870 ambience of the place. Ava Gardner, with her entourage of bullfighters, used to patronize this establishment, but that was long ago, before La Bola became so well known to tourists.

A specialty is the sopa Wamba, which is soothing to those who have had too much rich fare, made as it is with ham and rice in a broth over which chopped hard-boiled eggs are sprinkled. The roast chicken (*pollo asado*) is always reliable, as is the sole (*lenguado*) meunière. Depending on your selections, the cost of a complete meal ranges from 2,200 pesetas ($19.75) to 3,500 pesetas ($31.50). The restaurant is open from 1 to 4 p.m. and 9 to 11:45 p.m. daily.

El Mesón de San Jávier, 3 Calle del Conde (tel. 248-09-25), has a long history going back to the 16th century, when it was owned by a secretary to Philip II. Bandits, musicians, and composers of famous zarzuelas met here under the tavern's various ownerships. Clients of yore have included Ava Gardner and Frank Sinatra, but today you are more likely to see Tony Curtis.

The walls are dotted with various food awards, unusual artifacts, hand-painted pottery, and an antique rifle. Specialties include tournedos Tour d'Argent, pepper steak in wine sauce, Madrileña tripe, and roast suckling pig. For an appetizer, try one of the shrimp-stuffed avocados, and, for dessert, one of various tempting concoctions, including raspberry crêpes.

The service is first-rate, and your meal is likely to be accompanied by music from a group of strolling minstrels known as "La Tuna." Expect to pay around 3,500 pesetas ($31.50) if you order the more expensive à la carte items; however, it's possible to dine here for around 2,800 pesetas ($25.25) by sticking to the menu of the day.

The well-concealed restaurant, open from 1:30 to 4 p.m. and 8:30 p.m. to midnight, may be difficult to find, as it's down a flight of steps off the Calle Sacramento, near the Puerta Cerrado.

El Pescador, 75 José Ortega y Gasset (tel. 401-12-90), is a well-patronized fish restaurant which has become a favorite of the Madrileños who appreciate the more than 30 kinds of fish prominently displayed in a glass case. Many of these are unknown in North America, and some originate off the coast of Galicia. Management air-freights them in, and prefers to serve them grilled (*à la plancha*).

You might precede your main course with a spicy fish soup, and accompany it with one of the many good wines served from northeastern Spain. If you're not sure of what to order (even the English translations might sound unfamiliar), try one of the many varieties and sizes of shrimp. These go under the name of *langostinos, cigalas, santiaguinos,* and *carabineros.* Many of them are expensive and priced by the gram, so be careful when you order. Expect to spend around 3,500 pesetas ($31.50) per person. Closed Sunday and early August to mid-September, but open otherwise from 1 to 4 p.m. and 8 p.m. to midnight.

The **Lhardy,** 8 Carrera de San Jerónimo (tel. 521-33-85), opened its doors in 1839. I'm told the food served today isn't as good as back then, but there's really no one around to verify that claim. This is a place with a great tradition as a gathering place of Madrid's literati, its political leaders, and the better-heeled members of the city's business community. Your consommé is likely to be presented in cups from a large silver samovar, if you drink it in the ground-floor tea room. This adjoins a deli shop, where you can buy some of the delicacies you tasted at the bar or in the restaurant upstairs. There, the décor, known as "Isabella Segundo," gives off a definite aura of another era. Specialties of the house include an excellent roast beef and a *cocido,* the celebrated stew of Madrid. This might be served with a selection from the extensive wine cellar. Meals range from around 3,500 pesetas ($31.50). It is open from 1 to 3 p.m. and 9 to 11 p.m. daily except Sunday (closed from the last week in July until around mid-September).

El Espejo, 31 Paseo de Recoletos (tel. 410-25-25), offers good-tasting food and one of the most perfectly crafted art nouveau décors in Madrid. If the weather is good, you can choose one of the establishment's outdoor tables, served by a battery of uniformed waiters who carry food across the busy street to a green area flanked with trees and strolling pedestrians. I personally prefer a table inside, within view of the tile maidens with vines and flowers entwined in their hair, who stare calmly out at the Belle Époque lighting fixtures, sculptured plaster, brass railings, and bentwood chairs of the sophisticated décor. You'll pass through a charming café/bar, where many visitors linger before walking down a hallway toward the spacious and alluring dining room. Dishes include vichyssoise, codfish omelet, shellfish terrine, grilled sole, escargots bourguignons, and crêpes Suzette. Full à la carte meals begin at 2,600 pesetas ($23.50) and are served every day of the week from 1 to 4 p.m. and 9:30 p.m. to midnight.

BASQUE SPECIALTIES
(MODERATE)

Alkalde, 10 Jorge Juan (tel. 276-33-59), has been known for decades for serving top-quality Spanish food in an old tavern setting. It's decorated like a Basque inn, with beamed ceilings and hams hanging from the rafters. The gambas à la plancha (grilled shrimp) is excellent, but you may prefer the cigalas (crayfish). Another fish dish is mero salsa verde (that is, brill in a green sauce). Two other well-recommended main dishes include trout Alkalde and chicken steak Alkalde. The dessert specialty is a copa Cardinal. For around 3,500 pesetas ($31.50) and up, you can enjoy a very satisfying meal.

Upstairs is a large, *típico* tavern. Downstairs is a maze of caves, pleasantly cool in the summer, although the whole place is air-conditioned anyway. The service is efficient. Open from 1 to 4 p.m. and 9 p.m. to midnight, it's closed Saturday night and all day Sunday.

Gure-Etxea (Restaurant Vasco), 12 Plaza de la Paja (tel. 265-61-49), is housed in a stone-walled building that was the convent for the nearby Church of San Andrés before the Renaissance. Today, amid a décor enhanced by Romanesque arches, vaulted tunnels, and dark-grained paneling, you can enjoy selections from a small but choice menu. Specialties include vichyssoise, rape (a whitefish) in green sauce, and various other dishes, sometimes served with sautéed green beans along with regional cheeses. Full meals, which cost 2,500 pesetas ($22.50) to 4,000 pesetas ($36), are served from 1:30 to 4 p.m. and 9 p.m. to midnight every day of the week except Sunday and in August.

BEST FOR SEAFOOD

O'Pazo, 20 Reina Mercedes (tel. 253-23-33), is a deluxe Galician restaurant, considered by the local cognoscenti as one of the top seafood places in the country. The fish is flown in daily from Galicia. It is decorated in a tasteful style for the distinguished clientele it caters to. In front is a cocktail lounge and bar, all in polished brass, with low sofas and paintings—in all, the feel of a private seignorial living room. The restaurant has carpeted floors, cushioned Castilian furniture, soft lighting, and colored-glass windows.

Most diners begin with assorted smoked fish or fresh oysters. The house specialty is hake Galician style, but you may prefer the sea bass, baked in the oven, and served with a mustard sauce. O'Pazo sole is also recommended. Your tab for a full meal is likely to be about 4,500 pesetas ($40.50). Open from 1 to 4:30 p.m. and 8:30 p.m. to midnight, it is closed Sunday and in August.

Bajamar, 78 Gran Vía (tel. 248-59-03), is one of the best fish houses in Spain, and it's right in the heart of the city, near the Plaza de España. Both fish and shellfish are shipped in fresh daily by air from their points of origin, the prices depending on what the market charges. Lobster, king crab, prawns, soft-shell crabs and the like are all priced according to weight. There is a large array of reasonably priced dishes as well. The setting is contemporary and attractive, the service is smooth and professional, and meals are served from noon to 4 p.m. and 8 p.m. to midnight daily. The menu is in English. For an appetizer, I'd recommend half a dozen giant oysters or half a dozen rover crayfish. The special seafood soup is a most satisfying selection, a meal in itself. Try also the lobster bisque. Some of the more recommendable main courses include turbot Gallego style, the special seafood paella, even baby squid cooked in its ink. Desserts are simple, including the chef's custard. Seafood dinners begin at 5,000 pesetas ($45).

FOR VALENCIAN PAELLA (MODERATE)

La Barraca, 29-31 Reina (tel. 232-71-54). Like a country inn —right off the Gran Vía—this Valencian-style restaurant is a four-fork establishment recommendable for its tasty provincial cooking. There are eight dining rooms, all on different levels, and they're colorfully cluttered with ceramics, paintings, photographs, Spanish lanterns, flowers, and local artifacts. The house specialty is paella a la valenciana, made with fresh shellfish. The portions are enormous— only the most ravenous will clean out the skillet. Other recommendable main dishes include roast suckling pig and the roast leg of lamb. The sorbet makes a good finish. A complete meal, served from 12:30 to 4 p.m. and 8:30 p.m. to midnight, daily, will cost about 3,000 pesetas ($27).

DINING IN OLD MADRID (BUDGET TO MODERATE)

Right on or near a corner of the historic and immense square, the **Plaza Mayor,** are clustered fine typical restaurants and taverns, as well as *tascas,* all of which quickly capture the spirit of Madrid's past. No matter which restaurant you favor with your patronage you're likely to be entertained by the strolling bands of *tuna,* students dressed in Castilian capes with ribbons fluttering, guitars by their sides and tambourines for after-the-songfest collections.

The **Mesón del Corregidor,** 8 Plaza Mayor (tel. 266-50-56), shares the best vantage point on the Habsburg plaza. Tables are set out in fair weather, providing an unobstructed view of the entire square. Flowers are placed on the tables, the lighting is soft—an ideal background for an operetta scene. In winter, you enter first a *típico tasca,* with hanging smoked hams, wrought-iron chandeliers, vintage wine bottles, and ceramics. It's a well-tended slice of the past, with stone and cobbled floors, stained glass, and a fireplace. The specialty of the house is a shellfish paella for two people. The chef also prepares a succulent, spicy roast suckling pig. Other typical dishes include baby eels, hake wrapped in ham, and tripe Madrid style. For 3,600 pesetas ($32.50) you can enjoy a complete à la carte dinner. A set menu goes for 1,800 pesetas ($16.25). Hours are 1 to 4 p.m. and 8 p.m. to midnight daily.

Right down the steps is the even better-known **Las Cuevas de Luís Candelas,** 1 Cuchilleros (tel. 266-54-28). It is entered through a doorway under an arcade on the steps leading to Calle de Cuchilleros, the nighttime street of Madrid, teeming with restaurants, flamenco clubs, and rustic taverns. The restaurant is named after the legendary Luís Candelas, a bandit of the 18th-century—sometimes known as "the Spanish Robin Hood." He is said to have hidden out in this maze of *cuevas*. Although the menu is in English (the restaurant is very "touristy"), the cuisine is authentically Spanish. Specialties include the chef's own style hake. To being your meal, another house dish—for garlic lovers only—is sopa de ajo Candelas, a garlic soup. Roast suckling pig and roast lamb, as in the other restaurants on the Plaza Mayor, are the featured specialties. This one can be expensive, with meals, served from 1 to 4 p.m. and 7 p.m. to 1 a.m. daily, averaging from 3,000 pesetas ($27) to 4,500 pesetas ($40.50).

THE FOREIGN COLONY

Once upon a time a foreign restaurant was hard to find in Madrid. It seemed the Spanish were perfectly content with their own cuisine. However, in recent decades a noticeable change has occurred. For change-of-pace dining, today's restaurant shopper will find a fair selection of German, Italian, Chinese, French, Mexican, even Argentine and Japanese establishments. You'll even find American food.

Edelweiss, 7 Jovellanos (tel. 521-03-26), is a German standby that has provided good-quality food and service at moderate prices since the war. You are served hearty portions of food, mugs of draft beer, and fluffy pastries. That's why there's always a wait at lunch (1 to 4 p.m.) and dinner (7 p.m. to midnight). Tip: To beat the crowds, go for dinner at un-Spanish hours, say around 8 or 9 p.m. when tables are not at a premium. But even when it's jammed, service is almost always courteous. You can start with Bismarck herring, then dive into goulash with spätzle, or eisbein (pigs' knuckles) with sauerkraut and mashed potatoes, the most popular dish at the restaurant. Finish with the homemade apple tart. A complete meal is likely to cost 2,200 pesetas ($19.75) to 3,500 pesetas ($31.50). The décor

HEMINGWAY'S ROAST SUCKLING PIG: "I would rather dine on suckling pig at Botín's than sit and think of casualties my friends have suffered," Ernest Hemingway told his mythical "Old Lady" in *Death in the Afternoon*. For countless thousands of Americans, Papa made **Sobrino de Botín**, 17 Calle de Cuchilleros (tel. 266-42-17), famous. In the final two pages of his novel *The Sun Also Rises*, he had Jake invite Brett there for the Segovian specialty, washed down with Rioja Alta.

By merely entering its portals, you step back to 1725, the year the restaurant was founded. You'll see an open kitchen, with a charcoal hearth, hanging copper pots, an 18th-century tile oven for roasting the suckling pig, and a big pot of regional soup, the aroma wafting across the tables. The dining tables sit under time-aged beams, the wall literally covered with a mishmash collection of photographs, engravings, paintings, and bullfight memorabilia. Your host, Don António, never loses his cool—even when he has 18 guests standing in line waiting for tables.

The *menú de la casa* is priced in autumn and winter at 3,000 pesetas ($27). The two house specialties are roast suckling pig and roast Segovian lamb. From the à la carte menu, costing from 4,000 pesetas ($36), you might try the "quarter-of-an-hour" soup, made with fish. Good main dishes include the baked Cantabrian hake and filet mignon with potatoes. The dessert list features strawberries (in season) with whipped cream. You can wash down your meal with Valdepeñas or Aragón wine, although most guests order sangría. Hours are 1 to 4 p.m. and 8 p.m. to midnight daily.

is vaguely German, with travel posters and wood-paneled walls. It's air-conditioned in summer, but closes in August and always on Sunday.

A popular hangout for locals and visiting Yanks is **Hollywood,** 1 Calle Magallanes (tel. 448-91-65). It's a California-style hamburger extravaganza, a fashionable place to eat and be seen, serving, according to many travelers, "the best American food in Europe." It is owned and operated by an American couple from Detroit. Outside, you can sit in a director's chair on the terrace, with the name of a movie star on the back. You will find this one of the most comfortable and best people-watching sites in Madrid, while you enjoy sangría or your back-home favorite beverage. Inside, it's nostalgia time, with bentwood chairs and many framed photographs and posters. Some Spaniards have encountered problems in eating the hamburgers, as indeed would anyone not familiar with devouring

THE BEST STEAKS IN MADRID: Madrileños defiantly name **Casa Paco,** 11 Puerto Cerrada, just beside the Plaza Mayor (tel. 266-31-66), when someone has the "nerve" to put down Spanish steaks. They know that here you can get the thickest, juiciest, most flavorsome steaks in Spain—and at half the price you'd pay in Chicago. Señor Paco was the first Madrid restaurateur to seal steaks in boiling oil before serving them on plates so hot that the almost-raw meat continues to cook, preserving the natural juices. In business for more than 50 years, Paco is more or less retired now, though his son and daughter carry on his traditions.

Casa Paco isn't just a steakhouse. You can start with a fish soup and proceed to such dishes as grilled sole, baby lamb, Casa Paco cocido, or callos a la madrileña. You might top it off with one of the luscious desserts, but you can't have coffee here. Paco won't serve it, not necessarily for health reasons but because customers used to be inclined to linger over their cups, keeping tables occupied while people had to be turned away for lack of space.

In the Old Town, the two-story restaurant offers three dining rooms, and reservations are imperative. Otherwise, you face a long wait, which you can while away sampling the *tapas* (hors d'oeuvres) in the *tasca* in front. Around the walls are autographed photographs of such notables as Frank Sinatra. A typical meal will run about 3,800 pesetas ($34.25) and up. The tourist menu is 1,950 pesetas ($17.50), but the reason most people come here is to order one of the deliciously thick steaks, priced according to weight, and served sizzling hot on a wooden board. Food is served from 11:30 a.m. to 4 p.m. and 8:30 p.m. to midnight daily.

food five inches high. Hamburgers weigh in at one-half pound, and they vary from simple and unadorned to one with cheese, bacon strips, and Russian dressing. They are served with french fries and salad. Other Stateside treats are chili con carne, homemade apple pie, cheesecake, and, as once reported in the *New York Times,* "probably the best onion rings in the world." Tabs begin at 600 pesetas ($5.50). Hours are 1 p.m. to 1:45 a.m. daily.

The same food is also available at Hollywood's other locations at 3 Apolonia Morales (tel. 457-79-11) in the Castellana area near the Eurobuilding, 16 Avenida de Brasil (tel. 455-16-88) for the Melia Castilla hotels, at 80 Velázquez (tel. 435-61-28) in the Serrano shopping area, at 1 Tamayo y Baus (tel. 231-51-15) close to Plaza de Cibeles and the Prado, and at 16 Calle del Cristo in Majadahonda (tel. 638-67-94), one of Madrid's best suburbs.

Casablanca, 29 Calle del Barquillo (tel. 231-12-47), named after the famous movie whose principal role was rejected by Ronald Reagan, is a multilevel restaurant within walking distance of the Gran Vía and the Prado. The walls of the restaurant are decorated with cinematic blowups of Bogart and Bergman emoting with one another in scenes from the cult film. An international cuisine served at the umbrella-covered tables is a combination of northern Spanish, continental, and Japanese. The personable owner is Dick Angstadt, an American. The restaurant is open every day from 1:30 to 4 p.m. and 9 p.m. to 12:30 a.m. (till 1 a.m. on weekends), charging around 2,800 pesetas ($25.25) and up for an average meal. Casablanca has a *tapas* bar also.

The **Hostería Piamontesa,** 18 Costanilla de Los Angeles (tel. 248-34-14), is my recommendation for those seeking good, rib-sticking Italian cooking. Although there is a menu of the day for 1,850 pesetas ($16.75), you'd be better advised to order à la carte, paying about 2,500 pesetas ($22.50) for a meal. For an appetizer, try the stracciatella or perhaps a shrimp cocktail. Main-course specialties include lasagne and saltimbocca alla romana. The pasta is homemade. With main platters, the waitresses bring an accompaniment of five vegetables. For dessert, I'd suggest the zuppa inglese. The restaurant, open from 1 to 4 p.m. and 9 p.m. to midnight, is closed in August, Sunday night, and all day Monday.

The **Kuopin Restaurante Chino,** 6 Valverde (tel. 232-34-65), is an interesting Chinese restaurant, only 100 long strides from the busy Gran Vía. It's approached through a long hallway in an old Madrid building. Inside you'll find the usual Chinese décor with large lanterns. Many of your fellow diners will be Chinese, a fairly good gauge of authenticity and value. The chef offers a special budget dinner for 495 pesetas ($4.50) including, for example, egg-drop soup, sweet-and-sour pork, and ice cream with walnuts. Bread and a beverage are included. À la carte temptations are sweet corn, egg, and chicken soup, Cantonese shrimp, and roast pork Cantonese style. You can expect to pay about 1,200 pesetas ($10.75) for a complete à la carte dinner. Kuopin is open from noon to 4 p.m. and 8 p.m. to midnight daily.

The **Chez Lou Crêperie,** 6 Pedro Muguruza (tel. 250-34-16), near the Eurobuilding Hotel in the northern sector of Madrid, stands near the huge mural by Joan Miró, which alone would be worth the trek up here. In this intimate setting, you get well-prepared and reasonably priced French food. The restaurant serves pâté as an appetizer, then a large range of crêpes with many different fillings. Folded envelope style, the crêpes are not tea-room size, and they're perfectly adequate as a main course. I've sampled several variations on the crêpe theme, finding the ingredients nicely blended yet distinct enough to retain their identity. A favorite is the large crêpe stuffed with minced onions, cream, and smoked salmon. The ham and cheese is also tasty. Crêpes cost from 450 pesetas ($4) up, and the price of your dessert and drink is extra.

Come here if you're seeking a light supper when it's too hot for one of those table-groaning Spanish meals. Chez Lou is open from 8 p.m. to midnight and it also serves lunch from 1 to 4 p.m. except on Saturday. It closes up completely on Monday.

VEGETARIAN FARE

La Galette, 11 Conde de Aranda (tel. 276-06-41). Madrid doesn't have the number of vegetarian restaurants that Barcelona does, but the Spanish capital nevertheless has a few good ones. La Galette was one of the first, and it remains one of the best. Small and charming, it lies in a residential and shopping area in the Salamanca district, near the Plaza de la Independencia. Its hours are 2 to 4 p.m. for lunch and 9 p.m. to midnight for dinner; closed Saturday and Monday. For meat eaters, the kitchen prepares a number of dishes. However, vegetarians can enjoy such dishes as baked stuffed peppers, omelets, eggplant croquettes, and even a vegetarian "hamburger." Some of the dishes are macrobiotic. The place is noted for its mouthwatering pastries. A *menú de la casa* costs 1,535 pesetas ($13.75).

CHAPTER XII

THE ATTRACTIONS OF MADRID

□ □ □

Tourist officials in Madrid often confide, "We spend so much fuss to get people to visit Madrid. But when we get them here, and they've seen the Prado, and a bullfight, we send them off to El Escorial or Toledo."

Too true—and regrettably so, as Madrid is filled with many nuggets for the digger willing to pan for them.

As European capitals go, Madrid is hard to know. Her mainstream attractions—tree-shaded parks, wide *paseos*, bubbling fountains, the art treasures of the Prado—are obvious. And, of course, it is this Madrid that the routine visitor sees quickly before striking out on his next adventure, usually to one of the satellites such as Segovia.

But for the more determined traveler, willing to invest the time and stamina, the Spanish capital tucks away many hidden treasures behind her fan, discreetly revealing them to the courtier of her choice.

This grande dame of Spain is well worth the pursuit.

I don't believe in saving the best for last, so I'll lead off with:

THE TWO TOP ATTRACTIONS

SPAIN'S GREATEST MUSEUM—THE PRADO: A. E. Hotchner wrote of "Papa Hemingway": "Ernest loved the Prado. He entered it as he entered cathedrals." More than any other, one picture held him transfixed, "the girl whom he had loved longer than any other woman in his life," Hotchner relates—Andrea del Sarto's *Portrait of a Woman*.

The late American author wasn't alone in his passionate devotion to the Prado. Numerous citizens of Madrid go once or twice a month every month of their lives just to gaze upon their particular favorites (the reproductions at home are never adequate).

But first-time visitors, with less than a lifetime to spend, will have to limit their viewing. That task is difficult, as the Prado owns more than 7,000 paintings and is ranked among the top three art museums of the world.

In an 18th-century neoclassic palace designed by Juan de Villanueva, the Prado has been considerably improved in the past few years, especially in its lighting. There will be work in progress for some time to come.

The most hurried trekker may want to focus his attention on the output of three major artists: the court painters Velázquez and Goya, plus El Greco, who was in fact a Greek (born in Crete in 1541 or 1542).

But don't overlook the exceptional visions of Hieronymus Bosch, the 15th-century Flemish artist who peopled his canvases with fiends and ghouls and conjured up tortures that far surpassed Dante's Inferno. In particular, seek out his triptychs, *The Hay Wagon* and *The Garden of Earthly Delights*.

Most of the products of these artists are on the second floor. However, on the ground floor you'll find Goya's "black paintings" and his remarkable drawings.

The Prado's single most famous work is *Las Meninas*—the maids in waiting—the masterpiece of Velázquez.

In the Goya room is displayed his *Naked Maja*, certainly one of the most recognizable paintings in the West—said to have been posed for by the woman the artist loved, the Duchess of Alba. As a court painter to Charles IV and his adulterous queen, María Luisa, Goya portrayed all their vulgarity of person and mind—and got them to pay for the results.

Other paintings, by Raphael, Botticelli, Correggio, Titian, (Titzano), Pieter Brueghel, Murillo, Ribera, and Fra Angelico, will make the morning fade quickly into dusk.

The painting stirring up the most excitement in recent years is Picasso's *Guernica*. Long banned in Spain, the painting rested for years in the Museum of Modern Art in New York before it was returned to Spain. The Prado houses it in one of its satellites. Picasso's work reflected his sadness at Generalissimo Franco's bombing of Guernica, a little Basque town. Picasso requested that *Guernica* not be returned to Spain until the death of Franco and the "reestablishment of public liberties."

Expansion has increased the museum's space for display of treasures, including acquisition of the spacious Villahermosa Palace in 1985, a 17th-century building diagonally across the Plaza Cánovas del Castillo from the main Prado premises.

The Villahermosa Palace will be the home for at least the next ten years of what is considered to be the most important privately owned art collection in the world, that of Dutch-born Baron Hans Heinrich Thyssen-Bornemisza, which was formerly housed in the baron's residence/museum in Lugano, Switzerland. The collection includes works by El Greco, Velázquez, Goya, Frans Hals, Hans Memling, Rubens, Rembrandt, Sebastiano del Pompo, Watteau, Canaletto, and John of Flanders, as well as the only privately owned Dürer painting, *Christ Among the Doctors*. Picasso's *Harlequin with Mirror* is among that artist's important works in the collection, and there are also pictures by impressionist and post-impressionist painters, among them Degas, Renoir, Sisley, Van Gogh, Gauguin, Chagall, Monet, Cézanne, Toulouse-Lautrec, and Gris. Modern art is represented by such expressionists as Vlaminck, Pechstein, Heckel, Kirchner, Feininger, Nolde, and Kandinsky. The baron's recent acquisitions are concerned with American artists.

The museum, on the Paseo del Prado (tel. 239-80-23), is open from 9 a.m. to 7 p.m. all year. On Sunday and holidays, except Christmas and New Year's, it is open from 9 a.m. to 2 p.m. The entrance fee is 400 pesetas ($3.50). Metro stations Banco and Atocha. Buses going to the museum are numbered 10, 14, 27, 34, 37, and 45. Closed Monday.

The second major attraction in the capital is:

THE BULLFIGHT, A SPECTACLE OF DEATH: In art, literature, and life, the Spaniard is urgently concerned with the subject of death. The ritual killing of the bull, as reenacted in countless seasons of *corridas* from early spring till late October, sustains the Spanish soul. Perhaps it is in the back of the mind of some aficionados that the bull may not be the only one killed, that the matador may meet his "death in the afternoon."

Despite the fanfare and the fiesta mood enveloping the Plaza de Toros, bullfighting is a deadly serious business. Like a major industry, it supports a goodly number of the Spanish population—from the promoters, the *apoderados* biting down on their Havana cigars, to the poor soul who cleans up the horse dung and sells it as fertilizer.

In the way Americans growing up in the '40s and '50s dreamed of becoming movie stars, the Spanish boy often fantasizes about the acclaim, the shouts, and the cheers ringing in his ears in the bullring. For many a peasant boy born in poverty, bullfighting is his way to break out of the role life cast him in. A case in point is former matador El Cordobés, a poor boy who rose to become a symbol of wealth and glamour throughout Spain.

An aficionado, Ernest Hemingway wrote: "The bullfight is not a sport in the Anglo-Saxon sense of the word, that is, it is not an equal contest or an attempt at an equal contest between a bull and a man. Rather, it is a tragedy; the death of the bull, which is played, more or less well, by the bull and the man involved and in which there is danger for the man but certain death for the bull."

Fortified by that definition, you may be ready to attend your first bullfight.

The day of the corrida is Sunday afternoon, although Madrid may also hold fights on Thursday. It's becoming an increasing practice to stage an 11 p.m. Saturday *novillada,* in which amateur or inexperienced bullfighters test their skill against often "defective" bulls.

The spectacle of the bullfights opens with a parade—an exciting, dramatic experience, as the bullfighters stroll in their "suits of lights." This is followed by a matador's preliminary capework, often a *verónica,* in which he faces the bull for the first time. This act appears almost to be choreographed, and has been compared to a ballet.

The fight begins as *picadores* on horseback charge the bull to "pic" him with lances. The *banderilleros* are next, jabbing the beast with brightly ornamented *banderillas,* preparing the animal for the kill. A fight is considered much more enthralling if the bullfighter himself sticks in the darts.

After this ceremony, the matador faces the bull armed with a sword and a *muleta,* a scarlet cloth. The challenging of the bull— most hazardous—is a *natural.* After a series of such passes, the matador is ready for the kill, the so-called moment of truth.

Hopefully, he will kill the bull in one quick thrust, although many a leading matador has been forced to make repeated thrusts like a *novillero.* The more thrusts, the more hostile grows the reaction of the crowd toward the bullfighter. If he shows skill, the "lucky" matador will be rewarded with an ear (*òreja*) of the bull. The amateurish performer is likely to get a rotten tomato thrown in his face.

Madrid attracts the most skilled matadors in Spain to its 26,000-seat **Plaza de Toros,** 237 Calle de Alcalá (tel. 232-67-99). The height of the corrida season is the week of festivities on May 10, honoring San Isidore, patron of the city.

Major hotels sell bullfighting **tickets,** and you can also go to the "official" agency at **3 Victoria,** reached by heading east from the Puerta del Sol, then walking two blocks down the Carrera de San

Jerónimo, turning south onto Victoria. In a district of *tascas* and cheap restaurants—especially popular with aspiring matadors and their promoters, or would-be promoters—the agency saves you about 20% of the price of the ticket. But make absolutely sure it's the "official" agency, and not one of the other offices lining the street.

You can save an additional 25%, approximately, if you request *sombra y sol* (shade and sun) seats—meaning that for part of the fight you'll be in the sun. Prices vary from fight to fight. The tariffs to follow are only a general guideline—and may not apply to the actual fight you attend.

Front-row seats are called *barreras*. *Delanteras* or third-row seats are available in both the *alta* (high) and the *baja* (low) sections. You can also request quite passable *filas,* which are adequate seats (but not special). The cheapest seats, not really recommended, are of the *sol* variety, in which you're exposed to the hot sun during the entire fight.

When a top-flight matador is performing, tickets disappear quickly—only to be resold at scalper's prices. Tickets cannot be obtained weeks in advance. As for ticket prices, they vary. Count on spending at least 250 pesetas ($2.25) for a just-passable seat, all the way up to 7,000 pesetas ($63) or more for the more desirable seats in the shade.

If you're attending a fight on Sunday, it's best to go to 3 Victoria from 10 a.m. to 1 p.m. or 5 to 9 p.m. on the Saturday before the corrida. The office is also open on Sunday from 10 a.m. to 5 p.m.

You can take the Metro tube to Ventas to reach the Plaza de Toros. To avoid a stampede, try to arrive at the ring early, and while you're at it, visit the Bullfight Museum (see below). After the fight, it's virtually impossible to get a taxi back into the city. Why not wait, having a coffee at a nearby sidewalk table?

FIVE TOP SIGHTS

After wandering through the Prado and watching the blood and gore of the Plaza de Toros, you may be in a mood for more relaxed browsing through Madrid. What follows is a subjective listing of five additional attractions.

In order of importance, I'd rate them as follows: (1) the Royal Palace, (2) the Royal Factory of Tapestries, (3) the Lázaro Galdiano Museum, (4) the Convent of Las Descalzas Reales, and (5) the Goya Pantheon.

THE ROYAL PALACE: Alfonso XIII, grandfather of King Juan Carlos, and his queen, Victoria Eugénie, were the last to use the

Palacio Real as a royal abode, in 1931, before they fled into exile. Franco used the Royal Palace (also known as the Palacio de Oriente) for state functions and elaborate banquets for foreign dignitaries. But guides like to point out that he never sat on the king's chair in the Throne Room.

King Juan Carlos and Queen Sofia are more modest in their requirements. They have turned the Royal Palace over to history, choosing not to live there but in their much smaller suburban palace, the Zarzuela, named after the Spanish operetta or musical comedy.

On the landmark site of the former Alcázar of Madrid (destroyed by fire on the Christmas of 1734), the Royal Palace was launched in 1737. Its first tenant was Charles III, the "enlightened despot" of the House of Bourbon. In all, the number of rooms—many added at a later date—total around 1,800. Not all are open to the public, of course. Nor need they be, as it would then take a week to tour the entire enclave.

Visitors are conducted on a guided tour of the **State Apartments,** the Tapestry Room, the Reception Salons, the Royal Armory, the Royal Pharmacy, and the Royal Library. If you're rushed —and want just a quick glimpse of the grandeur of the palace— then you'll want to confine your sightseeing to the state apartments and the reception rooms. Metro stop: Opéra.

After your tour, you can skip across the courtyard to the **Royal Armory,** considered one of the most impressive in Europe. Recalling the days of jousting and equestrian warfare, many of the exhibits date from the reign of Charles V (Charles I of Spain) of the Habsburg Empire. Roughly, the collection spans about 200 years of the Spanish Empire.

Afterward, you can visit the **Royal Library,** with its leather-bound volumes—at least 190,000 different editions, many belonging to Spain's most famous kings and queens, such as Isabella I. Although seemingly ignored, the **Royal Pharmacy** merits a visit. It was, in its heyday, the "cure-all" source for any ailment that plagued the royal family.

If you wish to visit the Gallery of Tapestries (*tapices*), the State Apartments, Reception Salons, Armory, and Library, you'll pay a total admission fee of 500 pesetas ($4.50). If you don't want to see everything, you can visit only what you wish. For example, a single ticket to the Armory costs 100 pesetas (90¢).

The Palacio Real (tel. 248-53-50), on the Plaza de Oriente, is only a short walk from the Plaza de España. Hours in summer are 9:30 a.m. to 12:45 p.m. and 4 to 5:45 p.m. (on Sunday from 9:30 a.m. to 12:30 p.m.). In winter, hours are 9:30 a.m. to 12:45 p.m. and 3:30 to 5:15 p.m. (on Sunday from 9:30 a.m. to 12:30 p.m.).

Worth a detour, the **Carriage Museum** on the grounds charges an entrance fee of 100 pesetas (90¢). It's not as impressive as its more famous counterpart in Lisbon, but you can view the *carruajes* that Spanish royalty and aristocrats used in the days when a person was judged solely on appearance.

After your whirlwind tour, you can wind down by strolling through the **Campo del Moro,** the gardens of the palace.

LÁZARO GALDIANO MUSEUM: Deserving of far more visitors than it receives, this remarkable, compact, and art-stuffed museum at 122 Serrano (tel. 261-60-84) spans the centuries of artistic development with seeming ease.

An elevator takes you to the top floor of what was once one of the great mansions of Madrid; then you weave your way from room to room (37 in all), descending the stairs as you go.

The collection begins with vestments, some dating from the 15th century. Along the way, you can stop and stare at an assemblage of weapons, daggers, and swords, some with elaborate handles dating from the 15th century. Seals, such as one belonging to Napoleon, are displayed; and there is a rare exhibition of Spanish fans, one possessed by Isabella II.

In Room XX are two Flemish paintings by the incomparable Bosch—rats crawling through the eyes of humans, and so on. In the following room (XXI) is a portrait of Saskia signed by Rembrandt, dating from 1634. In other salons, several of the major artists of Spain are represented: Velázquez, Zurbarán, El Greco, Valdés Leal, Murillo, and Ribera. Room XXV is the salon of English-speaking portraitists: Gainsborough, Sir Joshua Reynolds, Gilbert Stuart, and Constable. Many well-known works by Goya are in his salon (XXX), including some of the "black paintings" and portraits of Charles IV and his voluble spouse.

Other intriguing showcases are filled with 16th-century Limoges crystal, French and Italian ivory carving from the 14th and 15th centuries, and a 15th-century Maltese cross. In Room VI hangs a small portrait of the Savior as an adolescent, encased in green velvet. Although the museum attributes this painting to Leonardo da Vinci, some art historians dispute this claim.

The museum is open daily except Monday from 10 a.m. to 2 p.m. The admission fee is 150 pesetas ($1.35). It is closed in August and on Monday. Metro stop: Rubén Dario.

THE PANTHEON OF GOYA: Emulating Tiepolo, Goya fres-

coed the **Church of San António de la Florida** in 1798. Although he depicted in part the miracles of St. Anthony of Padua, his work was nearly secular in its execution. Mirrors are placed to allow you to capture the beauty of the ceiling better. The figure of a woman draped in a cape is one of the most celebrated subjects in Goya's work.

Beyond the North Station, the hermitage is at Glorieta de San António de la Florida (tel. 247-07-22). Goya died in exile in Bordeaux, France, in 1828, but his bones were later removed from there and interred here in the memorial that he unknowingly created for himself.

Some church officials once considered Goya's frescoes irreverent—hence, the hermitage not a fit place of worship. A twin of the 18th-century church was erected alongside it, and services are conducted there now. Facing both of them, go into the one on the right to pay your respects to Goya.

THE ROYAL FACTORY OF TAPESTRIES: The making of tapestries—based on original designs by Goya, Francisco Bayeu (Goya's brother-in-law), and others—is still a flourishing art in Madrid. You can actually visit the factory where the *tapices* are turned out, and chat with the workers. Some of the hand-looms on which they work date back to the days of Goya.

The great Spanish artist sketched numerous cartoons that were converted into tapestries to adorn the walls of the Royal Palace not only in Madrid, but in Aranjuez and La Granja. One of the most famous, reproduced hundreds of times, is *El Cacharrero* (The Pottery Salesman).

Some craftspeople have copied the same design all of their lives, so that now they can work on it casually—perhaps with a cigarette dangling out of the corner of their mouth. Others, less cavalier, prefer to watch the design carefully through a mirror.

The factory—called **Real Fábrica de Tapices**—is at 2 Fuenterrabia (tel. 251-34-00). It may be visited daily except Saturday and Sunday, from 9:30 a.m. to 12:30 p.m. Admission is 50 pesetas (45¢) per person. Closed August 1 to September 1. Metro stop: Atocha or Pelayo.

The pantheon is open from 10 a.m. to 2 p.m. and 4 to 8 p.m. Tuesday to Friday, from 10 a.m. to 2 p.m. on Saturday and Sunday; closed Monday. Entrance is free.

CONVENT OF LAS DESCALZAS REALES: What would you do if you were a starving nun surrounded by a vast treasure house of paintings, gold, jewelry, and tapestries? Sell them? Not possible. The order of the Franciscan Clarissas threw themselves upon the mercy of the government, which in turn opened the doors of the convent to the general public as a museum (with the pope's permission, of course). It's still an operational convent of approximately 30 sisters.

The collection includes tapestries based on Rubens's "cartoons," 16th- and 17th-century vestments, a silver forearm said to contain bones of St. Sebastian, and a statue of the Virgin wearing earrings, as is the custom in Andalusia. The most interesting chapel is dedicated to Our Lady of Guadalupe (the statue of the Virgin is made of lead).

One of the best paintings here is a *Virgin and Child* by Bernardino Luini of northern Italy; but the most valuable oil is Titian's *Caesar's Money,* worth millions of pesetas. The Flemish Hall contains other superb canvases—for example, one of a processional by Hans Baker.

The Convent of Las Descalzas Reales is open from 10:30 a.m. to 12:30 p.m. and 4 to 5:15 p.m. Tuesday through Saturday from 11 a.m. to 1:15 p.m. on Sunday in summer; closed Monday. In winter, hours are 10:30 a.m. to 12:30 p.m. and 4 to 5:15 p.m. on Tuesday, Wednesday, Thursday, and Saturday. Admission is 300 pesetas ($2.75). From the Plaza de Callao, a satellite square of the Gran Vía, walk down a narrow street, Postigo de San Martín to the Plaza de las Descalzas Reales, one of the most charming squares in Madrid, and you'll find the convent (tel. 522-06-87) on your left. You must wait for a guided tour. Metro stop: Plaza del Sol.

OTHER SIGHTS

For the visitor who'd like to know Madrid more intimately, I've compiled the following list of museums, a park, and even a flea market.

FINE ARTS MUSEUM: Right on Madrid's busy boulevard, an easy stroll from the Puerta del Sol, the **Museo de la Real Academia de Bellas Artes de San Fernando,** 13 Calle de Alcalá (tel. 232-15-46), is considered second only to the Prado in importance as a leading Spanish museum. It houses more than 1,500 paintings and 800 sculptures by such masters as Goya, Murillo, and El Greco, plus drawings by Rubens, Ribera, and Velázquez. The collection ranges from the 16th century to the present, and was started in 1744 when the academy was founded during the reign of King Phil-

ip V. The emphasis is on works of Spanish, Flemish, and Italian artists, and you can see masterpieces by the artists mentioned above,
plus Zurbarán, Sorolla, Cano, and Coello. The museum is in the restored and remodeled palace of Juan de Goyeneche, a banker who
had it constructed in 1710 in the baroque style, later redone in the
neoclassical style. It's open from 9 a.m. to 7 p.m. Tuesday to Saturday, to 2 p.m. on Sunday and Monday. Admission is 200 pesetas
($1.80). Metro: Sol or Sevilla.

THE MUSEUM OF BULLFIGHTING: At the Plaza de Toros de
las Ventas, in the Patio de Caballos, this **Museo Taurino** (tel. 255-
18-57) ideally should be visited before you see your first Spanish
bullfight, as it serves as a good introduction to "the tragedy" in the
arena. The complete history of the *torero* is traced in pictures, historic bullfight posters, and scale models.

Works of art include a Goya painting of a matador, plus an exquisite bust, sculpted in bronze, of Manolete. The museum may
be visited from 9 a.m. to 3 p.m. Tuesday to Friday and on Sunday for
an admission fee of 175 pesetas ($1.60). You can take the subway to
the Ventas stop.

THE HOUSE OF LOPE DE VEGA: Ironically, the Casa de Lope
de Vega (tel. 429-92-16) stands on a street named after Cervantes
(no. 11), his competitor for the title of the greatest writer of the
Golden Age of Spain and a bitter enemy. The house is considered a
perfecta reconstruction of the casa in which Lope de Vega lived, and
it is furnished with pieces indigenous to his time (1562–1635). The
Spanish writer, the major dramatist of Habsburg Spain, wrote more
than 1,000 plays, many of which have been lost to history.

You'll be shown through the house, with its volumes upon volumes of manuscript reproductions, and then allowed to roam at
random in the garden in back. The museum and memorial to Lope
de Vega is open from 11 a.m. to 2 p.m. on Tuesday and Thursday,
and the price of admission is 125 pesetas ($1.15). From mid-July to
mid-September, the house is closed to the public. Metro: Antón
Martín.

MUNICIPAL MUSEUM: After years of restoration, the **Museo
Municipal,** 78 Fuencarral (tel. 522-57-32), is open with collections
on local history, archeology, art, porcelain, plans, engravings, and
photographs, all depicting the history of Madrid. In a churrigueresque baroque structure, the museum displays deal especially with
the Bourbon Madrid of the 18th century, whose paseos with strolling couples are shown on huge tapestry cartoons. Paintings from
the royal collections are here, plus period models of the best-known
city squares and a Goya that was painted for the Town Hall. The mu-

seum is open from 10 a.m. to 2 p.m. and 5 to 9 p.m. Tuesday through Saturday and from 10 a.m. to 2:30 p.m. Sunday; closed Monday. Admission is free. Metro: Tribunal.

THE WAX MUSEUM: A museum like London's Madame Tussaud's or the Musée Grevin in Paris, the **Museo de Figuras de Cera** (Waxworks Museum), 41 Recoletos (tel. 419-26-49), charges 500 pesetas ($4.50) for adults, 300 pesetas ($2.75) for children. There are scenes depicting events in Spanish history, such as Columbus calling on Ferdinand and Isabella. Twentieth-century international figures aren't neglected either. Thus we see Jacqueline Onassis having champagne at a supper club and Garbo all alone. The heroes and villains of World War II—everybody from Eisenhower to Hitler—are enlivened by the presence of the "Blue Angel," Marlene Dietrich, singing "Lili Marlene." Out-of-work filmmakers created the 400 figures in 38 tableaux, succeeding best with backdrops, falling shortest in the depiction of contemporary celebrities. Two new galleries contain historical figures of Romans and Arabs from the ancient days of the Iberian peninsula, and a new show in multivision gives a 30-minute recap of Spanish history from the time of the Phoenicians to today. Admission to the small theater to see this show is 100 pesetas (90¢). The museum is open from 10:30 a.m. to 2 p.m. and 4 to 9 p.m. daily. Metro: Colón.

THE CHURCH OF SAN FRANCISCO EL GRANDE: In lieu of a great cathedral, Madrid possesses this church (tel. 265-38-00), with a dome larger than that of St. Paul's in London. Constructed on the site of a much earlier church, San Francisco dates from the latter 18th century, owing much of its appearance to Sabatini, a celebrated architect of his day.

Its interior of Doric columns and Corinthian capitals is cold and foreboding, although 19th-century artists labored hard to adorn its series of chapels flanking the nave. The best painting—that of St. Bernardinus of Siena preaching—is by Goya.

You are conducted through the church by a guide, who notes the most outstanding artwork, especially the choir stalls dating from the 16th century. The church dominates its own square, the Plaza de San Francisco El Grande (1 San Buenaventura), and it may be visited from 11 a.m. to 1 p.m. and 4 to 7 p.m. daily, except Sunday and Monday. Admission is 50 pesetas (45¢). In summer, the afternoon hours are 5 to 8 p.m. Metro: La Latina. You can also take bus 3 from the Plaza de España, which goes right to the church.

THE RETIRO: This was formerly a much larger royal park through which the Habsburg Philips romped. But after 1868 it was largely reforested and turned over to the people of Madrid. Sprawling across more than 350 acres, it opens onto the eastern side of the Calle de Alfonso II. Near the center is a lake, **Estanque,** with a poorly designed monument to King Alfonso XII. All is tranquil in summer. You can rent rowboats, slowly traversing the waters.

Across the Calle de Alfonso XII in the southwestern part are the **Botanical Gardens.** The fountains of the Retiro, one honoring an artichoke, are handsomely sculpted and displayed. It is pleasant to stroll from one to another.

THE RASTRO (FLEA MARKET): This hillside market will warm the heart of anyone attracted to a mishmash of fascinating junk interspersed with bric-a-brac and paintings (don't expect to find a Goya). It's open every day of the week, but most popular late Sunday morning (go before 2 p.m.) when seemingly half of the Madrileños and many people from the nearby countryside jostle each other through the narrow streets, searching for bargains, real and imagined. Roughly, the flea market occupies a triangular district of streets a few minutes' walk south of the Plaza Mayor. The main center of the permanent antique shops—open daily—is on the **Plaza Cascarro** and the **Ribera de Curtidores.**

Much of the merchandise is displayed in open stalls, although many vendors simply spread their wares on patches of canvas on the street. The incongruity of merchandise and nonmerchandise offered may astonish and amuse: bits of ecclasiastical wooden statuary, such as armless madonnas and saints with missing halos, rusty keys large enough to fit that "castle in Spain," World War II motorcycle parts, brass scales, ornate antique watches, Victorian bureaus, umbrella stands, and second- (or third-) hand clothing. You name it! The nearest Metro station is La Latina, less than two blocks away. You can also take bus 3 or 17.

A WALKING TOUR

New Madrid is strictly for cars, buses, and trains, as it sprawls for miles in all directions. But in the center of Madrid cars get in the way. Old Madrid is strictly for walking, the only way to savor its unique charm.

The tour begins on the **Gran Vía,** a street whose position as *the* boulevard of Madrid is being fast overtaken by the Paseo de la Castellana. Still the busiest street in Madrid, the shop-flanked Gran Vía was opened at the end of World War I. Until recently it was called Avenida de José António. Long before deluxe hotels started to sprout up on the Castellana, the hotels of the Gran Vía were the most expensive and elegant in the Spanish capital. The street ends at the **Plaza de España,** a vast square overshadowed by one of the tallest skyscrapers in Europe.

From the square, you can walk up Calle de la Princesa, turning to your left down the Ventura Rodríguez. At 17 Ventura Rodríguez is the **Cerralbo Museum** (tel. 247-36-46), which gives you a rare glimpse into the life of one of the most prestigious Spanish families. The museum is open daily except Monday from 10 a.m. to 2 p.m. and 4 to 6 p.m., charging an admission of 200 pesetas ($1.80). Closed Sunday afternoon and in August. Metro stop: Plaza de España or Ventura Rodríguez.

Returning to the Plaza de España, head down Calle de Bailen until you reach the semicircular **Plaza de Oriente,** created in 1840. From that vantage point, you can explore the **Palacio Nacional** (Royal Palace), described above.

After your tour, if you take a tiny side street to the northeast, Calle Pavia, you'll arrive at the **Plaza de la Encarnación,** one of the most charming squares in Madrid. Sitting on this plaza is the **Convent de la Encarnación** (tel. 247-05-10), finished in 1616 in the reign of Philip III and his queen, Margaret (sister of Emperor Ferdinand II). This convent and adjoining church can be visited from 10:30 a.m. to 1:45 p.m. and 4 to 5:30 p.m. on Tuesday, Wednesday, Thursday, and Saturday. Admission is 250 pesetas ($2.25). Metro: Opera. From the square, walk down Calle de Arrieta to the Plaza de Isabel II. There you can connect with Calle del Arenal, leading to the **Puerta del Sol,** the "gateway to the sun," the historic heart of Madrid.

ORGANIZED TOURS

A large number of agencies in Madrid offer organized tours and excursions. Among them is **Viajes Marsans,** with offices at 15 San Nicolás (tel. 542-55-00). The most popular full-day excursion is to the imperial city of Toledo, the complete jaunt costing 4,800 pesetas ($43.25). Other heavily booked full-day treks encompass El Escorial and the Valley of the Fallen for 4,100 pesetas ($37); or Ávila, Segovia, and the summer palace of the Bourbons at La Granja, for 7,450 pesetas ($67). Full-day tours include lunch at a restaurant along the way. Half-day tours of Madrid include an artistic tour costing 2,950 pesetas ($26.50) which covers entrance to museums, and a panoramic tour for 1,950 pesetas ($17.50). On the nighttime circuit, a flamenco tour with dinner goes for 7,800 pesetas ($70.25).

CHAPTER XIII

SHOPPING IN MADRID

□ □ □

Practically everything is available in Madrid, which 17th-century playwright Tirso de Molina called "a shop stocked with every kind of merchandise." Thousands of tourists pass through the Spanish capital yearly; and, frankly, many shops are designed chiefly for what the proprietors think the well-heeled foreigner will like.

On the other hand, Madrid is chiefly an industrial and commercial capital, in which the majority of the stores and shops exist primarily for the patronage of Spaniards. As the average income of a Spanish family is far below that of an American, Canadian, English, or Scandinavian, managers or shopkeepers must keep prices in line with what they think the local traffic will bear. Consequently, the city offers some of the most moderately priced merchandise of any European capital.

HANDCRAFTS: Entrepreneur of Spanish decorative handcrafts Edward Kreisler from Akron, Ohio, owns and operates **Kreisler, 19** Serrano (tel. 276-53-38). Through his grapevine, he keeps in touch with artisans in obscure villages and towns, presenting their wares in his jam-packed galleries in the Serrano shopping district. Encased within are most of the Spanish items that the North American markets want, including olive-wood articles, "El Greco chairs," mantillas, Toledo damascene work, woodcarvings, Spanish fans, purses in grained leather, and a line of Spanish soaps and dolls. Kreisler is also an official agency for Majorcan pearls and Lladró porcelain. Prices are competitive because Kreisler doesn't add on any percentage for commissions to guides. Purchases can be packed and shipped anywhere in the world.

At the **Galería Kreisler,** in a separate section, some of the fine painters and sculptors in the country have found an important showcase for their talents. Here you'll find both the old master and the avant-garde artist. The Art Gallery features Spain's most reputable artists, whose works generally are in the permanent collection of the National Museum of Contemporary Art.

SPANISH ART: Another Kreisler enterprise (see above), **Kreisler Galería de Arte,** 8 Hermosilla (tel. 276-16-62), presents contemporary paintings, sculpture, and prints. It is open from 10 a.m. to 2 p.m. and 5 to 9 p.m. It's about 75 yards around the corner from 19 Serrano.

WOMEN'S CLOTHING: One of the most popular retail outlets for women's clothing is **Herrero,** 49 and 60 Gran Vía (tel. 521-29-90), on the main street of Madrid. Other stores are found at 7 Preciados (tel. 521-27-22), 23 Preciados (tel. 521-29-90), and 76 Serrano (tel. 421-85-80). They feature an especially good line of suede and leather dresses and coats—custom-made, if you desire.

Modas Gonzalo, 43 Gran Vía (tel. 247-12-39), is a boutique with a baroque and gilded atmosphere reminding you of the 1940s. However, its fashion designs for women are strictly up-to-date. A few might even suggest tomorrow.

PERFUMES: One of the best selections is found at **Perfumería Padilla,** 7 Carmen (tel. 522-68-33). It has many imported scents for women and also a good choice of costume jewelry.

Urquiola, 1 Mayor (tel. 521-59-05), has one of the most complete stocks in Madrid, with both national and imported brands. It also has a wide, tasteful selection of gifts and costume jewelry.

BOUTIQUE CLOTHING: On the best street for elegant shopping in Madrid, **Don Carlos,** 92 Serrano (tel. 275-75-07), is a boutique featuring an excellent selection of clothing for both women and men.

FANS AND UMBRELLAS: The best and most complete of Spanish fans and umbrellas in Madrid is found at **Casa de Diego,** 12 Puerta del Sol (tel. 522-66-43). It stands in the very heart of Madrid.

MADRID'S LEADING DEPARTMENT STORES: Right off the Gran Vía, **Galerías Preciados,** 28 Preciados (tel. 232-64-10), is really two stores connected by an underground passageway. But it's more Macy's than Lord & Taylor, with quite presentable ready-made clothing for men, women, and children. There's a top-floor snackbar and restaurant. Some good buys I recently noted include guitars, men's suede jackets, Spanish capes for men, and women's full-length suede coats in such exciting colors as royal blue, kelly green, olive, and violet.

For men's suits, in the second-floor tailoring department, you can have a suit made to order. You're fitted with one of the basic "try-on" suits. The goodly selection of fabrics—plaids, solids, herringbones—are made into whatever style you prefer.

The other big department store chain is **El Corte Inglés,** with outlets all around the country, including Málaga. At present, branches are on Calle Preciados (tel. 232-81-00), near the Puerta del Sol in the center of the city; on Calle Goya, where it crosses Calle de Alcalá (tel. 448-01-11); on Calle Raímundo Fernández Villaverde (tel. 456-50-20), next to the Paseo de la Castellana; and on Calle Princesa (tel. 242-48-00). Rather than running about from boutique to tourist shop to boutique, many visitors will find it easier and often cheaper to make all their purchases in a department store. For example, at El Corte Inglés you can buy all types of souvenirs, such as swords from Toledo, typical flamenco dolls, the well-known Spanish shawls, and Lladró sculptures. The store has a multitude of special services available for tourists—interpreters, currency exchange, and parcel delivery to their hotels or overseas—and it arranges for all the necessary formalities regarding the VAT refund, which can be up to 33% of the marked price according to law.

CUSTOM TAILORING: A tried and tested establishment, **Valdivia,** 86 Gran Vía (tel. 247-96-40), is in the Edificio España (the Plaza Hotel building) at the Plaza de España. It turns out skillfully tailored suits for men. Mariano Valdivia has won the respect and patronage of many a Spanish businessman or diplomat, inheriting his skill and business from his father. His staff can produce a suit in four or five working days, if you're available for fittings. Their shop offers an excellent choice of fabrics in all weather weights. Everything is made by hand, even the buttonholes. They can give you a conservative banker's look or outfit you in more stylish clothing. Señor Valdivia has expanded his shop to include women's clothing, blouses, and overcoats, many haute-couture garments shipped in from Paris. The prices are quite reasonable for this ready-to-wear.

HEADGEAR: Founded in 1894, **Casa Yustas,** 30 Plaza Mayor (tel. 266-50-84), is an extraordinary hat emporium, especially popular in this day of strange headgear. If your sessions with the analyst have revealed a hang-up for unusual hats, you can satisfy your inclinations here. Picture yourself as a Congo explorer, a Spanish sailor, an officer in the kaiser's army, a Rough Rider, a priest, even Napoleon. A straw sombrero is a conversation piece. Black berets are also sold here. One reader, a devotee of things Spanish, asserts that the beret, or *boiña*, is used extensively in Spain. "France has stolen many ideas from Spain," the reader, a former travel agent, claims.

ELEGANT LEATHER GOODS: For fine leather articles, **Loewe,** 8 Gran Vía (tel. 251-68-00), since 1846 has been the most elegant store in Spain. Its gold-medal-winning designers have always kept abreast of changing tastes and styles. For the latest in luggage, handbags, jackets for both men and women (in leather or suede), along with stylish accessories, come here or to one of their branches, such as that at 26 Serrano (tel. 435-06-45). If you miss the Madrid store, you'll find outlets in such major tourist towns as Barcelona, Palma Majorca, San Sebastián, Seville, and Valencia, as well as at the Hotel Alhambra Palace in Granada.

MAJORCAN TEXTILES: You're welcomed at **Casa Bonet,** 76 Calle Nuñez de Balboa (tel. 275-09-12), by the friendly staff. The store's specialty is the hand-worked textiles of Majorca, where women are famous for the quality of their needlework. A few examples are displayed on the walls, but a true concept of the establishment's inventory comes only when tablecloths, sheets, and pillowcases are unrolled on Spanish tables covered with velvet. You'll find a full range of cottons, linens, and polyesters here, embellished with either hand-embroidery or fancy machine stitching. English is spoken, and prices are usually competitive.

BOOKSTORES: There are many all over the city, selling both English- and Spanish-language editions, along with touring maps. **Aguilar** has three outlets: 24 Serrano (tel. 435-36-42), 18 Goya (tel. 275-06-40), and 154 Paseo Castellana (tel. 250-36-39).

   Casa del Libro, 9 Gran Vía (tel. 521-66-57), is considered the best bookshop in Madrid. One of the most visited shops on the Gran Vía, it contains five floors with various sections devoted to such special interests as travel, for instance.

MUSICAL INSTRUMENTS: With a wide selection of records and music scores, **Real Musical,** 1 Carlos III (tel. 241-30-09), is a music lover's dream house. All kinds of instruments are sold here, including pianos, Spanish guitars, and violins.

FOR CHILDREN: One of the largest selections of dolls and other toys to be found in the capital is at **Sánchez Ruíz,** 47 Gran Vía (tel. 241-53-13). The store also sells fancy dress for children.

A HOUSE OF CERAMICS: Called "the first house of Spanish

ceramics," the **Antiqua Casa Talavera,** 2 Isabel la Católica (tel. 247-34-17), has wares that include a sampling of regional ceramic styles from every major area of Spain, including Talavera, Toledo, Manises, Valencia, Puente del Arzobispa, Alcora, Granada, and Sevilla, among other sources. Sangría pitchers, dinnerware, tea sets, plates, vases—everything is handmade. Inside one of the showrooms there's an interesting selection of tiles, ranging from reproductions of scenes from *El Quijote,* bullfights, dances, and folklore, to scenes from famous paintings at the Prado. At its present location for more than 60 years, the shop is only a short walk from the Plaza de Santo Domingo and the subway station there.

ROPE SOLES: Selling shoes and other items made from rope, **Casa Hernanz,** 18 Calle de Toledo (tel. 266-54-50), has been in business more than 150 years. Madrileños pack the store to buy rope-soled espadrilles, stylish and well made, shoes in other styles, and hats. The staff is cordial, but they don't speak English.

CHAPTER XIV

MADRID
AFTER DARK

□ □ □

The Madrileños are called *gatos* (cats) because of their excessive fondness for prowling around at night. If you're going to see a show, the later you go, the better. Unaware of this, two American tourists once arrived at a restaurant at 10 p.m. for dinner, hoping to hear a young French singer. After their last brandy, they sat through a long, dreary revue, followed by routine dancing to orchestra music, then another drawn-out revue. Finally, the management announced the appearance of the headliner. The hour was 1:30 a.m., and this was his first show of the evening.

In spite of the late hours, the people of Madrid begin their evening as early as 8 p.m. by *tasca*-hopping (see below). For the younger crowd, many discos open around 6 p.m., remaining open till 9 p.m., when they usually shut down for dinner. Later, at about 11 p.m., they reopen and stay that way until early in the morning.

TASCA HOPPING

As mentioned earlier, dinner is fashionably served in Madrid at 10:30 p.m. But this late hour requires no iron will on the part of the Madrileño. From 8 p.m. on, you'll find him or her in the *tascas* (taverns), drinking a *chato* (small glass of vino) and eating *tapas,* literally "covers." Tapas are Spanish hors d'oeuvres, usually displayed on the counter of the bar. Most often they are crunchy fried fish, cold tortillas (omelets), squid, *gambas* (shrimp), olives, sausages, salads, mushrooms, even the tail of a bull. Each of the major tascas is noted for one or two specialties, which you'll usually find prominently displayed or advertised. Most of these taverns have waiter service at the tables, although the least expensive way to visit them is to order your tapas and drinks at the bar. Some of my favorite taverns—scattered about in interesting and colorful parts of Madrid—are the following:

António Sánchez, 13 Mesón de Parades (tel. 239-78-26), was named in 1850 after the founder's son who was killed in a bullfight ring. Memories of the bullfighter abound here, chief of which is the stuffed head of the animal that gored young Sánchez. Also featured on the darkly paneled walls are three valued works by Spanish artist Zuloaga, who had his last public exhibition in this restaurant shortly before he died. A limited array of tapas, including garlic soup, is served with the Valdepeñas wine that a barman will draw from a barrel. However, many guests ignore the edibles in favor of smoking endless cigarettes and arguing the merits of this or that bullfighter. A restaurant in the back serves Spanish food with a vaguely French influence. Tapas generally cost 70 pesetas (65¢) to 300 pesetas ($2.75). Hours are noon to 4 p.m. and 8 p.m. to midnight Monday through Saturday, from noon to 4 p.m. on Sunday. The establishment lies in a warren of narrow streets near the Plaza Tirso de Molina.

The **Taberna Toscana** (Tuscan Tavern), 22 Ventura de la Vega (tel. 429-60-31), doesn't look like much on the outside. But inside its theme is that of a country inn, with terrazzo floors, regional stools and tables, plus hand-hewn beams from which hang hams, sheaves of wheat, and garlic pigtails. Nearly two dozen tapas are set out at the bar. Tasty and recommended are kidneys in sherry sauce and snails in hot sauce. Tapas average 400 pesetas ($3.50) each. A jug of wine costs 250 pesetas ($2.25). The place is open from noon to 4 p.m. and 8 p.m. to midnight daily.

The **Café Bar Los Galayos,** 1 Plaza Mayor (tel. 265-62-22), with rows of outdoor tables, occupies one of the prime locations on the Plaza Mayor, right at one of the inside corners. If you prefer to drink inside, away from the streams of sunlight, there's a popular stand-up bar of elaborately molded hardwoods. You'll recognize the place by its forest-green façade which, even under the weathered arcades of 16th-century Spain, looks somewhat like a Victorian storefront in England. A beer costs 125 pesetas ($1.15) at the stand-up bar and a few pesetas more at one of the tables. Other than a selection of tapas, no food is served here. The place is open from 8 a.m. to 2 a.m.

THE BARS

Some visitors can't quite get into the hustle-bustle of the *típica tasca,* preferring the more sedate elegance of a bar. What follows is a random sampling of some of the most interesting bars—each one attracting a widely diverse clientele, many quite fashionable. The Palace, the Pickwick, and the Oliver are all suitable for two women traveling together . . . but if a woman drops in at Chicote alone, or on the arm of a girlfriend, only one assumption will be made.

The **Palace Bar,** 7 Plaza de las Cortes (tel. 429-57-51), basks in its tradition as *the* place in the capital for upper-crust Madrileños and international travelers from around the globe. In his Hemingway biography, A. E. Hotchner called it "the nerve center of Madrid social intrigue, where every woman looks like a successful spy." In the final chapter of *The Sun Also Rises,* Jake told Brett: "It's funny what a wonderful gentility you get in the bar of a big hotel." The panels of grained marble, the soft lounge chairs, the alert and polite waiters, are appropriate for the turn-of-the-century glamour of the Palace. Many a governmental policy has been made here; and many a female film star has preened her feathers in front of an admiring audience. The atmosphere is deliberately relaxed and cordial. A brand-name scotch costs 650 pesetas ($4). Open daily from 11 a.m. to 2 a.m.

A FAMOUS OLD COFFEEHOUSE: All old European capitals have a coffeehouse that traditionally has attracted the literati. In Madrid, the counterpart of Les Deux Magots in Paris or the Antico Caffè in Rome is the **Gran Café de Gijón,** 21 Paseo de Recoletos (tel. 231-91-21), which opened in 1890 in the heyday of Madrid's *bella época.* Artists and writers (some look like Spanish versions of Tennessee Williams) patronize this venerated old café on one of Madrid's major boulevards. Many of them spend hours over one cup of coffee. The coffeehouse has open street windows looking out onto the wide paseo as well as a large terrace for sun worshippers and birdwatchers. Along one side of the café is a stand-up bar, and on the lower level is a restaurant. In summer, you can sit in the garden, enjoying, say, a blanco y negro (that's black coffee with ice cream). Mixed drinks cost from 400 pesetas ($3.50), and meals start at 2,000 pesetas ($18). Hours are noon to midnight daily.

The **Nuevo Oliver,** 3 Calle del Conde Xiquena (tel. 521-01-47), only a minute from Calvo Sotelo, attracts a youthful, sophisticated crowd to its drawing-room atmosphere, like that of a private club. The street-floor room evokes a stage setting by one of London's gifted designers, what with its paneled scenic setting on the ceiling, the formal fireplace, and recessed alcoves containing shelves of art and theater books and record album covers. On the walls are old paintings and engravings, the color theme Mediterranean: faded red, sienna, bronze, and gold. You sit on upholstered chairs and sofas. Reached by a winding stairway, the lower level is more intimate, decorated with shades of Toledo red and sienna and furnished with sofas arranged for intimate get-togethers. Often someone plays the piano softly in the background. You pay 450 pesetas ($4) for an average drink. Tapas (hors d'oeuvres) are available. The bar is open from 8 p.m. till 3 a.m.

Balneario, 37 Juan Ramón Jiménez (tel. 458-24-20), serves gratifyingly potent drinks to a sophisticated clientele within an enclave of fresh flowers, white marble, and the kind of stone bathtub (filled with plants) that might have been used by Josephine Bonaparte. Near the Chamartín Station in one of the capital's sought-after northern edges, it's one of the most stylish and upmarket bars in Madrid. Many guests precede a meal at the previously recommended Cabo Mayor restaurant with a drink here. The two establishments share a portion of the well-tended garden a few steps away. Tapas such as endive with smoked salmon, asparagus mousse, and anchovies with avocados cost 350 pesetas ($3.15) to 1,300 pesetas ($11.75). Drinks go for 600 pesetas ($5.50) and are served daily except Sunday from 2:30 p.m. to 3 a.m.

Chicote, 12 Gran Vía (tel. 532-67-37). Whatever happened to Chicote, another favorite—some say *the* favorite—bar of "Don Ernesto"? Created by the now-legendary Señor Chicote, it once attracted thousands of English-speaking readers, fans of Hemingway. The writer used it as a setting for his only play, *The Fifth Column.* Hemingway would sit here night after night entertaining his friends with such remarks as "Spain is a country for living and not for dying." The bar still attracts writers, musicians, and artists. Drinks cost from 350 pesetas ($3.75). Open daily from 12:30 p.m. to 3 a.m.

Mr. Pickwick's, 48 Paseo Pintor Rosales (tel. 248-51-85), is a re-creation of the world of Dickens: timbered ceilings, highbacked settles, framed prints of the author's most famous characters, hunting horns, tiny nooks with a china collection, pewter mugs, an English fireplace, even a brass horse collection. It's a pleasant place at which to have a mug of beer—either at the tiny bar or at one of the small tables. Most drinks, accompanied by olives and peanuts, are 400 pesetas ($3.50). The pub is open from 6 p.m. till 1:30 a.m. It's in a corner building where its *paseo* meets the Calle del Marqués de Urquijo.

The **Sportsman British Pub,** 65 Alcalá (tel. 276-69-08). There are literally thousands of pubs in Madrid, as a quick review of the "bar" section of the telephone book will reveal. Many of them are recently established and pander to the modern taste of Madrileños. One of the most attractive is near the central post office in a beautifully paneled English-style club, ringed with banquettes and dotted with velvet. At the section near the entrance is a long bar area with comfortable, padded elbow rests. The walls are covered with photographs of celebrities, especially Rita Hayworth and Ava Gardner.

Beer costs 300 pesetas ($2.75). The pub is open from 10 a.m. to 4 a.m. Monday to Friday and from noon to 4 a.m. on Saturday and Sunday. The restaurant, the Paddock, is in back, with a bulletin board which seems to indicate that this is a gathering place for British expatriates in Madrid.

FLAMENCO CLUBS

By now, Americans are somewhat familiar with flamenco. Carmen Amaya toured the U.S.A. during most of World War II; Carmelita Maracci made her unique comment; through endless TV appearances, José Greco popularized the art form even more. The only catch is, Mr. Greco isn't from Spain. As one dance critic put it, he was "born in Italy, raised in Brooklyn, and is a great Spanish dancer."

Flamenco personifies the blood and guts of Andalusia, where it originated. Nowadays the gypsies have virtually taken over the art form, making flamenco part of their own folklore. Their basic fire and flair do add another dimension.

The performers sit in a half circle around the stage, with the lead or head dancer on the end. At the left and right rear, the male singers and dancers await their turn. To the accompaniment of guitars, castanets, and rhythmic clapping, each performer does a solo, occasionally uniting with another partner—strutting, tapping, clapping, and stamping their feet with inner tension and pride. The songs are chanted in a passionate, tense tone, almost Arabic in origin. Age doesn't keep an artist off the center stage. Flamenco singers (*cantores*) seem to perform forever, until the lid on their coffin is lifted for a farewell olé.

Before you leave Madrid, you may want to attend at least one show at one of the many *tablaos* throughout the city. Usually, you pay no cover charge, but the price is stiff for your first drink. The tabs are lowered for subsequent libations. My specific recommendations follow.

The **Café de Chinitas,** 7 Torija (tel. 248-51-35), is one of the swankiest and most expensive flamenco spots in town. In the old part of Madrid, between the Opera and the Gran Vía, it features dancer La Chunga, as well as guitarist Serranito. They join with 37 others to make up the *cuadro*. The show starts at 11 p.m., running until 3:30 a.m. The minimum, which entitles you to a drink at a table is 3,000 pesetas ($27). You can also go for dinner at about 9:30 p.m., and then stay on for the flamenco. Meals cost from 7,500 pesetas ($67.50). The café is open daily except Sunday all year. You sit in an elongated room at tables with fair visibility. The stage is at the far end of the room. The décor is amorphously elegant, sometimes in questionable taste, and doesn't quite live up to the promise of the street exterior. You enter through a staircase lined with old bullfighting engravings, posters, and pictures, which takes you to two glass doors with bronze hands on them for handles.

The **Corral de lo Morería,** 17 Morería (tel. 265-84-46). In the Old Town, the Morería—meaning a quarter where Moors reside—sizzles more in its flamenco than in its skillet. The place is open from 9 p.m. to 3 a.m. daily. Strolling performers, colorfully costumed, get the proceedings under way around 11 p.m., but they are there only to warm up the audience. A flamenco showcase follows, with at least ten dancers—the women have Gloria Vanderbilt waistlines. The star always appears late. The management has devised ways of putting tables in the most unlikely places; reserve near the front and go early if you really want a ringside table. The show and an à la carte dinner is 5,000 pesetas ($45) to 6,000 pesetas ($54). The cost of the show and one drink is 2,240 pesetas ($20.25).

Zambra, in the Hotel Wellington, 8 Velázquez (tel. 435-51-64), is a subterranean supper club in the hotel premises. Some of the best flamenco singers and dancers of Spain appear here every night in front of enthusiastic audiences. The doors open at 9:30 p.m. for dinner daily except Sunday, although the show doesn't begin until 10:30 p.m., continuing until closing at 3 a.m. With dinner included the price is 5,000 pesetas ($45). Without dinner, a view of the show costs 3,000 pesetas ($27). Reservations are a good idea. If no one answers at the number given above, call the reception desk at the Hotel Wellington (tel. 275-44-00) for information.

If you're still on the flamenco trail, then you might try the **Arco de Cuchilleros,** 7 Cuchilleros (tel. 266-58-67), near the Botín Restaurant. Lots of single men and women come here. A flamenco show with a girlie twist is often presented. All in all, it's fun to be here if you don't take the proceedings too seriously. The one-drink minimum will cost you 2,000 pesetas ($18). Shows are presented at 10:30 p.m. and 12:30 a.m.

SPECTACLES

Madrid's nightlife is no longer steeped in conservatism, as it was in the Franco era. You can now see glossy cabarets and shows with lots of nudity.

Scala Melia Castilla, 43 Calle Capitan Haya (entrance at 7 Rosario Pino; tel. 450-44-00), serves meals, but few of the patrons show up for the food. The allure is the girls, the glitter, and the gloss of the in-house ballet, a gaggle of musicians, and a graceful duo of ice skaters whose gyrations almost make an audience wish for real snow. The first show begins around 10 p.m.; the second starts at midnight Sunday to Thursday and at 1 a.m. on Friday and Saturday.

The first show and dinner costs 4,384 pesetas ($57.50). The second show, with one drink, costs 3,024 pesetas ($27.25) Sunday to Thursday, 3,248 pesetas ($29.25) on Friday and Saturday. If your Spanish is fluent, you may appreciate the observations of the stand-up comedian, but if is isn't, you'll probably find the flesh and finery enough. Reservations are needed.

CULTURAL ATTRACTIONS

For an authentic Spanish experience, you can attend a *zarzuela,* a Spanish musical variety show with turn-of-the-century music enlivened by bright costumes. Often these vaudevillian presentations sandwich flamenco numbers and musical revues between their regular acts.

One of the best places to view this musical theater is the **Monumental Theater,** 60 Calle de Atocha (tel. 227-12-14). Even non-Spanish-speaking visitors seem to enjoy performances here, with dancing, ballet, and musicals scheduled daily except Monday, at 7 and 10:30 p.m. Tickets cost 500 pesetas ($4.50) to 1,200 pesetas ($10.75).

The **Teatro Nuevo Apolo,** 1 Tirso de Molina (tel. 227-38-16), is devoted to zarzuela, serving as the permanent home of the renowned Antologia de la Zarzuela company. It is on the restored site of the old Teatro Apolo, where zarzuelas were performed more than 50 years ago. The new theater company is directed by José Tamayo.

Ballet, Spanish style, is presented at the **Centro Cultural de la Villa,** Plaza de Colón (tel. 275-60-80).

PARQUE DE ATRACCIONES

The "Park of Attractions" is a combination of Coney Island and Copenhagen's Tivoli Gardens. Madrileños speak of it as "Disneylandia." Created almost overnight in 1969 to amuse the young at heart, it lies in the former royal hunting grounds of the Casa de Campo. The park is open all year from 3 to 9:30 p.m. Monday to Friday, from noon to 10 p.m. on Saturday, and from 11 a.m. to 10 p.m. on Sunday. Admission is 120 pesetas ($1) for adults, 30 pesetas (25¢) for children up to 9 years old. Tickets for rides cost 45 pesetas (40¢), and a ride may take one, two, three, or four tickets. However, you can purchase a pass for 900 pesetas ($8) which entitles you to go on all the rides for one day.

At the core of the park is an illuminated tower; you can take the elevator up to its observation platform. The tower is surrounded by a large reflection pool. From the tower, water drops into a *cascadas* of pools and falls, all brilliantly lit at night.

Numerous attractions interest young and old: a toboggan slide, a carousel, pony rides, an adventure into "outer space," a walk through a maze of glass, a super-dash in a racing car, a jaunt in an antique automobile, a visit to "jungleland," a sound-and-light spectacle, a leisurely trip in a motorboat on a circuitous canal, a motor-propelled series of cars disguised as a tail-wagging dachshund puppy, and a gyrating whirl clutched in the tentacles of an octopus, "El Pulpo." The most popular rides are the roller coasters, "7 Picos" and "Jet Star."

You may also want to attend a performance at the open-air Greek-style *teatro,* where a one-hour show is presented nightly at 8 from May till the end of September, weather permitting. No admission is charged. The theater is a well-designed structure, with cast-cement seats facing a bowl-like shell and stage. The apron has a reflecting pool and fountains for a colored water display. The popular entertainment is strictly potluck—everything from Spanish ballet to a flamenco singer.

How to get to the park: A cable car leaves for the park from the intersection of the Paseo del Pintor Rosales and the Calle Marqués de Urquijo. At the terminus of the *teleférico,* a line of micro-buses awaits to complete the journey to the entrance to the park. An alternative approach is via a suburban train from the Plaza de España, which stops near an entrance to the park (the Entrada del Batán). Of course, the easiest way to get there is by taxi.

THE DISCOS

Some discos are spectacular, complete with the latest gimmicks and live combos. Others are little cellar dives where the owner plays records to special but fickle claques who desert him the next day for a newer club. As earlier mentioned, the disco evening is broken into two cycles: one a before-dinner session, another a post-dinner frolic. Before dinner, prices and admission tabs are usually lower. Of general interest are the following recommendations:

Bocaccio, 16 Marqués de la Enseñada, off the Plaza Colón (tel. 419-10-08), created a sensation when it opened in Barcelona, and an offshoot has survived a successful transplant to Madrid. It is now the most elegant disco in the Spanish capital. Everything is free form and stylized, a triumph of art nouveau. Tufted red-velvet crescent-shaped banquettes seat the most attractive young people in Madrid today. Serving them are catfooted, regally attired bartenders who become part of the show. They pour your drinks—and powerful ones at that—with one hand elaborately positioned behind their backs. The establishment is open from 7 to 10 p.m. when admission is only 650 pesetas ($5.75). It reopens at 11:30 p.m., with admission raised to 1,350 pesetas ($12.25) until closing time at 5 a.m.

Joy Eslava, 11 Arenal (tel. 266-54-40), may be one of the most electronics-conscious nightspots in Madrid. It's filled with up-to-date lights and sound equipment, with imitation lasers that fill the corners of this converted movie theater. If you don't feel like dancing, a collection of comfortable chaise longues is scattered throughout the establishment to help you forget how much you might be drinking. Libations range from 600 pesetas ($5.50) to 1,400 pesetas ($12.50), depending on the day of the week and the time you enter. It's slightly more expensive on weekends, although that's when it might be the most fun. The place is closed Monday, but open other days from 7 to 10 p.m. and 11:30 p.m. to 5 a.m.

Mau-Mau, José Lazaro Galdiano (tel. 457-94-23), in the Eurobuilding complex, is a leading nightspot of Madrid in the fickle world of discomania. Anyone with hopes of being included in the *tout Madrid* category will eventually show up or apply for membership in what is almost considered a private club, especially on those evenings when it's reserved for private parties. It's open from 11 p.m. to 5 a.m. daily except for about a week at the end of March or the first of April and for three days in mid-August. Drinks cost 1,800 pesetas ($16.25) to 2,500 pesetas ($22.50). The manager, Paco de Riveria, requires men to wear jackets and ties except on Sunday and from the first of July to the end of September.

JAZZ CLUBS

Clamores, 14 Calle Albuquerque (tel. 445-79-38), is the largest jazz club in Madrid, accommodating some 450 people. With dozens of small tables and a huge bar in its somewhat dark interior, the club specializes in the best Catalán champagne to go with the music of bands that come on at 11:30 p.m. and at 1:30 a.m., with closing at 3 a.m. If you come early, you can see young jazz buffs playing dominoes. During the jazz performances there is a 100-pesetas (90¢) surcharge on your first drink.

Whisky Jazz, 7 Diego de León (tel. 261-11-65), is a hideaway for jazz enthusiasts just a block away from the U.S. Embassy. Once inside, if you've appeared at the right moment, you'll be presented with one of the best showcases of jazz in all of Spain. In the interior of the two-story brick building is a stairway leading to an open mezzanine which projects out over a downstairs bar. The walls and especially a glass case contain intriguing jazz memorabilia, including autographs and photos of its heyday in Chicago and New Orleans. The entrance price begins at 650 pesetas ($5.75), but could go much higher depending on which group is appearing. Hours are midnight to 3 a.m. daily.

THE ART OF CIDER DRINKING: In an old tavern, just a short way from the Goya pantheon, **Casa Mingo**, 2 Paseo de la Florida (tel. 247-79-18), for decades has been known for its Asturian cider, both the still and the bubbly kind. There's no formality here, with customers sharing big tables under the vaulted ceiling in the dining room. Cider is served at Casa Mingo in the old manner. The waiter or bartender holds the glass as low as he can in the left hand, and the bottle of still cider as high as he can in the right, and then pours the cider (*echa la sidra*). A few drops may fall on the ground, but it's all part of the rite. The perfect accompanying tidbit is a piece of the local Asturian *cabrales* (goat cheese), but the roast chicken is *the* specialty of the house, with an unbelievable number of helpings served daily. Casa Mingo started roasting chicken when it was an uncommon delicacy in Spain. The price of chicken and cider is 800 pesetas ($7.25). In summer, the staff places some tables and wooden chairs outdoors on the sidewalk. Or if you prefer, you can stand at the bar, under the huge casks of wine lining the walls. Open from 10 a.m. to midnight daily. Metro: Norte.

BELLE ÉPOQUE CABARET

Las Noches de Cuple, 51 Calle La Palma (tel. 232-71-15). If you don't mind going to bed as the rays of an Iberian sunrise filter through the narrow streets of the surrounding neighborhood, you might enjoy this updated version of the once-celebrated Madrileño cabaret. Its entrance is on a crowded street barely wide enough for the pedestrians and cars that compete for space. Inside, a long room with a vaulted ceiling and a tiny stage are the forum for the still-charming former beauty, Señora Olga Ramos, who conducts an evening of Iberian song with (and sometimes without) a mantilla. The charm of her all-Spanish act is increased by the discreet humor of an octogenarian accompanist with an ostrich-feather tiara and a fuchsia-colored boa. Your first drink will cost 2,000 pesetas ($18), plus a 400-pesetas ($3.50) supplement for brand-name liquors. Each additional drink costs from 800 pesetas ($7.25). The restaurant opens at 9:30 p.m., and the show, in theory, begins at 11:45 p.m. Dinner is offered at 4,200 pesetas ($37.75).

"CUEVAS" HOPPING

Throughout Old Madrid—and especially south of the Plaza Mayor (head down Calle de Cuchilleros)—are gypsy-like *cuevas* (caves) where for a *chato* of wine you can join in spontaneous song-fests. One of the most famous establishments (recommended just to get you started) is the following:

Sesamo, 7 Príncipe (tel. 429-65-24), is a *cueva* both *cosmopolita y bohemio.* It has hosted Truman Capote and many other celebrated persons. Styles and cultural heroes change, but Sesamo goes on forever. Its two cellar rooms—beneath a snackbar—are reached via a long flight of steps. Downstairs you'll find seats gathered around tiny tables. The action warms up to a high level around 11 p.m. Guests often bring their guitars or banjos, spontaneously singing folk songs, laments of love and protest. And there's always a piano player. It's customary to order a pitcher of sangría for four at 575 pesetas ($5.25). Hours are 6:30 p.m. to 3 a.m. daily.

Mesón del Champiñon, 17 Cava San Miguel (tel. 248-67-90), is a place where the barmen keep a brimming bucket of sangría behind the long stand-up bar as a thirst-quencher for the many people who crowd in. The name of the establishment translates as "mushroom," and that is what you see delineated in various sizes along sections of the vaulted ceilings. A more appetizing way to experience a champiñon is to order a *ración* of grilled, stuffed, and salted mushrooms, served with toothpicks and accompanied by beer, costing 225 pesetas ($2). Sangría costs 300 pesetas ($2.75). Strange as it may seem, the pair of tiny, slightly dank rooms in the back is where Spanish families jam in for the organ music produced by a stalwart musician performing in one corner. Unless you want to be exiled to the very back, don't expect to sit down here. Practically everyone prefers to stand, anyway. Hours are 6 p.m. to 2 a.m. daily.

CASINO ACTION

The **Casino Gran Madrid,** Torrelodones (tel. 859-03-12). Even non-gamblers sometimes make the trek here from the capital, considering the casino's many entertainment facilities to be the most exciting thing around. Its scattered attractions include a trio of restaurants, four bars, and a nightclub. The casino is open from 5 p.m. to 4 a.m. Sunday to Thursday, to 5 a.m. on Friday, Saturday, and holiday eves. For an entrance fee of 500 pesetas ($4.50) you can sample the action in the gaming rooms, including French and American roulette, blackjack, punto y banco, and baccarat y chemin de fer.

An à la carte restaurant in the French Gaming Room offers international cuisine, with dinners costing from 5,000 pesetas ($45). A buffet in the American Gaming Room will run from 1,800 pesetas ($16.25). In the Grill/Barbecue Restaurant, independent of the gaming rooms, meals cost around 3,500 pesetas ($31.50). The three restaurants are all open from 9 p.m. to 2 a.m. The casino is about 17 miles northwest of Madrid, along the Madrid–La Coruña N-VI highway.

CHAPTER XV

ONE-DAY TRIPS FROM MADRID

□ □ □

Imperial cities . . . El Greco masterpieces . . . a monastery considered the eighth wonder of the world . . . castles that "float" in the clouds . . . the palaces of the Bourbon dynasty . . . the snow-capped Guadarrama mountains.

Some of the most interesting and varied scenery and man-made attractions in Europe lie in the satellite cities and towns ringing Madrid. Each of the cities, like Segovia and Toledo, knew former glory in separate and individualized ways.

If your time is pressed, go at least to **Toledo,** which captures the ages of Spain in miniature. Many tourists combine the tour of Toledo with a stopover at the royal palace of **Aranjuez.**

Ranking second is the day trip to **El Escorial,** the monastery built by Phillip II—combined with a side trip to the **Valley of the Fallen.** This is followed by a trek the third day to **Segovia,** with a side visit to nearby **La Granja,** the summer palace of the Bourbons.

These cities of Old and New Castile are appropriately called "monumental."

TOLEDO

The ancient capital of Spain looms on the horizon like an El Greco painting, seemingly undisturbed by the ages. The See of the Primate of Spain, the ecclesiastical center of the country, Toledo is medieval, well preserved. (For a preview of the city much as it is today, see El Greco's *View of Toledo* at the Metropolitan Museum of Art in New York City.)

The Tagus River loops around the granite promontory on which Toledo rests, surrounding the Imperial City on three sides like a snake.

Toledan steel, known as early as the 1st century B.C., has sliced its name down through the ages. Many a Mexican or Peruvian—if he had lived—could attest to the deadly accuracy of a Toledan sword.

But except for its steel and damascene work, the lack of major industrial activity has kept Toledo a virtual museum. Many of its buildings are intact, having survived countless battles, the most recent being the bloody fighting the city witnessed in the Spanish Civil War. It is not uncommon for mansions to preserve their original coats-of-arms in their façades.

The natural fortress that is Toledo is a labyrinth of narrow and precipitous streets, decaying palaces, towers, and squares—all of them tourist-trodden.

The Spanish government has seen fit to preserve all of Toledo as a "national monument." One critic labeled the entire city "a gallery of Art," with every style represented from Romanesque to Moorish to Gothic (best exemplified by the cathedral) to Renaissance.

Essentially, Toledo is a blending of the widely diverse cultures that made Spain what it is today: Roman, Visigothic, Moorish, Jewish, Christian. Perhaps for that reason, Tirso de Molina, the 17th-century dramatist, called Toledo "the heart of Spain." He named three of his dramas *Los Cigarrales de Toledo,* which brings us to a most important suggestion:

Before you leave the Imperial City, you should—preferably in the late of the afternoon—traverse the **Carretera de Circunvalación,** that most scenic of roads across the left bank of the Tagus. Along the slopes of the hills, you'll find the *cigarrales,* the rustic houses. From this side of the river, you can obtain the best panorama, seeing the city in perspective as El Greco did. With luck, you'll be perched on some belvedere as the sun goes down. Then you'll know why Toledo's sunsets are called violet.

Toledo lies 44 miles south of Madrid. You can reach it by car, of course, although public transportation includes both train and bus. However, the train delivers you outside the city, and you must take a bus into the heart of Toledo, depositing yourself at the Plaza of Zocodover.

You can see all of the major sightseeing attractions in one day, providing you arrive early and stay late.

THE CATHEDRAL: Built at the flowering peak of the Gothic era of architecture, the Cathedral of Toledo (tel. 22-22-41) is one of the greatest in Europe. It was erected principally between the years 1226 and 1493, although there have been later additions. The monument is a bastion of Christian architecture, but a great deal of the actual construction work was carried out by the Moors, master builders themselves.

The cathedral witnessed many prime moments in Spanish

history—such as a proclamation naming "Juana la Loca" (the insane daughter of Isabella I) and her husband, Philip the Handsome, heirs to the throne of Spain.

Inside, the Transparente—the altar completed in 1732 by Narciso Tomé—is considered a landmark in European architecture. It has been called "unheard-of pomp." Lit by a "hole" cut through the ceiling, this production includes angels on fluffy clouds, a polychrome "Last Supper," and a Madonna winging her way to heaven.

Dating from the 16th century, the iron gate of the cathedral is in the plateresque style. Works of art include the *Twelve Apostles* by El Greco; paintings by Velázquez, Goya, Morales, and Van Dyck. El Greco's first painting in Toledo was commissioned by the cathedral. Called *El Expolio,* it created a furor when the devout saw the vivid coloring of Christ's garments. The artist was even hauled into the courts. Many elaborately sculpted tombs of both the nobility and ecclesiastical hierarchy are sheltered inside.

Don't fail to visit the Gothic cloister, the Capilla Mayor, and the Renaissance-style Choir Room (elaborate woodcarvings), and you should see the rose windows, preferably near sunset. In the Treasure Room is a 500-pound monstrance, dating from the 16th century and said to have been made, in part, from gold that Columbus brought back from the New World. To celebrate Corpus festivities, the monstrance is carried through the streets of Toledo. The Mozarabic Chapel dates from the 16th century and contains paintings by Juan de Borgoña (a mass using Mozarabic liturgy is still conducted here).

The treasures of the cathedral can be visited in summer from 10:30 a.m. to 1 p.m. and 3:30 to 7 p.m., costing 300 pesetas ($2.75) for admission. Off-season, the cathedral closes an hour earlier in the evening.

THE MUSEUM OF SANTA CRUZ: Dating from the 16th century and built in the form of a Greek cross, this plateresque hospice has been turned into a **Museum of Fine Arts and Archeology,** Calle de Cervantes. As a hospital, it was originally founded by Cardinal Mendoza. It is of such beautiful construction—especially its paneled ceilings—that it's a question of the "frame" competing with the pictures contained inside.

In the Fine Arts Museum are 18 paintings by El Greco (*The Burial of Count Orgaz* is a copy of his masterpiece). *The Assumption of the Virgin* is his most important canvas here. Other works are by Ribera and Goya. Flemish tapestries, antique furnishings, and jewelry round out the exhibit.

In the Archeological Museum the past ages of Toledo are

peeled away: prehistoric, Iberian, Roman (note the mosaics), Moorish, Visigothic, and Gothic. The museum is an easy walk from the Plaza de Zocodover.

Santa Cruz is open daily from 10 a.m. to 6:30 p.m., and charges 200 pesetas ($1.75) for admission. Using the same ticket, you can visit the nearby **Museo de los Concilios y de la Cultura Visigoda.**

EL GRECO'S HOUSE AND MUSEUM:
The famous painter, Domenico Theotocopouli, called El Greco because he was born in Crete, arrived in Toledo in 1577, living there with Doña Jerónima, a noted beauty (wife or mistress?), until his death in 1614. His house, the Casa del Greco, stands in the *antiguo barrio judío,* or the old Jewish quarter, of the monumental city on Calle Samuel Levi.

It is believed that in 1585 the painter moved into one of the decaying palace apartments belonging to a Marqués de Villena. The chancellor of the exchequer to Pedro the Cruel, Samuel Ha-Levi, is said to have built a home on the same spot in the 14th century. He had subterranean passages dug to hide his treasury. The house was eventually occupied by Don Enrique de Villena, who is believed to have practiced alchemy in the underground cellars.

El Greco rented the main part of the palace. From the palace windows, the Greek painter could look out onto views of the Tagus.

The Villena apartments were torn down in this century, but the Marqués de la Vega-Inclán was responsible for saving El Greco's dwelling place, a small Moorish house, probably also once the house of Samuel Ha-Levi. Eventually a neighboring house was incorporated to house the museum with 19 pictures by El Greco.

Visitors are admitted into the studio of El Greco, containing a painting by the artist. Especially interesting are the garden and kitchen. Except on Sunday afternoon and Monday, the house may be visited from 10 a.m. to 2 p.m. and 3:30 to 7 p.m. in season. Off-season times are from 10 a.m. to 2 p.m. and 3:30 to 6 p.m. The admission fee is 200 pesetas ($1.75).

THE CHURCH AND CLOISTERS OF SAN JUAN DE LOS REYES:
This church at 21 Calle de los Reyes Católicos (tel. 22-38-02), was founded by King Ferdinand and Queen Isabella to commemorate their triumph over the Portuguese at Toro in 1476. Its construction was started in 1477, according to the plans of architect Juan Guas. It was finished, together with the splendid cloisters, in 1504, dedicated to St. John the Evangelist, and used, from the very beginning, by the Franciscan Friars. It is a perfect example of Gothic-Spanish-Flemish style.

San Juan de los Reyes has been restored after being damaged in the invasion of Napoleon and abandoned in 1835. Actually, the national monument has been entrusted again to the Franciscans since 1954. The price of admission is 60 pesetas (55¢). You can visit the church from 10 a.m. to 2 p.m. and 3:30 p.m. to 7 p.m. daily (it closes an hour earlier in winter).

THE CHURCH OF SANTO TOMÉ: Except for its mudéjar tower, this little 14th-century chapel, on Calle de Santo Tomé (tel. 21-02-09), is rather unprepossessing. But by some strange twist it was given the honor of exhibiting El Greco's masterpiece, *The Burial of Count Orgaz*. Long acclaimed for its composition, the painting is a curious work in its blending of realism with mysticism. To view the painting, you have to purchase a ticket for 85 pesetas (75¢).

The church is open daily from 10 a.m. to 1:45 p.m. and 3:30 to 6:45 p.m. in summer, closing an hour earlier in winter. Closed on Christmas Day and New Year's Day.

THE ALCÁZAR: The characteristic landmark dominating the skyline of Toledo is the Alcázar, on the Plaza de Zocodover. It attracted worldwide attention during the siege of the city in 1936. Nationalists held the fortress for 70 days until relief troops could respond to their plea for help, arriving on September 27, 1936.

The most famous event surrounding that battle was a telephone call the Republicans placed to the Nationalist leader inside. He was informed that his son was being held captive and would be executed if the Alcázar were not surrendered. He refused to comply with their demands, and his son was sacrificed.

The Alcázar was destroyed, and the one standing in its place today is a reconstruction, housing an **Army Museum** with a monument out front to the heroes of that 1936 siege. The price of admission is 100 pesetas (90¢). Entrance is from 9:30 a.m. to 7 p.m. daily March through August, to 6:30 p.m. in September and October, and to 6 p.m. in winter.

THE TRÁNSITO SYNAGOGUE: Down the street from El Greco's museum on the Paseo del Tránsito is the once-important worshipping place for the large Jewish population that used to inhabit the city, living peacefully with both Christians and Arabs. This 14th-century building is noted for its superb stucco and its Hebrew inscriptions. There are some psalms along the top of the walls and on the east wall a poetic description of the temple. The building of the synagogue was ordered by the chancellor of the exchequer to King Pedro el Cruel (Peter the Cruel), Don Samuel Ha-Levi. The name of the king appears clearly in a frame in the Hebrew inscription.

The synagogue is the most important part of the **Sephardic Museum** (Museo Sefardí), which was inaugurated in 1971 and contains in other rooms the tombstones with Hebrew epigraphy of the Jews of Spain before 1492, as well as other art pieces. The museum and synagogue can be visited from 10 a.m. to 1:45 p.m. and 4 to 5:45 p.m. daily except Sunday afternoon and Monday. Admission is 200 pesetas ($1.75). For information, telephone 22-36-65.

ARANJUEZ

On the Tagus River, 29 miles south of Madrid, Aranjuez strikes visitors as a virtual garden. It was mapped out by the royal architects and landscapers of Ferdinand VI in the 18th century. The natural setting has been blended with wide boulevards and fountain- and statuary-filled gardens.

And what a setting! Surrounded in late spring by beds of asparagus and heavily laden strawberry vines, Aranjuez exudes the spirit of May. But for some visitors autumn best reveals the royal town. It is then that the golden cypress trees cast lingering shadows in countless ponds, evoking a painting by Santiago Rusiñonly Prats.

Once at Aranjuez, you can buy a ticket for 265 pesetas ($2.40), entitling you to visit the three most important sights in the town, the **Royal Palace** and the adjoining **Jardín de la Isla** (Garden of the Island), and the **Casa del Labrador** in the Jardín del Príncipe.

THE ROYAL PALACE: Since the beginning of a united Spain, the climate and natural beauty of Aranjuez have attracted Spanish monarchs, notably Ferdinand and Isabella, as well as Philip II, who managed to tear himself away from El Escorial. But the Royal Palace in its present form dates primarily from the days of the Bourbons, who used to come here mainly in the autumn and spring, reserving La Granja, near Segovia, for their summer romps. The palace was also favored by Philip V and Charles III.

Fires have swept over the structure numerous times, but most of the present building was finished in 1778. William Lyon, writing in the Madrid weekly, the *Guidepost,* called "its dominant note" that of ". . . deception: in almost each of its widely varying rooms there is at least one thing that isn't what it first appears." Among other examples, Mr. Lyon cites assemblages of mosaics that look like oil paintings; a trompe-l'oeil ceiling that seems three-dimensional, although in fact it is flat; and a copy of a salon at the Alhambra Palace at Granada.

In spite of these eye-fooling tricks, the palace is lavishly and elegantly decorated. Especially notable are the dancing salon, the throne room, the ceremonial dining hall, the bedrooms of the king and queen, and a remarkable Salón de Porcelana (Porcelain Room). Paintings include works by Lucas Jordán and José Ribera.

The palace is always open in the morning from 10 a.m. to 1 p.m. However, its afternoon hours are as follows: 3 to 5 p.m., October through February; 3 to 6 p.m., March through May; and 4 to 7 p.m., June through September.

EL ESCORIAL

In the Guadarrama mountain resort of El Escorial, about 30 miles northwest of Madrid, stands the imposing **Monastery of San Lorenzo el Real del Escorial.** Many refer to it as the eighth wonder of the world. Both a palace and a monastery, it was ordered built by Philip II to commemorate the triumphs of his forces at the Battle of San Quentín in 1557. Escorial was dedicated to St. Lawrence, the martyred saint burned to death.

The original architect in 1563 was Juan Bautista de Toledo. After his death the monumental task was assumed by the greatest architect of Renaissance Spain, Juan de Herrera, who completed it in the shape of a gridiron in 1584.

The severe lines of the great pile of granite strike many as being as austere as the pious Philip himself. The architectural critic, Nikolaus Pevsner, called it "overwhelming, moving no doubt, but frightening."

The Palace, Pantheon, Chapter House, and Library, as well as the satellite Casita del Príncipe and the Casita del Infante, may be visited daily except Monday from 10 a.m. to 1:30 p.m. and 3:30 to 6 p.m. The general-admission ticket costs 350 pesetas ($3.25).

In the **Charter Hall** is one of the greatest art collections in Spain outside of the Prado, the canvases dating primarily from the 15th to the 17th centuries. Among the most outstanding works are El Greco's *The Martyrdom of St. Maurice,* Titian's *Last Supper,* Velázquez's *The Tunic of Joseph,* Van der Weyden's *Crucifixion,* and another version of Bosch's *The Hay Wagon* (see also a remarkable tapestry based on a painting by "El Bosco"); there are also works by Ribera, Tintoretto, and Veronese.

The **Biblioteca** contains one of the most important libraries in the world, its estimated number of volumes in excess of 50,000. The collection, started by Philip II, ranges far and wide: Muslim codices; a Gothic "Cántigas" of the 13th century from the reign of Alfonso X (known as "The Wise King"); and signatures from the Carmelite nun, St. Teresa of Jesús, who conjured up visions of the devil and of angels sticking burning hot lances into her heart.

For many sightseers, the highlight of the tour is a visit to the **Apartments of Philip II,** containing many of the original furnishings of the monarch. He died in 1598, in the "cell for my humble self" that he ordered built. He desired quarters that were spartan, and so they remain today—graced by a painting by Bosch, a copy he made of his *The Seven Capital Sins,* now at the Prado.

The **Apartments of the Bourbons** reflect different tastes and style, a complete break from the asceticism imposed by the Habsburg king. They are richly decorated, with a special emphasis on tapestries (many resembling paintings), based on Goya and Bayeu cartoons at the Royal Factory in Madrid.

From a window in his bedroom, a weak and dying Philip II could look down at the services being conducted in the **Basilica.** As the dome clearly indicates, the church was modeled after Michelangelo's drawings of St. Peter's in Rome. Works of art include a crucifix by Benvenuto Cellini, choir stalls by Herrera, and sculpted groups of father and son (Charles V and Philip II), along with their wives, flanking the alter.

The **Royal Pantheon,** burial place of Spanish kings from Charles V to Alfonso XII, is under the altar. (The Bourbon king, Philip V, is interred at La Granja, and the body of Ferdinand VI was placed in a tomb in a Madrid church). In the octagonal mausoleum you'll see the tombs of queens who were mothers of kings.

On the lower level rests one of the curiosities of El Escorial: a "Wedding Cake" tomb for royal children. The Whispering Hall, with its odd sound effects, is also intriguing.

THE VALLEY OF THE FALLEN

The Spanish call it the *Valle de los Caídos.* Inaugurated near El Escorial by Generalísimo Franco in 1959, it is a heroic-size monument to the Spanish dead of the Civil War, both the Nationalists and the Republicans. "El Caudillo" had wanted to honor only the Nationalist soldiers, but was prevailed upon to change his mind in the interest of the country's unity.

For two decades workmen tunneled out an already-existing gorge in the Guadarrama mountains, making room for a basilica and a mausoleum. Crowning the Rock of Nava is a gargantuan cross, nearly 500 feet high, stretching its crossbars a distance of 150 feet.

Directly below the cross is the underground basilica, decorated with mosaics. The body of José António, the founder of the Falangist party, was finally interred here. His burial at the monastery of El Escorial sparked a wave of protests from the monarchists, who objected to the Spanish leader's "nonroyal" birth. To reach the basilica, you must first walk through a series of six chapels.

SEGOVIA

In Old Castile, Segovia is one of the most romantic of Spanish cities, its glory of another day. Isabella I was proclaimed Queen of Castile here in 1474. Segovians live with the memory of the time when their star was in the ascendancy.

The capital of a province of the same name, it lies on a slope of the snow-capped Sierra de Guadarrama mountains, between two ravine-studded valleys and the Eresma and Clamores Rivers (actually streams). As it appears on the horizon, dominated by its Alcázar and its Gothic cathedral, Segovia is decidedly of the Middle Ages.

The city was of strategic importance to the Roman troops, and one of its greatest monuments, the Aqueduct, dates from those times. The skyline is characterized by the Romanesque belfries of the churches and the towers of its old and decaying palaces.

The Upper Town is mainly encased by its old walls; but the part outside the walls is of interest too, especially for views of the Alcázar and visits to the Church of Vera Cruz and the Monastery of El Parral.

THE TOP SIGHTS: Many of the charms of Segovia are obvious. Merely strolling its narrow winding streets and stumbling upon a secluded plaza forgotten by time is a fit and proper reward to any traveler. More so than any other competitor, Segovia captures and maintains the pristine look of an ancient Castilian city. But the capital contains three sights that are the front rank: (1) the **Alcázar,** (2) the **Aqueduct,** and (3) the **cathedral.**

WHERE TO DINE: One reason the Spanish go to Segovia is to dine on cochinillo oasado, or roast suckling pig. Everyone from Hemingway to King Hussein has been drawn to the landmark **Mesón de Cándido,** 5 Plaza Azoguejo (tel. 911/42-81-02), a 15th-century inn presided over by the *mesonero mayor de Castilla.* Near the Aqueduct, the classic Castilian restaurant, the finest in Segovia, offers a choice of six dining rooms in an antique motif. Those who don't order the roast suckling pig ask for the cordero asado (roast lamb). Both seem equally good. For a complete repast, including the specialties, expect to pay 2,500 pesetas ($22.50) to 3,500 pesetas ($31.50). Hours are 12:30 to 4:30 p.m. and 8 to 11:30 p.m. daily.

LA GRANJA

This was the summer palace of the Bourbon kings of Spain, who imitated the grandeur of Versailles in Segovia province. Set against the snow-capped Guadarrama mountains, the slate-roofed palace dominates the village that grew up around it (nowadays a summer resort).

The founder of La Granja was Philip V, grandson of Louis XIV and the first Bourbon king of Spain (his body, along with that of his second queen, Isabel de Fernesio, is interred in a mauseoleum in the Collegiate Church). Philip V was born at Versailles on December 19, 1683, which partially explains why he wanted to re-create that atmosphere at Segovia.

At one time a farm stood on the grounds of what is now the palace—hence the totally inappropriate name *granja,* meaning farm in Spanish.

The palace was built in the first part of the 18th century. Inside you'll find valuable antiques (many in the Empire style), paintings, and a remarkable collection of tapestries of Flemish design and others based on Goya cartoons from the Royal Factory in Madrid.

Most visitors, however, seem to find a stroll through the gardens more to their liking, so allow adequate time for it. The fountain statuary is a riot of gods and nymphs cavorting with abandon, hiding indiscretions behind jets of water. The gardens are studded with chestnuts and elms.

Charging an admission fee of 300 pesetas ($2.75), the royal palace can be visited from 10 a.m. to 1:30 p.m. and 3 to 4:30 p.m. daily. A spectacular display comes when the water jets are turned on.

CHAPTER XVI

SPAIN IN A NUTSHELL

□ □ □

Before leaving the Spanish capital, why not take the extra time at least to skim the surface of some of the most rewarding targets on the Iberian peninsula?

CENTRAL SPAIN

ÁVILA: One of the great medieval centers of Europe, Ávila is forever associated with St. Teresa of Jesús, the mystic Carmelite nun about whom a number of legends arose after her death. The loftiest city in Spain, Ávila is completely encircled by its 11th-century walls.

While there, visit the 17th-century **Convent of St. Teresa;** a Romanesque and Gothic cathedral that once doubled as a fortress; and the 15th-century Gothic-style **Church and Monastery of St. Tomás,** burial place of Torquemada, prosecutor of "heretics."

Avila lies 71 miles west of Madrid, reached in about two hours by train from Madrid's North Station.

SALAMANCA: Once one of the most prestigious university centers of Europe, this golden city of plateresque buildings is wonderfully preserved. It was the home of the great Spanish philosopher Unamuno, who died there in 1936. Salamanca is a virtual museum of architectural monuments: its **Old** and **New Cathedrals,** the 13th-century **University** (oldest in Spain), the **Casa de las Conchas** (house of shells), the **Convent of San Esteban** (late Gothic, high altar by Churriguera), and the **Plaza Mayor.**

From Madrid, Salamanaca is traditionally visited after a stopover in Ávila. Salamanca lies about 131 miles west of Madrid, in the direction of the Portuguese frontier. Many motorists leave Madrid in the morning and spend the night in Salamanca. Trains bound for the city depart Madrid's North Station.

ANDALUSIA

SEVILLE: The unofficial capital of Andalusia, Seville is the most festive city in Spain—but also one of the most dangerous. Because of high unemployment, its crime rate is among the highest in Spain. Purse-snatching is now commonplace, and cars left unguarded on the street are often broken into. Take caution whenever and wherever you travel, but be extremely careful in visiting this city, the legendary home of Carmen.

The city is wealthy in sights, including a Gothic **cathedral,** among the largest in the world, and an **Alcázar** that was a 14th-century mudéjar palace (former tenants: Ferdinand and Isabella). The landmark of the city is **La Giralda Tower,** built as a minaret in the 12th century. But it is the city itself—especially the **Santa Cruz** district of narrow streets and bougainvillea-draped balconies—that intrigues the foreign wanderer. However, don't go wandering alone there at night. Its April Fair and Holy Week draw visitors from all over Europe.

Seville is 334 miles southwest of Madrid. It's customary for drivers to make it to Córdoba for the first night's stopover, then head on to Seville the following day, a distance of 86 miles. The fast TALGO train leaves Madrid's Atocha Station.

From Seville, the most interesting day trip is to **Jerez de la Frontera,** surrounded by its aristocratic vineyards that produce sherry. Connected by bus and rail to Seville, it lies 60 miles to the south of that city.

GRANADA: The legacy of the vanquished Moors, the **Alhambra Palace** is the most celebrated architectural site in Spain. Stroll through its patios, past its bubbling fountains where harem girls danced, and relive Washington Irving's *Tales of the Alhambra*. The 13th-century Muslim palace stands alongside an incongruously placed Renaissance structure, ordered erected by the Habsburg king Charles V. Isabella and Ferdinand, the "liberators" of Granada, are buried in the Gothic-style **Royal Chapel,** in back of the ornate Renaissance Cathedral of Granada.

Granada is 2,200 feet above sea level, spread over two hills, the Albaicín and the Alhambra. It lies at the foothills of the Sierra Nevada and their snow-capped peaks. A colorful city of Andalusia, it attracts tourists at night to its gypsy caves of **Sacro-Monte,** where *zambras* (Moorish festivals) are staged. However, these are often unabashed tourist traps. Go if you must, but hang on to your valuables. Recently when one light-fingered performer couldn't pick my pocket, she chased me down the hill yelling, "Money, money, money."

Granada is 269 miles south of Madrid, a long day's drive. A fast TER train leaves Madrid's Atocha Station, the trip taking approximately seven hours.

CÓRDOBA: This Andalusian city enjoyed its greatest prosperity under the Moors when it was the seat of the Western Caliphate. In the middle of the 10th century it was the largest city of Europe, a focal point of culture, with mosques, libraries, and palaces. Today, after much destruction and rebuilding, it is still characterized by narrow streets, flower-filled patios, whitewashed houses, and Moorish, Romanesque, and Gothic sightseeing attractions.

The most important sight is the **Mezquita,** a mosque founded in the 8th century, the crowning architectural achievement of the Muslims in the West, who adorned it with peppermint-stripe pillars, a forest of jasper and marble. See also the **Alcázar** of the Christian kings, built in the 14th century, and the **Museum of Julio Romero de Torres,** a memorial to the Córdoba-born artist who delighted in painting nude women.

The distance from Madrid to Córdoba is 248 miles and can be traversed in a day's drive. You can also take a TER train from Chamartín Station, leaving Madrid in the morning and arriving in midafternoon.

CATALONIA

BARCELONA: The capital of Catalonia in the northeastern part of the country, Barcelona is Spain's "second city." The largest port on the Mediterranean, it will introduce you to a way of life and culture far removed from that of the cliché-ridden Spain of mantillas and Carmens.

Barcelona is often referred to as the most European of Spanish cities; it's graced (critics say marred) by some of the most curious architecture in the world, the work of the incomparable Gaudí. See, in particular, his Catalán landmark, the uncompleted **Temple of the Sacred Family,** as well as his **Parque Güell,** a surrealist park on the slope of Tibidabo Mountain.

Tibidabo, a sort of Coney Island in the sky, is one of the more intriguing man-made attractions, as is the **Pueblo Es-**

pañol in Montjuich Park (built in 1929 for the World's Fair). The **Gothic Quarter,** dominated by its historic **cathedral,** is the aristocratic sector of the city, characterized by narrow streets and squares. Other sights include the **Picasso Museum** and, in contrast, the **Museum of the Art of Catalonia,** unique in the world.

The denizens of Barcelona promenade up and down the **Ramblas,** and so will you. But do so with care. One local woman confided to me that she considers the Ramblas unsafe after noon!

TRANSPORTATION

Barcelona is 385 miles east of Madrid. Many make-it-or-die motorists attempt to drive this long, difficult route in one day. More prudent trippers stop over in **Saragossa,** the capital of Aragón, for the night.

Iberia Airlines flies directly between Madrid and Barcelona; there is train service as well. Avoid the slow coaches that stop at every olive grove en route; instead, take the *Costa Brava Express,* leaving Madrid's Chamartín Station.

EXCURSIONS

Like Madrid, Barcelona is the hub for some of the most interesting excursions in Spain. Chief among them is the world-famed benedictine monastery of **Montserrat,** 38 miles to the northwest (it can be explored on an organized tour). A large number of tourists are learning that it's better to visit the **Costa Brava** on a one-day excursion than to attempt to fight the French for the limited number of hotel accommodations in summer. The jagged coastline begins about 43 miles north of Barcelona at **Blanes,** a fishing village. It runs along a serpentine 95-mile trail, racing toward the French frontier. The most popular resorts are **Tossá de Mar** and **Lloret de Mar.**

Gaining in importance is the resort to the south of Barcelona, **Sitges,** on the "Gold Coast" (especially frequented by the beautiful people of Scandinavia). For historic interest, **Tarragona,** about 59 miles south of Barcelona, was an old Roman city (visit its "Cyclopean" city walls, its 12th-century cathedral, Roman amphitheater, and Necropolis).

THE LEVANTE

VALENCIA: Dominating southeastern Spain, known as the

Levante, this Mediterranean port city is belatedly gaining recognition as a tourist center. El Cid liberated the city from Moorish domination in 1094, but the Arabs regained possession in 1101 following the death of the warrior king.

Encircling the city is the **Huerta,** studded with orange trees and rice paddies (paella is a specialty of Valencia). The capital of its province, Valencia is Spain's third city, ranking after Madrid and Barcelona. The Valencian beach, **Playa de Levante,** is about two miles from the city proper.

In Valencia, visit the 13th-century **cathedral** (it claims to possess the Holy Grail, used by Christ at the Last Supper). See also its **Generalidad,** built in the 15th and 16th centuries in the Mediterranean Gothic style, plus the **Ceramics Museum,** housed in a rococo and churrigueresque palace.

The city is 218 miles southeast of Madrid, easily reached by car (one day) or by rail. If you prefer the latter, take a TALGO train from Madrid's Atocha Station.

THE BALEARICS

MAJORCA: The largest land area in the Balearic archipelago, Majorca is the most popular tourist island in the Mediterranean. It's characterized by sandy beaches, windmills turning in the wind, olive and almond trees, mountains and winding roads, little harbors, small villages, and thousands upon thousands of visitors.

Its capital is **Palma** in the western part of the island—a big, bustling seaport with an old quarter and the greatest number of modern hotels of any city in Spain. Swimming is possible from late April through October. While on the island, you may want to take a 31-mile jaunt east to **Mancor** where the artificial Majorca pearls are made, continuing on till you reach the underground forest of stalactites and stalagmites, **Las Cuevas del Drach.** In a different direction, you can explore **Valldemosa,** where George Sand and Chopin wintered, and the artist colony of **Deyá,** long associated with Robert Graves (now deceased).

Iberia Airlines and Aviaco fly to Palma from Madrid, Barcelona, and Valencia. In addition, the **Compañía Transmediterránea** offers regular motorboat service between Palma and Barcelona, and Palma and Valencia.

IBIZA: The easy life holds forth at Ibiza, the second major Balearic island. Some 85 miles from Majorca, Ibiza is reached by boat or air.

The chief center is the port of **Cuidad de Ibiza,** but the resort of **San Antonio Abad** holds more appeal for most visitors. However, those who really want to get away from it all should head for **Santa Eulalia del Río,** five miles north of Cuidad de Ibiza.

THE BASQUE COUNTRY

SAN SEBASTIÁN: This international beach resort on the Atlantic is the capital of the Basque province of Guipúzcoa, about 13 miles from the French frontier. In August it becomes the summer capital of Spain, when a retinue of government officials moves here from Madrid. **La Concha Beach,** its major attraction, is one of the finest in Spain.

San Sebastián also makes a good base for excursions into the Basque country: the nearby fishing villages known as the **Pasajes;** the sanctuary of **Loyola;** the once-destroyed town of **Guernica,** subject of Picasso's most famous painting, now housed in the Prado in Madrid. Many prefer to locate in San Sebastián and commute to **Pamplona** for the week-long July festival of San Fermín, highlighted by the running of the bulls through the streets. Some 56 miles away, Pamplona is tied to San Sebastián by rail and bus connections.

In hotels, San Sebastián never has enough in July and August. Don't arrive without a reservation nailed down.

San Sebastián is reached principally by rail or car from Madrid, a distance of 291 miles. Because the resort is such a long drive from Madrid, an overnight stopover in **Burgos,** the city of "El Cid Campeador," is recommended. A TALGO train departs from Madrid's Chamartín Station.

GALICIA

SANTIAGO DE COMPOSTELA: A National Monument cathedral city, Santiago de Compostela is the most ancient—and most famous—pilgrimage city of Spain.

A university town and market center for Galician farmers, Santiago is considered the third Holy City of the Christian world. Begun in the 11th century, the **cathedral** is the most splendid achievement of the Spanish Romanesque style of architecture. The **Hostal de los Reyes Católicos,** founded by Isabella and Ferdinand, has been converted into one of the most spectacular hotels in Europe by the government.

AFTER MADRID——WHERE TO?: If you're flying or driving to the Costa del Sol (next chapter), read on. However, if you want a deeper look at Spain, and plan to visit its other fascinating cities, including Granada, Córdoba, Seville, and Barcelona, you'll need our companion guide, *Spain and Morocco on $40 a Day*. This larger guide is devoted to the country's many sightseeing attractions, and provides wide coverage of hotels and restaurants. It explores the country in depth, and its philosophy is to help you get the most for your dollar. Special features of the book include detailed sections on the Balearic Islands (including Majorca, Ibiza, and Minorca), Gibraltar, the Canary Islands, and even more exotic, the mysterious country of Morocco on the northwest coast of Africa.

CHAPTER XVII

THE COSTA DEL SOL

□ □ □

The most popular beach strip in Spain—and Europe's most spectacular real-estate boom—begins at the port of Algeciras and stretches eastward all the way to Almería. Against the backdrop of once-pagan Andalusia, the Sun Coast curves gently along the Mediterranean, studded with beaches, sandy coves, lime-washed houses, high-rise apartments, olive groves, tennis courts, golf courses, swimming pools, and hotels of every type and description.

Sun-seekers from all over Europe and North America are drawn to the mild climate and virtually guaranteed sunshine. You can bathe in the sun year round, but in January and February only the Scandinavians dare the sea. The less hardy splash in sheltered, heated pools. The mean temperature in January, the coldest month of the year, is 56° Fahrenheit. In August, the hottest month, the mean temperature is about 75° Fahrenheit, as prevailing sea breezes mercifully keep the heat down.

Once the Sun Coast was only a spring-to-autumn affair. Now, so many shivering refugees have descended from the cold cities of northern Europe that the strip is alive year round. From June through October, however, "alive" isn't the half of it. All year, bullfights, flamenco, and fiestas crowd its calendar. Holy Week in Málaga, for example, is among the most stunning celebrations in Spain, rivaling that of Seville. And then there's Málaga's colorful winter festival, packed with cultural and sporting events ranging from horse racing to folk songs and dances. On August fiesta days, Málaga's bullfights are second to none.

MÁLAGA

One of the most important seaports on the Mediterranean, Málaga is the queen of the Costa del Sol and the second-largest city of Andalusia. At the foot of Mount Gibralfaro, it is marked by orange trees, flower markets, and fishing boats. The best way to see the city in true 19th-century style is in a horse-drawn carriage. If possible, visit the vegetable and fish markets.

Málaga's winter climate ranks as one of Europe's most idyllic, perhaps sufficient explanation for the luxuriant vegetation in the city's parks and gardens. Truly, **El Parque,** dating from the 19th century and filled with many botanic species, ranks among the handsomest parks in Spain.

The **telephone area code** for Málaga is 952.

SIGHTS 'N' THINGS: Málaga is not especially known for its art treasures, even though Pablo Picasso was born here in 1881. The **Fine Arts Museum** (Bellas Artes), 6 San Agustín, owns two of his works, an oil painting and a watercolor, both done when he was a teenager. The museum is open Tuesday to Sunday from 10 a.m. to 1:30 p.m. and 5 to 6 p.m. Cost of admission is 250 pesetas ($2.25).

The city proudly possesses a trio of historical sights, however, including the **Alcazaba,** the remains of the ancient palace of Málaga's former Moorish rulers. Towers encircle two walled precincts. In ruins, it is considered an outstanding example of Moorish-Spanish architecture. Troops loyal to Isabella and Ferdinand fought a savage battle with the Arabs to take it. When the Catholic monarchs conquered Málaga, they lodged at the castle. Right in the center of town, it offers spectacular views. Wander at your leisure through the open patios, tile-lined pools, and flower gardens. Inside is an **Archeological Museum,** containing artifacts found in prehistoric caves in Málaga province. Other exhibits document cultures ranging from Greek to Phoenician to Carthaginian. Hours are 10 a.m. to 1 p.m. and 5 to 8 p.m. Monday through Saturday, from 10 a.m. to 2 p.m. on Sunday. Admission is 20 pesetas (20¢).

The **cathedral** of Málaga was begun in 1528. Its 300-foot tower stands as a lone sentinel, without a mate. Although never finished, the cathedral took so long to build that it's a mélange of styles, roughly classified as "Spanish Renaissance." Inside, seek out in particular its ornate choir stalls. It is open from 10 a.m. to 1 p.m. and 4 to 7 p.m. daily, charging an admission of 75 pesetas (70¢).

Finally, as the sun is setting, head for **Gibralfaro Castle,** on a hilltop over the Mediterranean bay. It, too, is what's left of an ancient Moorish fortress. Originally, it is believed, the Phoenicians built a fortress on this site, but the present castle is of Arab construction and dates from the 7th century.

At Pizzara, about 25 miles northwest of Málaga, the **Museo Hollander** (tel. 48-31-63), operated by New York natives Gino and Barbara Hollander, contains a wealth of material, ranging from tools and weapons from neolithic and paleolithic sites in Spain to Iberian, Visigothic, and Roman days on the peninsula, plus historic clothing. The Hollanders built their own palatial home and museum here, using bricks, tiles, and carved ceiling beams from a 15th-century palace in Córdoba. The 40 massive doors date mostly from 1492. The museum can be visited by appointment, as the Hollanders take turns guiding visitors through the house and the stables in which a series of small rooms and artisan's shops show what life was like in other days. Admission is free.

So much for sightseeing. Now head back to town and do some shopping on Calle Larios and its satellite alleys, all containing stores brimming with Spanish handcrafts.

A TRAVELER'S ADVISORY: Málaga is the unfortunate winner of a recent survey which declared it to have the highest crime rate in Spain. By far the most common complaint is purse-snatching, with an estimated 75% of the crimes committed by juveniles. The related problem of stolen passports reported to the U.S. consular office in Fuengirola has become a common story in this town where the pickings are rich from a floating population serviced by an understaffed police force.

As a warning to travelers, I stress that all precautions should be taken, including buttoning wallets and valuables into pockets (a money belt might be an even better idea). Drive with your doors locked and your windows rolled up (many incidents occur while motorists are waiting at traffic signals with their windows down).

In an era of changing social structures, when you are likely to be perceived as a "have" traveling in an area of "have-nots," it is wise to take special care of your valuables. Don't flaunt your possessions, especially jewelry. With the right precautions taken, you can still have a pleasant, carefree holiday, and the crime wave sweeping across Málaga need not darken the spirit of your traveling time spent there.

WHERE TO STAY: For such a large city, Málaga has a surprising lack of hotels. The best ones in all price ranges are documented below.

The Upper Bracket

The **Málaga Palacio,** 1 Cortina del Muelle, 29015 Málaga (tel. 21-51-85), is the leading five-star hotel of Málaga, a city which, frankly, lags behind in its innkeeping. The deluxe hotel is thrust right in the core of the city, opening directly on a tree-lined esplanade, near the cathedral and harbor. The building, containing 224 rooms, is built flat-iron style, rising 15 stories and crowned by an open-air swimming pool and refreshment bar. Most of the balconies open onto views of the port. Down below you can see graceful turn-of-the-century carriages pulled by horses. In high season, a twin or double rents for 10,000 pesetas ($90), 8,000 pesetas ($72) in a single, including a continental breakfast. Rooms contain private bath, phone, bar, and piped-in music; they are air-conditioned and traditionally furnished. The street-floor lounges mix antiques with more modern furnishings. Parking is available next to the hotel, and other facilities include hairdressers for both men and women, a cafeteria, boutiques, and a beauty salon.

The **Hotel Guadalmar,** Urbanización Guadalmar, Carretera de Cádiz, km 238/9, 29080 Málaga (tel. 31-90-00), is a nine-story resort hotel at the edge of the city with its own private beach, about a mile from the airport. All the rooms open onto a swimming pool and garden. Each well-furnished accommodation is spaciously designed, with a private sea-view balcony. From June 21 to September 30 one person pays 5,900 pesetas ($53); two people, 8,500 pesetas ($76.50). Children under 12, in addition to staying free in the same room with their parents, are provided with such extra advantages as a swimming pool and playground, plus babysitters and cribs, even a special menu. Take your meals in the dining room, La Bodega, which opens onto the sea and is decorated in a rustic theme. But for a live combo to listen and dance to, go straight to La Corrida.

Medium-Priced Hotels

The **Parador Nacional de Gibralfaro,** Monte Gibralfaro, 29016 Málaga (tel. 22-19-02), is a government-owned hotel/restaurant perched high on a hill near the ancient castle, with a view of the sea, the city, the mountains, and beaches. It's an unusual combination of taste, beauty, moderate cost, and comfort. To get the picture, imagine a building of rugged stone with long arched open corridors and bedrooms furnished with cowhide upholstery and draped in hand-loomed fabrics. Moreover, each of the bedrooms comes with a private bath, a sitting area, and a terrace bedecked with garden furniture. The price for all this in a double is 8,500 pesetas ($76.50), 7,000 pesetas ($63) for single occupancy. To reach the parador, take the coast road, Paseo de Reding, which becomes Avenida Casa de Pries and finally Paseo de Sancha. Turn left onto Camino Nuevo and follow the small signs the rest of the way. Do not attempt to walk down to the heart of Málaga, however. It's not safe: many readers have been mugged. (*Note:* Book well in advance for all paradores.)

The **Parador Nacional del Golf,** Torremolinos, 29000 Apartado 324 Málaga (tel. 38-12-55), is another tasteful resort hotel created by the Spanish government. Surrounded by an 18-hole

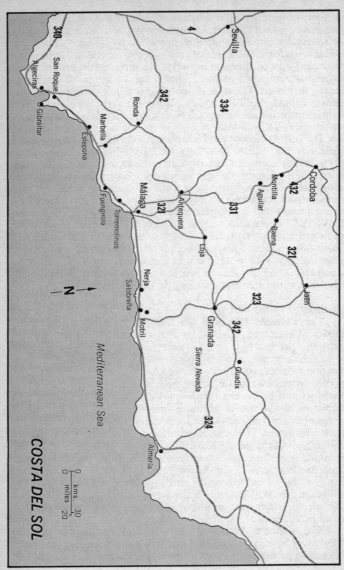

golf course on one side, the Mediterranean on another, it is arranged hacienda style, with several low, tile buildings. You're greeted by chirping birds and grounds planted with flowers. Here, too, all bedrooms have a private balcony, with a view of the green, the circular swimming pool, or the water. The furnishings are attractive. There are no single rooms, but you can rent doubles and twin-bedded rooms costing 8,000 pesetas ($72) to 10,000 pesetas ($90), depending on the season. Long tile corridors lead to the public rooms (air-conditioned, unlike the bedrooms); graciously furnished lounges, and a bar and restaurant. The parador is less than 2 miles from the airport, 6½ miles from Málaga, and 2½ miles from Torremolinos.

The **Las Vegas,** 28 Paseo de Sancha, 29016 Málaga (tel. 21-77-12), is in an eastern residential zone of Málaga, about ten minutes from the center of town. Its newness has long ago worn off, but it remains well kept and comfortable. The décor, not exactly stylish, combines traditional with contemporary pieces. Still, each of the spacious bedrooms has a private bath, piped-in music, phone, and central heating, and the rear rooms, with picture windows and private balconies, have a nice view of the swimming pool, garden, and sea. A double costs 5,500 pesetas ($49.50); a single 3,600 pesetas ($32.50). In the dining "room-with-a-view" (Spanish and French cuisine), a complete meal goes for an additional 1,800 pesetas ($16.25). Two American bars, one with a copper hood over its hearth, offer—you guessed it—good views.

NERJA

In 1959 five young men put Nerja on the map. At a point some 32 miles east of Málaga, near the hamlet of Maro, they discovered one of the great **prehistoric caves** of Europe. Nicknamed "the buried cathedral," the cave, about 350 yards long, is a series of intertwining galleries and passageways, reaching its highest point—about 200 feet—in what is called the Cataclysm Hall.

Paleolithic paintings of goats, deer, and horses were discovered here, as was a skeleton of a Cro-Magnon man. Rich in stalagmites and stalactites, the caves are open from 10 a.m. to 1:30 p.m. and 4 to 7 p.m. daily in winter. Summer hours are 9:30 a.m. to 9 p.m. Admission is 150 pesetas ($1.35). In August, music festivals are presented in the Hall of the Cascade, its floor the bottom of an ancient lake.

Before the discovery of the caves, the sleepy village of Nerja was known for its fabulous belvedere, the **Balcony of Europe,** commanding one of the most spectacular positions along the Costa del Sol. Nerja, perched on a cliff on the slopes of the Sierra Almijara, is a town of narrow streets and whitewashed houses. Below are plenty of hidden coves for swimming.

Nerja's **telephone area code** is 952.

MEDIUM-PRICED HOTELS: Outside of town, the **Parador Nacional de Nerja,** Playa de Burriana, 29780 Nerja (tel. 52-00-50), takes the best of modern motel designs and blends them with a classic Spanish ambience of beamed ceilings, tile floors, and hand-loomed draperies. It's built around a flower-filled courtyard with a splashing fountain. On the edge of a cliff, this government-owned hotel stands in a setting of lawns and gardens, its social life centering around a large swimming pool. There is, as well, a sandy beach below, reached by an elevator. The air-conditioned bedrooms are spacious and furnished in an understated but tasteful style. Maximum rates are charged from March 1 to October 31 and at the end of December: twin-bedded rooms with bath go for 9,500 pesetas ($85.50), and singles for 8,000 pesetas ($72).

The **Hotel Monica Playa,** Playa de la Torrecilla, 29780 Nerja (tel. 52-11-00), looks something like a three-pronged propeller if you view it from the air. At ground level as you approach the entrance, you see that it has North African arches and green-and-white panels. This is the newest and the most luxurious hotel in Nerja. You'll find this four-star establishment in an isolated position about a ten-minute walk from the Balcony of Europe, on a low-lying curve of beachfront. The glistening white marble in its imaginative lobby is highlighted with such neo-baroque touches as elaborately detailed cast-iron balustrades, gracefully curved marble staircases, and bas-reliefs, paintings, and sculptures. Some of the stairwells even contain oversize copies, set in tiles, of the beach scenes of Claude Monet. A nautical theme is carried out in the bar with brass navigational instruments, models of clipper ships, and comfortable sofas. Both of the hotel's restaurants have outdoor terraces or patios for indoor/outdoor dining. A gracefully curved swimming pool was built into a terrace a few feet above the beach.

The 234 comfortable bedrooms offer private balconies and numerous other amenities. In high season, doubles rent for 10,000 pesetas ($90), and singles go for 6,500 pesetas ($58.50). Fixed-price lunches and dinners cost 2,500 pesetas ($22.50).

AN INEXPENSIVE HOTEL: Comfortable accommodations at the **Hostal Fontainebleau,** Calle Alejandro Bueno, 29780 Nerja (tel. 52-09-29), are provided by three young people from England, sister and brother Kerry and Neil Anderson and Tania Boon, along with a Welsh partner, Leigh Anderson. All of them are in their early 20s, and they operate the hostal with a family atmosphere. Each of the 22 pleasantly furnished rooms has a bath with shower, wall-to-wall carpeting, local and Gibraltar radio, and tea- and coffee-making facilities.

Singles cost 2,900 pesetas ($26), doubles or twins run 3,900 pesetas ($35), and some family rooms suitable for three people are available for 4,900 pesetas ($44). All rooms open onto an attractive fountain patio. You can order a continental breakfast served on the patio, weather permitting, or have a cooked breakfast in the restaurant. The hostal has a clients' telephone booth for metered calls worldwide, plus laundry, drying, and ironing facilities, and a foreign-currency-exchange desk open seven days a week. You can watch satellite TV in the cozy lounge.

You can have drinks on the rooftop lounging terrace from May to October and in the Fountain Bar, resembling a British pub and selling pub food and snacks, any time. From the pub, you enter the Beefeater Steak Bar, which features English home-style cooking. A three-course table d'hôte daily menu costs 975 pesetas ($8.75), including bread and wine.

The hostal is about a ten-minute walk from the main beach, Playa Burriana, and a five-minute walk from the center of town. It's open all year except the first three weeks of December.

TORREMOLINOS

On a rocky promontory in the heart of the Costa del Sol, this resort dominates a magnificent bay at the foot of the Sierra Mijas. The around-the-clock international tourist center achieved such prominence because of its five-mile-long beach, one of the finest along the Mediterranean.

If you get up at daybreak and go to the beach, you'll see the fishermen bringing in their nets. But by 10 o'clock the sun worshippers have taken over. Many never leave the beach all day, depending on vendors who come around selling snacks and drinks. The once-sleepy fishing village pulsates with life in its high-rise apartments, hotels of every hue, discos, flamenco clubs, wine *bodegas,* boutiques, restaurants, and bars, bars, and more bars—some with such unlikely names as "Fat Black Pussycat."

The original village runs along **Calle de San Miguel,** still distinctively Andalusian despite its boutiques and restaurants. Reached past a zigzag of buildings leading down to the beach, **La Carihuela** was the old fishermen's village—it still is, if you ignore the hotels and apartments. Opposite is **Montemar,** a smart residential quarter of villas and gardens. For a slice of old Andalusia, see the **El Calvario** area, with its whitewashed houses, donkeys, and street vendors.

In the evening the sidewalk café life flourishes. Tanned blondes get inspected by retired English colonels in baggy pants—a happy melting pot of Europe (and now North America). You can spend an entire evening along the traffic-free **Calle del Cauce,** with its open-air restaurants and bars (sample before-dinner *tapas,* Spanish hors d'oeuvres, here).

If you want to do some shopping, you won't be disappointed: the best stores of Barcelona and Madrid operate branches in Torremolinos.

To sum up, the town has been called "Andalusian Miamic"— and that should give you some idea of what to expect.

The **telephone area code** for Torremolinos is 952.

HOTELS IN THE UPPER BRACKET: Considered the best ho-
tel in town, the **Castillo de Santa Clara,** 1 Calle Suecia, 29620 Torremolinos (tel. 38-31-55), is an angular modern palace built in 1975 above the cliffs that separate Torremolinos from its satellite village of La Carihuela. It was designed so that about half of the 288 accommodations lie below the terraced gardens. Into these gardens were sunk a pair of curvaceous swimming pools, whose waters are shaded with exotic cacti, lush palms, and well-maintained flowerbeds.

The public rooms are sheathed almost entirely in russet-colored marble, the expanses of which are relieved with sculpted terracotta bas-reliefs, scattered copies of Chippendale antiques, and nautical accessories. The bar area contains photos of award-winning sailboats, navigational accessories, and tortoise-shell trim. On the premises are a sauna, a gymnasium, a nightclub, a tennis court, and an elevator that takes you down the cliffs to the beach.

Each bedroom is air-conditioned and has a private bath and a wood-trimmed balcony. Single rooms rent for 10,500 pesetas ($94.50); doubles, 13,000 pesetas ($117).

The **Don Pablo,** Paseo Marítimo, 29620 Torremolinos (tel. 38-38-88), is one of the most desirable hotels in Torremolinos. It's a super-modern building, a minute from the beach, surrounded by its own garden and playground areas. There are two unusually shaped open-air swimming pools, with terraces for sunbathing and refreshments, and a large indoor pool as well. The surprise is the glamorous interior which borrows heavily from Moorish palaces and medieval castle themes. Arched tile arcades have splashing fountains, and life-size stone statues of nude figures in niches line the grand staircase. Several of the lounges have wooden paneled and painted ceilings. Other rooms have tufted leather sofas set around Oriental rugs. At lunch a help-yourself buffet is spread before you. The 443 bedrooms have air conditioning, phones, hi-fi channels, and sea-view terraces. Facilities include a tennis center with seven courts, floodlights, and top coaching. The hotel has a full day-and-night entertainment program, including keep-fit classes, dancing at night to a live band, and a disco, The Caprice. Piano music is also played in a wood-paneled English lounge, and the hotel has video movies shown on a giant screen every night. Highest tariffs are in effect from mid-July to mid-September. At that time most clients book in here on the half-board plan, paying from 6,750 pesetas ($60.75) per person in a double and from 8,250 pesetas ($74.25) in a single.

The **Cervantes,** Calle de las Mercedes, 29620 Torremolinos (tel. 38-40-33), is a four-star hotel a short walk from the beach. It has its own garden and swimming pool (and yet another pool on the roof). The hotel is adjacent to a maze of patios and narrow streets of boutiques and open-air cafés. The Cervantes is self-contained, with many facilities, including a sun terrace, sauna, massage, the two pools (one covered and heated), hairdressers, a gift shop, a garden, a TV and video lounge, games such as billiards, table tennis, darts, and American bowling, and a card room. A restaurant, a bar with an orchestra and entertainment programs, and a coffeeshop are among the attractions. The hotel is fully air-conditioned. The bedrooms have streamlined modern furniture, many with sea-view balconies. All the units have complete baths, phones, music, safes, TVs (on request), and spacious terraces. Singles rent for 6,490 pesetas ($58.50); doubles, for 10,130 pesetas ($91). You can enjoy lunch or dinner at the hotel for 1,750 pesetas ($15.75) and up. Los Molinos Grill on the top floor offers excellent grill meals.

The **Aloha Puerto Sol,** 44 Vía Imperial, 29620 Torremolinos (tel. 38-70-66), stands on the seashore in the residential area of El Saltillo. Away from the noise in the center of Torremolinos, it offers spacious rooms facing the sea and beach, protected by the Benalmádena Marina. One of the most modern hotels along the Costa del Sol, it contains 418 suites, each with a sitting room, a bar, and a terrace overlooking the sea. Air conditioning, radios, and phones are provided. Two people are charged 7,000 pesetas ($63) to 9,200 pesetas ($82.75). In this resort setting, guests are given a choice of two restaurants and four bars. During the day you can lounge around two swimming pools, one heated. Spanish evenings at El Bodegón, one of the bars on the premises, last well into the early morning.

BUDGET HOTELS: Near the coastal road, **Las Palomas,** 1 Carmen Montes, 29620 Torremolinos (tel. 38-50-00), is one of the most striking and attractive of the resort hotels built on the Málaga edge of Torremolinos. It has a formal entrance opening into spacious lounges. Tile corridors lead to dining rooms and cocktail lounges. Public rooms often utilize ceramic collections, stone sculpture, large urns, and stylized murals in the décor. Equally stylish are the all-white bedrooms, each with balcony and private bath. You pay 5,500 pesetas ($49.50) in a single room, 7,760 pesetas ($70) in a double. Lunch or dinner costs an extra 1,750 pesetas ($15.75). The hotel has dancing every night to records, and a tennis court, two pools (one heated), plus a sauna.

The **Miami,** 10 Calle Aladino, 29620 Torremolinos (tel. 38-52-55), near the Carihuela section, is like one of those houses movie stars used to erect in the '20s. It may even bring back memories of Vilma Banky and Rod La Rocque. Its swimming pool is isolated by high walls and private gardens. In the rear patio fuchsia bougainvillea climbs over arches. A tile terrace is used for sunbathing and refreshments. The country-style living room contains a walk-in fireplace, plus lots of brass and copper. In high season, doubles rent for 4,000 pesetas ($36); singles, for 2,500 pesetas ($22.50). The bedrooms are furnished with style, each traditional, each providing comfort. Every accommodation has its own balcony and private bath. Breakfast is the only meal served.

The **Amaragua,** Los Nidos, 29620 Torremolinos (tel. 38-47-00), is right on the beach in the middle of the residential area of Torremolinos-Montemar, with a total of 198 rooms (12 of which are suites), all with complete bath, terrace, and sea view. The hotel has lounges, television, a bar, three large swimming pools (one heated), gardens, water sports, a children's playground, a sauna, parking facilities, and a tennis court. In a double with private bath, the rate is 5,700 pesetas ($51.25), 3,800 pesetas ($34.25) in a single with shower bath.

BENALMÁDENA

Where Torremolinos ends and Benalmádena begins is hard to say. Benalmádena has long since become a resort extension of Torremolinos, and it's packed with hotels, restaurants, and tourist facilities.

The Benalmádena **telephone area code** is 952.

AN UPPER-BRACKET HOTEL: Less than two miles from Torremolinos, the **Tritón,** 29 Avenida António Machado, 29491 Benalmádena-Costa (tel. 44-32-40), is a seafront Miami Beach–style resort hotel colony in front of the marina of Benalmádena-Costa. It not only features a high-rise stack of air-conditioned bedrooms, but has the most impressive pool and garden area in the vicinity.

Surrounding the swimming pool are subtropical trees and vegetation, plus thatched sun-shade umbrellas. The 200 air-conditioned bedrooms have room-wide windows opening onto sun balconies, and each has a private bath. With breakfast, singles cost 10,800 pesetas ($97); doubles, 15,100 pesetas ($136). Half board is an additional 3,550 pesetas ($32) per person daily.

Among the public rooms are multilevel lounges and two bars with wood paneling and handmade rustic furniture (one has impressive stained-glass windows). For food, there's the main dining room with its three-tiered, mouthwatering display of hors d'oeuvres, fruits, and desserts; a barbecue grill; plus a luncheon terrace where ferns and banana trees form the backdrop. Not enough for you? Well, how about tennis courts, a Swedish sauna, even a piano player in the bar?

FUENGIROLA

This will be the Torremolinos of the future. It is already a formidable challenger. About ten miles to the west of its rival, Fuengirola and its adjacent resort village of Los Boliches are already deep into their development. Good sandy beaches against a hilly backdrop of pine woods couldn't escape attention for long—and didn't. Crowning the town are the ruins of the 10th-century **Sohail Castle,** built by the Caliphs of Córdoba and later rebuilt by Charles V as a defense against Berber pirates.

Fuengirola's **telephone area code** is 952.

FOOD AND LODGING: A luxurious new resort, the **Byblos Andaluz,** Urbanización Mijas Golf, 29640 Fuengirola (tel. 47-30-50), is a hotel and health spa with lavish rooms, in a magnificent setting. The grounds contain shrubbery, a white minaret, Moorish arches, tile-adorned walls, and an orange-tree patio inspired by the Alhambra grounds, 97 miles away. Two 18-hole golf courses designed by Robert Trent Jones (with a third to be completed soon), tennis courts, spa facilities, a gymnasium, and swimming pools bask in the Andalusian sunshine. The spa is a handsome classic structure, Mijas Thalasso Palace.

The 135 rooms and suites are elegantly and individually designed and furnished, in the Roman, Arabic, Andalusian, and rustic styles. Private sun terraces and lavish bathrooms add to the comfort. Singles cost 26,000 pesetas ($234); doubles, 35,000 pesetas ($315). Full board is offered at 25,000 pesetas ($225) to 38,000 pesetas ($342) per person daily.

The hotel has a restaurant, El Andaluz, serving low-calorie menus as well as regional cuisine, and Le Nailhac Restaurant featuring gourmet cuisine created from local products. If you're just visiting, dinners cost from 5,000 pesetas ($45). Terrace dining is available in both restaurants, and the San Tropez Bar, opening onto a poolside terrace, has music nightly, with flamenco dancers, singers, and musicians presenting programs weekly. The Byblos Andaluz is about ten minutes away from Fuengirola and the Mediterranean.

Las Pirámides, Paseo Marítimo, 29640 Fuengirola (tel. 47-06-00), is a complex under pyramidal roofs favored by travel groups from the north of Europe. It's a city-like resort on the beach, with seemingly every kind of divertissement: flamenco shows on the large patio, a cozy bar and lounge, traditionally furnished sitting rooms, a Belle Époque coffeeshop, a poolside bar, and a gallery of boutiques and tourist facilities, such as car-rental agencies. All bedrooms are air-conditioned, with slick modern styling, as well as private bath and terrace. Singles pay 7,500 pesetas ($67.50); doubles, 9,600 pesetas ($86.50).

MIJAS

It's called "White Mijas" because of its bone-white Andalusian houses. Just five miles from Fuengirola above the Costa del Sol, the village is a gem, standing at the foot of a sierra. From its lofty perches 1,400 feet above sea level, a panoramic vista of the Mediterranean unfolds. Along its narrow, cobblestone streets have walked Celts, Phoenicians, and Moors. You'll do better hiring a "burro-taxi." In a park at the top of Cuesta de la Villa, you see remnants of a Moorish citadel dating from 833. Shops threaten to inundate the village, selling everything from original art to olive-wood jewelry. Incidentally, Mijas possesses the only square bullring in Spain.

The **telephone area code** for Mijas is 952.

WHERE TO STAY: The only hotel in town of any significance is the **Hotel Mijas,** Urbanazción Jamisa, Carretera Benalmádena, 29650 Mijas (tel. 48-58-00). This is one of the special hotels along the coast, with a view of the sea and surrounding mountains. Designed hacienda style, it is perched on the side of a hill, with a semi-enclosed flower patio, a terrace with white wicker furniture and a view, a swimming pool, a tennis court, and a lounge that's Castilian in décor. The Andalusian drinking tavern is pleasant, with large kegs of wine. The living room is furnished with fine antiques and inlaid chests, even a framed fan collection. All the excellently furnished bedrooms contain a private tile bath and a small refrigerator. Doubles rent for 12,500 pesetas ($112.50) to 14,000 pesetas ($126); singles, 9,000 pesetas ($81). Other facilities include a sauna, gymnasium, and beauty parlor. Barbecues are held in the open air. Entertainment is provided (in season) in the evening, and during the day guests can play at the 18-hole Mijas golf course.

MARBELLA

In the shadow of what was once an Arab fortress, Marbella is definitely chic, attracting a fashionable crowd of movie people and socialites—and "ordinary" people. Many mansions and villas are found hereabouts.

About halfway between Málaga (37 miles to the east) and Gibraltar, Marbella is at the foot of the Sierra Blanca, which keeps the climate mild. Its best beaches are the 600-yard-long Fuerta and the 800-yard-long Fontanilla. Sports, such as waterskiing, shark-fishing, and tennis, are popular. The even more athletically inclined dance till dawn.

At some point, take a walk in the old part of town, still partially enclosed by walls. The whitewashed houses, studded with potted flowers, along narrow streets make for pleasant strolling. Then stop off at a café on the Plaza de los Naranjos (oranges) for a drink.

Marbella's **telephone area code** is 952.

WHERE TO STAY: Since the setting is so ideal—pure Mediterranean sun, sea, and sky, plus the scent of Andalusian orange blossoms in the air—some of the best hotels along the Costa del Sol are found in Marbella. I'll start with:

The Luxury Resort Hotels

Los Monteros, Carretera de Cádiz, km 187, 29600 Marbella (tel. 77-17-00), is one of the most tasteful and imaginative resort complexes along the Costa del Sol. Between the coastal road and its own private beach, it attracts those seeking intimacy and luxury. No cavernous lounges here; instead, many small, tasteful rooms, Andalusian/Japanese in concept. You'll find various salons with open fireplaces, a library, a bar, terraces, and four restaurants on different levels, opening onto flower-filled patios, gardens, and fountains.

The bedrooms are brightly decorated, with lightly colored lacquered furniture, air conditioning, private baths, and terraces. One is a duplex design with a stairway between the sitting room and bedroom. Half-board rates, in effect from July to the end of October, are 40,000 pesetas ($360) for two people, 23,750 pesetas ($214) in a single. Free to guests of the hotel is the nearby 18-hole golf course, Río Real. Other facilities include several swimming pools, plus a beach club, La Cabane (which has an indoor heated pool), ten tennis courts, five squash courts, a riding club and school, plus a fully equipped gymnasium with a sauna, massage, and a Jacuzzi.

Within the precincts, Grill El Corzo is one of the finest grill rooms along the coast. The grill, done up in Toledo red, is on the first floor. Wall-size scenic murals are in the background, and tables are bedecked with bright cloths and silver candlesticks. Soft, romantic music is played nightly. Meals cost from 6,000 pesetas ($54). The cuisine is a pleasing combination of French and Spanish.

The **Hotel Don Carlos,** Jardines de las Golondrinas, Carretera de Málaga, 29600 Marbella (tel. 83-11-40), one of the most dramatically alluring hotels along the coastline, rises on a set of angled stilts above a forest of pines. Between it and its manicured beach, considered the best in Marbella, are 130 acres of award-winning gardens replete with cascades of water, a full-time staff of 22 gardeners, and thousands of subtropical plants. There's far more to this hotel owned by Hotels Coach than the ultramodern tower that rises conspicuously above the eastern edge of Marbella. Its low-lying terraces and elegant eating and drinking facilities attract high-powered conferences from throughout Europe, as well as individual nonresident diners from along the Mediterranean coast.

You can dine amid splashes of bougainvillea beside an oversize swimming pool bordered with begonias and geraniums or in La Pergola, where ficus and potted palms decorate the hundreds of glistening lattices. The most sophisticated hideaway of all, Los Naranjos, has a sun-flooded atrium with exotic mosses and a quartet of orange trees. A grand piano on the marble dais provides pleasantly diverting music. Fixed-price meals here go for a reasonable 4,000 pesetas ($36) each. Meals in the other restaurants, including grills or elaborate buffets in the semi-outdoor beachfront cabaña, cost about half as much.

Among the bars scattered around the various terraces and marble-lined hideaways of the public rooms, the most popular offers an English-inspired décor of exposed hardwoods, a panoramic view of the sea, plenty of intimate sofas, a dance floor, and a well-rehearsed musical trio. After the show, residents can return to their air-conditioned bedrooms to watch one of ten European or North American TV stations clearly received via satellite.

Each air-conditioned accommodation has its own panoramic balcony, lacquered furniture, a private bath done in honey-colored marble, a phone, and a radio. Single rooms rent for 20,000 pesetas ($180), and doubles go for 25,000 pesetas ($225). The lush golf course, the saunas, the gym, and a dozen tennis courts are free for the use of hotel guests. A complete selection of water sports, plus horseback riding, is available at an extra charge to guests.

The **Hotel Puente Romano,** 2½ miles west of Marbella on Carretera de Cádiz, 29600 Marbella (tel. 77-01-00), was originally built as a cluster of vacation apartments, a fact which influenced the careful attention to detail and the lavish landscaping that surrounds it. In the early 1970s a group of entrepreneurs transformed it into one of the most unusual hotels in the south of Spain, sitting close to the frenetic coastal highway, midway between Marbella and Puerto Banús.

Once inside the complex, guests can wander happily through a maze of arbor-covered walkways. Along the route, they pass cascades of water, masses of vines, and a subtropical paradise. Nestled amid the carefully organized lushness are plushly upholstered indoor/outdoor bars and restaurants. Three of these overlook a terracotta patio, bordered at one end by the weathered stones of a reconstructed Roman bridge, the only one of its kind in southern Spain. The edges of a free-form swimming pool are bordered by trees and vines and a drain-away waterfall, making it look something like a Tahitian lagoon.

The arrangement of the 200 Moorish-style accommodations is a mini-study in urban planning. A decorator's dream of shiny fabrics, glossy accessories, and unusual furniture make all the units memorable and comfortable. Each of the air-conditioned units has a semi-sheltered balcony festooned with flowers, color TV, direct-dial phone, mini-bar, and an electronic safe. Depending on the season and the accommodation, singles cost 15,200 pesetas ($137) to 22,400 pesetas ($202), and doubles go for 19,000 pesetas ($171) to 28,000 pesetas ($252). Half board is an extra 6,300 pesetas ($56.75) per person per day.

If you're wondering who your fellow guests might be, the King of Spain, Barbra Streisand, Björn Borg, Stevie Wonder, Julio Iglesias, the Kennedys, and the President of Ireland have all enjoyed the pleasures of this establishment. Not the least of these are a sandy beach with an array of water sports, tennis courts, a glistening nightclub, and a cluster of chic boutiques.

The **Meliá Don Pepe,** Finca Las Merinas, 29600 Marbella (tel. 77-03-00), is impressive, occupying six acres of tropical gardens and lawns between the coastal road and the sea. Fully air-conditioned, its 218 lavishly furnished bedrooms, with private baths and wall-to-wall carpeting, face either the sea or the Sierra Blanca mountains. In high season, a single rents for 15,500 pesetas ($139.50), and a double goes for 25,000 pesetas ($225). Full board begins at 21,000 pesetas ($189) per person. The facilities are so vast you could spend a week here and not use them all. They include three swimming pools, tennis courts, a Swedish sauna, a collection of boutiques, even a bridge clubroom, along with lounges, bars, and restaurants. La Farola grill provides an international à la carte cuisine, with meals costing from 4,500 pesetas ($40.50). Other facilities include a yacht harbor along the beach and a golf course.

The **Marbella Club,** Carretera de Cádiz, km 178, 29600 Marbella (tel. 77-13-00), is a deluxe hotel with private beach club on the road from Marbella to Gibraltar. Begun in 1953 by Prince Alfonso von Hohenlohe, the hotel has grown into a luxurious holiday resort favored by people with taste from all over the world. It's a place of peace and quiet for guests seeking relaxation at the edge of the sea and for nature lovers. The 12 bungalows, between the beach and the organically structured green spaces, seem to be set in a park. The bungalows contain two or three bedrooms with living rooms, private gardens, and swimming pools. Other accommodations consist of 48 double rooms and 22 suites. All units have baths, phones, music, and mini-bars. The charge for single occupancy is 21,000 pesetas ($189); for two people, 26,000 pesetas ($234).

The club's gourmet restaurant serves international cuisine, the chef offering skillfully prepared fish dishes and soufflés. A breakfast buffet is served on the hotel patio, and lunch can be taken in the garden restaurant or at the Beach Club. The Beach Club is also the scene of after-dinner dancing. Daytime activities are windsurfing, waterskiing, boat trips, paddle tennis, and swimming in the pools or at the beach.

The **Andalucía Plaza,** Urbanización Nueva Andalucía, 29660 Apartado 21 Nueva Andalucia Marbella (tel. 81-20-40), is a resort complex on a grand scale. On the mountain side of the coastal road between Marbella and Torremolinos, twin buildings are linked by a reception lounge and formal gardens. On the sea side is the hotel's beach club. Far more than a 300-foot strip of sand, it has sunbathing terraces, a sauna, gymnasium, open-air swimming pool, even an enclosed all-weather pool. And there's a 1,000-yacht marina, where you can rent one of the vessels and go deep-sea fishing. The public rooms in the hotel buildings are spacious and lavishly decorated. Equally luxurious are the 418 air-conditioned bedrooms furnished in the classic Andalusian manner, utilizing reproductions. Lone travelers pay 10,000 pesetas ($90); two people, 13,000 pesetas ($117).

The Middle Bracket

The **Hotel El Fuerte,** Castillo de San Luís, 29600 Marbella (tel. 77-15-00), is the most recommendable hotel in the center of Marbella. With a balconied and angular façade, it's right on the waterfront, its palm-fringed swimming pools set across the street from a sheltered lagoon and wide-open beach. A handful of terraces, some shaded by flowering arbors, provide hideaways for quiet drinks. A restaurant with a panoramic water view and a bar are part of the facilities. The 262 comfortable, contemporary bedrooms all contain baths, mini-bars, TVs, piped-in music, and air conditioning, with terraces and sea views. Singles rent for 10,000 pesetas ($90); doubles, for 11,000 pesetas ($99). The hotel has a coffeeshop, two restaurants, and two bars. Leisure activities include two swimming pools, a floodlit tennis court, mini-golf, and a squash court.

The **Estrella del Mar,** Carretera de Cádiz, km 197, 29600 Marbella (tel. 83-03-63), is a tasteful resort hotel between Marbella and Torremolinos, with its own seafront swimming pool and sandy beach. The bedrooms of the Estrella del Mar, attractively furnished, have pleasant, flower-filled balconies. A single rents for 5,000 pesetas ($45); a double, for 7,800 pesetas ($70.25). For a room and full board, the charge is 8,800 pesetas ($79.25) per person. The main lounge, with its reproductions of Castilian antiques, is two stories high. Meals are taken in the informal dining room in the main building. You can try a dish created in the hotel. Called fondue Marbella, it features an assortment of Mediterranean fish served with sauces ranging from tartar to curry. The hotel is open only from March to November.

The **Marbella-Dinamar,** Nueva Andalucía, Carretera de Cádiz, km 175, outside Marbella, 29660 Puerto Banús (78-05-00), is an exotic resort oasis, right on the seafront. The architecture and décor are Moorish-inspired, with stark-white walls and arches. At the rear, the lounges, facing the sea, have a light, airy mood. The patio, adjoining the bar, is tropical Victorian, with ornate white wicker armchairs. The large swimming pool is oddly shaped and surrounded by a tile terrace, lawns, and palm trees. The bedrooms, conventionally furnished, contain all the modern necessities, including radio, phone, private bath, and air conditioning. Most of them open onto a sea view. Peak-season rates are charged from July 1 to September 30: 10,000 pesetas ($90) in a single, 13,000 pesetas ($117) in a twin-bedded room. Another facility is a heated and covered swimming pool directly connected to the main building. The tennis courts are floodlit at night, and nearby is one of the best all-around golf courses along the Costa del Sol.

The **Hotel Guadalpín,** Carretera 340 Cádiz-Málaga, km 186, 29600 Marbella (tel. 77-11-00), is right on the rugged coast, only 300 yards from the beach (a mile from the center of Marbella). You can live at this three-star hotel for 7,500 pesetas ($67.50) in a double room with private bath. For a single with a full bath the rate is 5,500 pesetas ($49.50), but only ten rooms are available in this category.

Guests spend many hours relaxing around two swimming pools, or they walk along a private pathway lined with fir trees to the Mediterranean. The dining room has large windows overlooking the patio and pool, and the main lounge has been designed in a ranch style with round marble tables and occasional leather armchairs arranged for conversational groups. The bar area of the spacious lounge is brick and natural wood, making it warm and attractive. Each room has not only two terraces, but a living room and bedroom combined. Most of the rooms are furnished in "new ranch" style. They have all the conveniences, such as telephones and central heating during the cooler months.

SAN PEDRO DE ALCÁNTARA

In a little resort suburb west of Marbella are found some of the most tranquil oases along the Costa del Sol. The Golf Hotel Guadalmina is moderately priced, the others falling into the budget categories, although they are definitely not second-rate.

The San Pedro de Alcántara **telephone area code** is 952.

The **Golf Hotel Guadalmina,** Hacienda Guadalmina, 29670 San Pedro de Alcántara (tel. 78-14-00), is a large country club–type resort, where the first tee and 18th green are both right next to the hotel. A friendly, informal place, it is really a private world on the shores of the Mediterranean. You reach it by a long driveway from the coastal road. Three seawater swimming pools (one heated for children) attract those seeking the lazy life; the tennis courts appeal to the athletic. The bedrooms—most of them opening onto the pool recreation area and the sea—are attractive in their traditional Spanish style. A single rents for 9,500 pesetas ($85.50); a double, for 12,000 pesetas ($108). Full board is 12,500 pesetas ($112.50) to 16,000 pesetas ($144) per person daily.

Tasty meals are served in the main dining room as well as in the woody grill, where a pianist plays nightly. The golf course is open to residents and nonresidents alike. The hotel offers two excellent dining choices, one a luncheon-only, reed-covered poolside terrace overlooking the golf course and the sea, the other an interior room in the main building, with a sedate clubhouse aura. Informality and good food reign. The set luncheon or dinner is priced at 3,500 pesetas ($31.50).

The **Pueblo Andaluz,** Carretera de Cádiz, km 172, 29670 San Pedro de Alcántara (tel. 78-05-97), is a self-contained resort, built Andalusian village style, with many patios and gardens lined with flowering trees and shrubbery. It's right on the coastal road, five miles from Marbella and a five-minute walk to the beach. Guests congregate in the tile bar and lounge, furnished with antiques, or else on the grassy lawn with its swimming pool. Families with children are welcomed, and there's a special paddling pool and playground. Bedrooms are consistently decorated in the Spanish style, a single costing 4,300 pesetas ($38.75); a double, 5,100 pesetas ($46). The regional dining room is built like a hacienda. The hotel is open from April 1 to October 31.

The **Cortijo Blanco,** Carretera de Cádiz, km 172, 29670 San Pedro de Alcántara (tel. 78-09-00), is a self-contained little world of whitewashed walls, tile roofs, fountains, courtyards, bell towers, wrought-iron balconies, and a maze of cottages linked by dozens of patios filled with tall subtropical vines and vegetation. All 162 bedrooms face the main garden, dominated by a good-sized swimming pool. Rates vary according to season, the highest prices in effect from mid-July to mid-September, at which time half board costs 6,650 pesetas ($59.75) in singles, 11,300 pesetas ($101.75) in doubles. Evening meals are a gracious affair, as you sit in high-backed, carved red-and-gilt Valencian chairs; lunch is quite pleasant, served around the covered pergola with its luxuriant vegetation.

SOTOGRANDE

Sotogrande, a residential tourist development, sprawls across 4,400 acres—certainly the most luxurious resort along the whole of the Costa del Sol. Across from the Rock of Gibraltar, it represents elegant Andalusia at its best.

The area appeals to the well-heeled sportsperson, one who doesn't mind crossing an ocean and/or a continent to play the two Robert Trent Jones golf courses. (There's a nine-hole executive course for the less energetic.)

Sotogrande's **telephone area code** is 956.

This is a large complex, with many facilities, some of which are in the membership-only category. However, the **Hotel Sotogrande,** Carretera N. 340, km 131, 11310 Sotogrande (tel. 79-21-00), is open to the general public, containing 46 handsomely furnished double rooms and two luxurious suites. On the half-board plan, the rate in a double room is 20,000 pesetas ($180) to 32,000 pesetas ($288), from 12,000 pesetas ($108) to 18,000 pesetas ($162) in a single.

The Hotel Sotogrande serves breakfasts, full luncheons, and dinners. Light snacks and bar service are available at the hotel as well as at the Golf Hotel restaurant, Beach Club restaurant, and New Golf restaurant.

Next to the hotel, there are six tennis courts, a large swimming pool, a children's play area, and a hairdressing salon. Guests may also hire horses from nearby stables, and polo is enjoyed throughout the summer season by players and spectators alike on Sotogrande's two polo grounds.

WHERE TO DINE

Most visitors to the Costa del Sol eat at their hotels. In fact, in high season many establishments require guests to take at least half board (breakfast, plus one main meal). But, even so, there are many good and independent restaurants along the Sun Coast for those desiring to escape from their hotel dining rooms. I'll preview only a sampling of the many, many possibilities.

First, a word about the food specialties of the area. In this part of the Mediterranean, fish (such as whitebait), chopitos, and anchovies are the major part of the banquet. Particular specialties include fish soup (sopa de pescado), a fisherman's rice dish of crayfish and clams (arroz a la marinera), and grilled sardines (espetones de sardinas). In all of Andalusia, soothing gazpacho is a refreshing opener to many a meal. Of course, everything's better when washed down with the renowned wines of Málaga, including Pedro Ximénez and Muscatel.

MÁLAGA: A waterside restaurant, **Antonio Martín,** 4 Paseo Marítimo (tel. 22-21-13), does better with the skillets than any other restaurant in town. On the eastern edge, close to the bullring, it is favored by knowing Spanish families, local executives, and the expatriate colony. Antonio, who opened the place in 1886, is gone now, but his children have kept alive his traditions and his name. Three dining rooms are clustered under a peaked wooden ceiling with natural brick walls. The most rustic dining room is Rincón de Ordóñez, in honor of one of Spain's top matadors. On the wall is the head of the last bull Ordóñez killed before his retirement, as well as the suit last worn by him. In summer, the shaded harborfront terrace is the ideal place to dine. Shellfish soup is the traditional opener, or else you might prefer the special hors d'oeuvres. A paella of shellfish, chicken, and meat is the chef's specialty. Other specialties include sirloin steak on a skewer and golden mackerel in salt. I also recommend the grilled swordfish and the stewed oxtail. Custard with whipped cream is the standard dessert. For a good meal, expect to pay anywhere from 1,800 pesetas ($16.25) to 3,000 pesetas ($27). Service is rapid and attentive. It's usually crowded, so reservations are necessary. Hours are 1 to 4 p.m. and 8 p.m. to midnight. It is closed Sunday night.

The **Parador Nacional del Gibralfaro,** Monte Gibralfaro (tel. 22-19-02), is preferred for its view. Government-owned, it sits on a mountainside high above the city. You can look down into the heart of the Málaga bullring, among other things. Meals are served in the attractive dining room, with a ceramic plate collection, or under the arches of two wide terraces, providing views of the coast. Featured are hors d'oeuvres parador—your entire table literally covered with tiny dishes of tasty tidbits. Another specialty is an omelet of chanquetes, tiny whitefish popular in this part of the country, or chicken Villaroi. If you stick to the set menu, a complete dinner will cost from 2,500 pesetas ($22.50). Food is served from 1 to 4 p.m. and 8:30 to 11 p.m. daily.

Another government-owned restaurant is the **Parador Nacional del Golf,** Apartado 324, Málaga (tel. 38-12-55). Its indoor/outdoor dining room opens onto a circular swimming pool, golf course, and private beach. The interior dining room, furnished with reproductions of antiques, has a refined country-club atmosphere. Pre-lunch drinks at the sleek modern bar tempt golfers and others, who then proceed to the covered terrace for their meals, served from 1:30 to 4 p.m. and 8:30 to 11 p.m. daily. A set meal costs from 2,400 pesetas ($21.50).

NERJA: Outside of town, the **Parador Nacional de Nerja,** Playa de Burriana (tel. 52-00-50), is the ideal choice for many diners. The dining room opens onto views of the Mediterranean at the bottom of the cliff. Good food is served in the hacienda-style beamed dining room, with wide glass sliding doors. The price for a full lunch or dinner is 2,500 pesetas ($22.50). Before or after dinner, you can go for a swim.

TORREMOLINOS: Right in the heart of Torremolinos, **El Caballo Vasco,** Calle Casablanca, La Nogalera (tel. 38-23-36), is the best place to dine among the independent restaurants. It serves the deservedly popular Basque cuisine from the top floor of a modern building complex which is reached by an elevator. Picture windows lead to a terrace. As a prelude to your repast, you might try melon with ham or fish soup. Generous portions of tasty, well-prepared seafood are served, including prawns in garlic sauce and codfish Basque style. Also good, if you have the taste for it, is squid in its own ink, and the Basque-style hake is excellent. The meat dishes are of uniformly good quality, and you get some imaginative interpretations, not usually found on menus along the Costa del Sol—pork shanks Basque style and oxtail in a savory sauce. For timid diners, one of the safest bets is chicken in sherry sauce. It's also one of the least expensive main courses. A complete meal, served from 1 to 3:15 p.m. and 7:30 to 11:15 p.m. daily, will cost from 2,200 pesetas ($19.75) to 3,500 pesetas ($31.50).

Casa Prudencio, 41 Carmen (tel. 38-14-52), is the leading seafood restaurant on the beach at Carihuela. It packs in diners like sardines, but its devotees don't seem to mind the wait. The décor is rustic, with indoor dining service. However, in summer the favored place is a reed canopy–covered open-air terrace where you dine elbow to elbow. The owner orchestrates and choreographs the waiters to a fast and nervous pace. Service is haphazard, but friendly. For an appetizer, a soothing gazpacho is ideal. Most diners are fascinated by the specialty of the house, lubina a la sal (salted fish). Cooked in an oblong pan, the fish is completely covered with white salt, which is then scraped away in front of the diner anxious to get to the well-flavored, tender white flesh inside. Other main-course dishes include swordfish, shish kebab, and a special paella. For dessert, try the fresh strawberries. A typical à la carte meal is likely to cost from 2,200 pesetas ($19.75), while a special budget menu goes for only 1,000 pesetas ($9). The restaurant is open from 1 to 4 p.m. and 8 to 12:30 p.m. daily except Wednesday.

The **Hong Kong,** Calle del Cauce (tel. 38-41-29), is the only restaurant along the Costa del Sol serving an Indonesian rijsttafel (literally, a rice table). You're served a large bowl of rice with a selection of seven highly spiced side dishes. Among the Chinese dishes offered are hot spiced pork with vegetables and chop suey. If you order à la carte, count on spending from 2,000 pesetas ($18). The Oriental restaurant, open from 1 to 4 p.m. and 7 p.m. to midnight daily, is on a busy street of milling visitors, virtually an open-air dining room.

FUENGIROLA (LOS BOLICHES): Widely known for good

food, **Don Bigote** (Mr. Mustache), 39 Francisco Cano (tel. 47-50-94), was a deserted century-old sardine factory and a row of fishermen's cottages before its transformation into one of the most popular restaurants in the area. In summer, a splashing fountain in the garden patio makes the right background for the well-prepared international menu. In cooler weather you have a choice of dining in one of the attractively decorated dining rooms, each furnished in a regional style. You might enjoy a before-dinner drink under the rafters in the lounge bar. The chefs turn out a most recommendable Spanish and continental cuisine. Meals begin at 3,000 pesetas ($27). The place is open only for lunch in summer, from 1 to 4 p.m. Other times of year, dinner is served from 8 p.m. to 1 a.m. daily.

MIJAS: An interesting stop, the **Club el Padrastro,** Paseo del

Compás (tel. 48-50-00), is aptly named. In Spanish *padrastro* is a curious word, meaning both "stepfather" and "hangnail." However, it also suggests height, a commanding position. You'll agree after climbing the 77 steps to reach it, although it's more sensible to take the elevator at the town parking lot. After you've scaled the heights, a swimming pool and an artfully decorated restaurant await you. Before dinner, take a drink under pine trees by the pool, enjoying the view. Inside, ten picture windows on two levels also open onto the panorama, and soft music helps too. The food is quite good. For openers, why not the pâté? Specialties include fish soup Padrastro, bass with fennel, and a special flambé Padrastro. The tab here is likely to run 2,200 pesetas ($19.75) to 3,300 pesetas ($29.75), although special budget meals are offered for 950 pesetas ($8.50) and 1,350 pesetas ($12.25). Hours are noon to 11 p.m. daily.

MARBELLA: A favorite place, the **Restaurante La Meridiana,** Camino de la Cruz, at Las Lomas (tel. 77-61-90), is inland from the coastal highway across from the Puente Romano complex. Here Italian-born Paolo Ghirelli has established a restaurant that has become famous for its cuisine, its service, and its intimate ambience. You enter through a tropical garden to reach the large restaurant, where you'll be seated in one of the elegant dining areas and greeted with a complimentary fish pâté and fresh bread. The dishes come from the kitchen temptingly presented, with colorful accompaniments, turning them into small works of art—some à la nouvelle cuisine, others from the chef's special repertoire—all aimed at pleasing the eye as well as the palate.

You can choose from a menu which offers many fish, game, beef, pork, and lamb courses, including hare stuffed with duck liver, raisins, and Málaga wine; filet of dorado with purée of green and red peppers; medallions of lobster Florentine with béarnaise sauce; partridge sausages with chestnut purée; and wild duck with shallots. For dessert, I suggest the capricho Meridiana, which varies through the "caprice" of the chef but is sure to have fine and fresh ingredients such as fruit of the season. Expect to pay from 5,000 pesetas ($45) per person.

Don't worry about your car: The restaurant has valet parking. It's open from 1:30 to 3:30 p.m. and 8:30 p.m. to midnight daily.

La Hacienda, Urbanización Hacienda Las Chapas, Carretera de Cádiz, km 193 (tel. 83-12-67), is a tranquil choice, enjoying a reputation for serving some of the best food along the Costa del Sol. In cooler months you can dine inside in the rustic tavern before an open fireplace. However, in fair weather meals are al fresco, served on a patio partially encircled by open Romanesque arches. Cutlery and silverware complement the good service. The chef is likely to offer calves' liver with truffled butter, lobster croquettes (as an appetizer), and roast guinea hen with cream, minced raisins, and port. A baked Alaska finishes the repast quite nicely, although you may prefer an iced soufflé. For such good food, the bill isn't exorbitant: 4,000 pesetas ($36) to 6,000 pesetas ($54) for a complete meal. In summer, only dinner is served, with reservations important. In winter, both lunch and dinner are offered. The restaurant, open from 1 to 3:30 p.m. and 8:30 to 11:30 p.m., is closed on Monday except in August and also on Tuesday all year.

La Fonda, 10 Plaza Santo Cristo (tel. 77-25-12), is run by Horchers of Madrid. The restaurant was the outgrowth of an inn, which had been created by connecting a trio of town houses in Old Marbella. Patios and colonnaded loggias are combined effectively, and the beamed ceilings, Moorish arches, checkerboard marble floors, fireplaces, and grilled windows have been retained. Considering the matchless art performed in the kitchen, the prices are reasonable. The tops in ingredients are used. You'll notice this right away when ordering an appetizer—perhaps avocado ceviche or vichyssoise. The main dishes are cooked with care and professionalism, and are a familiar array taken from an international repertoire—coq au vin, shrimp in dill sauce, veal scaloppine Don Quixote, a blanquette de veau, and chicken Kiev. A complete meal ranges in price from 3,500 pesetas ($31.50) to 6,000 pesetas ($54). Just as the food is international, so is the crowd. Some of the most beautiful faces of Marbella (and some of the richest) are seen here. It is closed on Sunday, but open other days from 8 p.m. to midnight.

Gran Marisquería Santiago, 5 Paseo Marítimo (tel. 77-00-78). As soon as you enter this seaside restaurant, the bubbling lobster tanks will give you an idea of the kinds of dishes available. The orange-and-green décor, the stand-up *tapas* bar near the entrance, and the summertime patio join together with fresh fish dishes to make this one of the most popular eating places in town. On my most recent visit, I arrived so early for lunch that the mussels for my mussels marinara were just being delivered. The fish soup is well prepared, well spiced, and savory. The sole in champagne comes in a large serving, and the turbot can be grilled or sautéed. On a hot day, the seafood salad, garnished with lobster, shrimp, and crabmeat and served with a sharp sauce, is especially recommended. For dessert, I suggest a serving of Manchego cheese. A complete meal, served from 1 to 5 p.m. and 7 p.m. to 1 a.m. daily, will cost 3,500 pesetas ($31.50) and up.

Calycanto, 9 Avenida Canovas del Castillo (tel. 77-19-59), at the west end of the bypass road, is a restaurant built in cortijo style, standing in its own grounds. The garden is the setting for meals in summer, while winter service is in a large room with a log fire. The menu offers a number of good dishes, and the wine list is extensive, with good table wines as well as vintage products. Vegetarians can be happy here, with such main dishes as vegetable mousse pudding and, of course, crisp salads and a smoked salmon salad served with tagliatelle, asparagus mousse, and endives roquefort. For your main course, you might choose guinea fowl or an interesting fish dish with grapes. Meals cost from 3,000 pesetas ($27). The restaurant is open from 1 to 4 p.m. and 8 to 11:30 p.m. daily, but only for dinner in July and August.

The **Marisqueria Marcuño,** 26 Calle Nuestra Sra. de Gracia (tel. 82-00-44), is a chic, romantic place serving high-quality cuisine in comfortable surroundings. The restaurant is decorated with plants, murals, aquariums filled with tropical fish, and waterfalls, all blending with the blues evoking the sea. The gazpacho you might select to begin your meal can be followed by such specialties as baked bass in salt (for two people), mixed grill of seafood or fish, paella, or lobster either thermidor or American style. In all, you can choose fish done about 30 different ways, or perhaps you will prefer tournedos Rossini, lamb chops, or beef tenderloin. The luscious desserts include banana flambé, crêpes Suzette, and ice-cream cake with whisky. Expect to pay around 3,000 pesetas ($27) for a complete meal with the house wine. The restaurant is open from 1 to 3:30 p.m. and 8:30 to 11:30 p.m. daily.

ESTAPONA: The wide-mouthed frog, **La Rana,** Carretera de Cadiz, km 162.5 (tel. 80-10-55), is across from Camping la Chimenea. The menu provided by Swedish chef Lars and his Finnish wife, Pico, is a refreshing change from the usual Spanish foods. Scandinavian dishes are interspersed with English offerings from partners Roger and Wendy, and international specialties are available as well, including frogs' legs à la Rana. In summer you can dine on a vine-covered terrace, and in winter in the cozy dining room. Meals average 3,000 pesetas ($27) per person. The restaurant is open only from 8 p.m. "till late," daily except Sunday.

PUERTO BANÚS: An excellent Italian restaurant is **Don Leone** (tel. 781-727). Puerto Banús is becoming one of the most popular and visited spots along the Costa del Sol, and many visitors drive over just for dinner. If you decide to do likewise, you'll find Don Leone right at dockside. The decoration is attractive, with many luxurious touches. The waiters have been carefully screened. You can dine inside or out. The wine list is one of the best along the coast. To begin your repast, you might order the house minestrone, which is invariably good. Pasta dishes, made on the premises, naturally are featured in various savory sauces, including bolognese and a clam sauce. Lasagne is also a regular item on the menu. Veal parmigiana and roast baby lamb are among the better meat courses, and there are also some well-prepared fish dishes. Count on spending about 4,000 pesetas ($36) or more for a meal. The restaurant is open from 1 to 4 p.m. and 8 p.m. to 12:30 a.m. daily. Closed from November 20 to December 20. It tends to get crowded, so try to reserve a table.

NIGHTLIFE ALONG THE COSTA DEL SOL

Along the Costa del Sol, nightlife consists mainly of hopping from bar to bar, occasionally to a flamenco club or disco. Without a car and a good sense of direction, you might want to cover the top spots by organized tour: for an all-inclusive price, you're picked up at your hotel and returned there, plus given one free drink at each spot visited.

Many organizations run these tours; one such is **Viajes Alhambra,** 514 La Nogalera (tel. 38-17-20) in Torremolinos, or 10 Calle Especerias (tel. 21-37-74) in Málaga. Its Torremolinos night tour costs from 4,000 pesetas ($36), 6,000 pesetas ($54) if you're staying in Marbella. The tour includes two top nightclubs with flamenco shows and other attractions, plus dancing to live bands. But if you want to go it alone, here are a few suggestions.

NERJA:
A family place for a night of Spanish fun, **El Colono,** 6 Calle Granada (tel. 52-18-26), is about a three-minute walk from the main-road bus stop at Nerja. Guitar music and flamenco dancing are the highlights of the entertainment, with original dancing and music. You can also dine here in a tavern atmosphere, either à la carte or from set menus, costing 1,850 pesetas ($16.75), 2,450 pesetas ($22), and 2,950 pesetas ($26.50). Local specialties are served. If you just want a glass of wine, you can still enjoy the shows (three different ones an evening, from 8 p.m. until "the wee hours"). El Colono is closed Sunday.

TORREMOLINOS:
Torremolinos stands in the eye of the nighttime hurricane. The earliest action is always at the bars, which are lively most of the night, serving drinks and *tapas* (Spanish hors d'oeuvres). Sometimes it seems there are more bars in Torremolinos than people—so you shouldn't have trouble finding one you like.

The **Bar El Toro,** 32 San Miguel (tel. 38-65-04), is for aficionados (the bullfight theme is everywhere). Kegs of beer, stools, and the terrace in the main shopping street make it perfect for drinking a before-dinner sherry or an after-dinner beer. As a special attraction, the staff prepares a bullfight poster, with your name between those of two famous matadors, for 500 pesetas ($4.50). Drinks at your table begin at 135 pesetas ($1.25). A special budget menu costs only 1,250 pesetas ($11.25).

Gatsby, 68 Avenida Montemar (tel. 38-53-72), stands on a major, traffic-choked boulevard, and, wisely, has its own private parking. Taking its theme from Fitzgerald's 1920s, Gatsby has a loud, distortion-free sound system. The illumination employs strobes and spots, as you dance to up-to-the-instant disc selections. Entrance for the "matinee," from 6 to 10:30 p.m., is 450 pesetas ($4). From 11:30 p.m. to 4:30 a.m., the price is 800 pesetas ($7.25). One drink is included in the price of admission.

Piper's Club, Plaza Costa del Sol (tel. 38-29-94), is more theatricalized, decorated tongue-in-cheek. It resembles a subterranean world, suggesting the caves at Nerja. Spread over many levels, with connecting ramps and tunnels, it has four dance floors, splashing water in reflecting pools, strobe lighting, and an aggressive set of international records to amuse its packed audience. It's very much the '60s in aura and ambience. The club is open from 6 to 10:30 p.m. daily, when admission is 400 pesetas ($3.50). It reopens at 11 p.m., closing at 4:30 a.m. and charging 900 pesetas ($8) Sunday to Thursday, 1,000 pesetas ($9) on Friday and Saturday. Your first drink is included in the prices.

The leading strictly flamenco club has been and remains **El Jaleo,** Plaza de la Gamba Alegre (tel. 38-12-84). Its *tablao flamenco* showcase of local singers, dancers, and guitarists performs nightly for a cover of 1,700 pesetas ($15.25), including the first drink. Go between 10:30 p.m. and 1 a.m.

Intermezzo Piano Club, 4 Plaza del Remo (tel. 38-32-67), is by far the most sophisticated bar in Carihuela. The sea is visible from the front door, and the interior opens generously into a large, almost square room whose focus is a shiny black piano. Its curves are repeated in the upholstered bar area, which is skillfully lit with a series of dramatically placed spotlights. The décor might be called a combination of Victorian with ultramodern, with dusty rose and black the main colors and English hunting scenes hanging on the walls. There's a small dance floor for those who want to follow the live music, which is presented from 10 p.m. to 3 a.m. every day of the week. Drinks range upward from 300 pesetas ($2.75).

MARBELLA: Long a leading disco along the Costa del Sol, **Pepe Moreno,** Carretera de Cadiz, km 186 (tel. 77-02-79), enlivens the Marbella nightlife scene with a little disco action. A disc jockey seems to play the right music at the right moment. It has a Spanish décor and ambience. Admission is 1,200 pesetas ($10.75), and it's usually open from 11 p.m. to 4 a.m.

PUERTO BANÚS: On the outskirts of Puerto Banús, the **Casino Nueva Andalucía Marbella,** Nueva Andalucía (tel. 81-40-00), is the most exciting nightlife complex along the Costa del Sol. To the west of Marbella, it offers about everything—including terrace dining, swimming pools, a beach, and a nightclub, as well as the gaming rooms. The casino features French roulette, American roulette, blackjack, punto y banco, craps, and chemin de fer. The club stays open all year. An admission card is available upon presentation of your passport and the payment of a fee—600 pesetas ($5.50) for one day. The casino is open from 9 a.m. to 5 p.m. daily. There's also a boîte offering recorded music from 10 p.m. to 1:30 a.m., charging an admission fee of 3,000 pesetas ($27). You can dine in the Casino

Restaurant, raised a few steps up from the gambling floor, for about 3,250 pesetas ($29.25), with wine and service included. Everybody should dress according to the high standards of the casino.

The **Casino Torrequebrada,** 266 Carretera de Cádiz, Benalmádena-Costa (tel. 44-25-45), is another casino in the region that offers blackjack, chemin de fer, punto y banco, and two kinds of roulette to its formally dressed clientele. On the premises are a restaurant, bar, disco, nightclub, and cinema. It is open from 8 p.m. till 4 a.m. daily.

For a much less formal evening than the gambling clubs already previewed, you might drop in at one of the popular piano bars in the heart of Puerto Banús. The most popular is **Duques,** Local 54, Muelle Ribera (tel. 78-35-38). It's owned by Duke Meeks, an American with a skill for booking good acts. A scotch and soda costs from 600 pesetas ($5.50). It's a lively place from 6:30 p.m. to 1:30 a.m. daily.

Index

NOW, SAVE MONEY ON ALL YOUR TRAVELS!
Join Frommer's™ Dollarwise® Travel Club

Saving money while traveling is never a simple matter, which is why, over 27 years ago, the **Dollarwise Travel Club** was formed. Actually, the idea came from readers of the Frommer publications who felt that such an organization could bring financial benefits, continuing travel information, and a sense of community to economy-minded travelers all over the world.

In keeping with the money-saving concept, the annual membership fee is low—$18 (U.S. residents) or $20 U.S. (Canadian, Mexican, and foreign residents)—and is immediately exceeded by the value of your benefits which include:

1. The latest edition of any TWO of the books listed on the following pages.

2. A copy of any Frommer City Guide.

3. An annual subscription to an 8-page quarterly newspaper *The Dollarwise Traveler* which keeps you up-to-date on fastbreaking developments in good-value travel in all parts of the world—bringing you the kind of information you'd have to pay over $35 a year to obtain elsewhere. This consumer-conscious publication also includes the following columns:

> **Hospitality Exchange**—members all over the world who are willing to provide hospitality to other members as they pass through their home cities.
>
> **Share-a-Trip**—requests from members for travel companions who can share costs and help avoid the burdensome single supplement.
>
> **Readers Ask . . . Readers Reply**—travel questions from members to which other members reply with authentic firsthand information.

4. Your personal membership card which entitles you to purchase through the club all Frommer publications for a third to a half off their regular retail prices during the term of your membership.

So why not join this hardy band of international Dollarwise travelers now and participate in its exchange of information and hospitality? Simply send $18 (U.S. residents) or $20 U.S. (Canadian, Mexican, and other foreign residents) along with your name and address to: Frommer's Dollarwise Travel Club, Inc., Gulf + Western Building, One Gulf + Western Plaza, New York, NY 10023. Remember to specify which *two* of the books in section (1) and which *one* in section (2) above you wish to receive in your initial package of member's benefits. Or tear out the next page, check off your choices, and send the page to us with your membership fee.

FROMMER'S™ CITY GUIDES

(Pocket-size guides to sightseeing and tourist accommodations and facilities in all price ranges.)

☐ Amsterdam/Holland $5.95	☐ Montreal/Quebec City $5.95
☐ Athens $5.95	☐ New Orleans $5.95
☐ Atlantic City/Cape May $5.95	☐ New York $5.95
☐ Boston $5.95	☐ Orlando/Disney World/EPCOT $5.95
☐ Cancún/Cozumel/Yucatán $5.95	☐ Paris $5.95
☐ Dublin/Ireland $5.95	☐ Philadelphia $5.95
☐ Hawaii $5.95	☐ Rio (avail. Nov. 1988) $5.95
☐ Las Vegas $5.95	☐ Rome $5.95
☐ Lisbon/Madrid/Costa del Sol $5.95	☐ San Francisco $5.95
☐ London $5.95	☐ Santa Fe/Taos (avail. Mar. 1989) $5.95
☐ Los Angeles $5.95	☐ Sydney $5.95
☐ Mexico City/Acapulco $5.95	☐ Washington, D.C. $5.95
☐ Minneapolis/St. Paul $5.95	

SPECIAL EDITIONS

☐ A Shopper's Guide to the Caribbean . . $12.95	☐ Motorist's Phrase Book (Fr/Ger/Sp) . . . $4.95
☐ Beat the High Cost of Travel $6.95	☐ Paris Rendez-Vous $10.95
☐ Bed & Breakfast—N. America $8.95	☐ Swap and Go (Home Exchanging) . . . $10.95
☐ Guide to Honeymoon Destinations	☐ The Candy Apple (NY for Kids) $11.95
(US, Canada, Mexico, & Carib) $12.95	☐ Travel Diary and Record Book $5.95
☐ Manhattan's Outdoor Sculpture $15.95	☐ Where to Stay USA (Lodging from $3
	to $30 a night) $10.95

☐ Marilyn Wood's Wonderful Weekends (NY, Conn, Mass, RI, Vt, NH, NJ, Del, Pa) $11.95
☐ The New World of Travel (Annual sourcebook by Arthur Frommer previewing: new travel trends, new modes of travel, and the latest cost-cutting strategies for savvy travelers) $12.95

SERIOUS SHOPPER'S GUIDES

(Illustrated guides listing hundreds of stores, conveniently organized alphabetically by category)

☐ Italy $15.95	☐ Los Angeles $14.95
☐ London $15.95	☐ Paris $15.95

GAULT MILLAU

(The only guides that distinguish the truly superlative from the merely overrated.)

☐ The Best of Chicago (avail. Feb. 1989) $15.95	☐ The Best of New England (avail. Feb.
☐ The Best of France (avail. Feb. 1989) . . $15.95	1989) $15.95
☐ The Best of Italy (avail. Feb. 1989) . . . $15.95	☐ The Best of New York $15.95
☐ The Best of Los Angeles $15.95	☐ The Best of San Francisco $15.95
	☐ The Best of Washington, D.C. $15.95

ORDER NOW!

In U.S. include $1.50 shipping UPS for 1st book; 50¢ ea. add'l book. Outside U.S. $2 and 50¢, respectively. Allow four to six weeks for delivery in U.S., longer outside U.S.

Enclosed is my check or money order for $_____

NAME _____

ADDRESS _____

CITY _____ STATE _____ ZIP _____